Mr. President

★

The Human Side of
America's Chief Executives

Mr. President

★

The Human Side of America's Chief Executives

David Rubel

TIME® LIFE BOOKS

Time-Life Books, Alexandria, Virginia

For Abigail

An Agincourt Press Book
President: David Rubel
Art Director: Tilman Reitzle

Contributors: Mary Collins, Doug Hill, Russell Shorto, Richard Steins,
    Sam Tanenhaus, Michael Weber
Copy Editor: Ron Boudreau
Proofreader: Laura Jorstad

Interior Design: Tilman Reitzle
Image Research: Diane Hamilton, Julia Rubel

Image credits appear on page 256.

Time-Life Books is a division of Time Life Inc.
President & CEO: George Artandi

Time-Life Books
President: Stephen R. Frary

Time-Life Custom Publishing
Vice President and Publisher: Terry Newell
Vice President of Sales and Marketing: Neil Levin
Director of Special Sales: Liz Ziehl
Managing Editor: Donia Steele
Project Manager: Jennifer M. Lee
Production Manager: Carolyn Bounds
Quality Assurance Manager: James D. King

Printed and bound in Canada

Library of Congress Cataloging-in-Publication Data

Rubel, David.
    Mr. President: The Human Side of America's Chief Executives / by
David Rubel.
    p. cm.
        ISBN: 0-7835-5253-X
    1. Presidents—United States—Biography—Miscellanea—Juvenile Literature. 2. Presidents—
United States—Psychology—Miscellanea—Juvenile Literature
I. Title.
E176.1.R877   1998
973'.09'9—dc21   97-41135
[B]   CIP

Books produced by Time-Life Custom Publishing are available at special bulk discount for promo-
tional and premium use. Custom adaptations can also be created to meet your specific marketing
goals. Call 1-800-323-5255.

Contents

★

Introduction

★

WHO CAN DOUBT THAT PERSONALITY INFLUENCES HISTORY? Abraham Lincoln's gritty frontier determination certainly altered the course of the Civil War, just as Theodore Roosevelt's matchless egotism guaranteed the United States control of the Panama Canal. To understand more fully the history of this country, therefore, it helps to understand the personalities of the men who have governed it.

The U.S. presidents have not been average men but extraordinary ones, whose careers have encompassed the highest power and the greatest stakes. Their dreams have shaped our history, and their flaws have troubled it. Yet, as the stories in this volume demonstrate, the presidents have been Americans just like us—or at least a little like us—with familiar hopes, fears, habits, and idiosyncrasies. Some have had an excellent sense of humor. Others drank too much. Many were inspiring. One or two were simply appalling.

Each presidential profile begins with a quotation from that president's inaugural address and ends with a highly selective survey of the major political and historical events of his time. In between is an attempt to reach beyond the political persona of the chief executive to capture his genuine personality: the Lincoln who never lost his strong frontier accent, the Calvin Coolidge who regularly slept ten hours a day, the Harry Truman who threatened to beat up a music critic who had panned his daughter's singing performance. "When I was a boy I was told that anyone could become president," Clarence Darrow once said. "I'm beginning to believe it."

The foundation of our national policy will be laid in the pure and immutable principles of private morality, and the preeminence of free government be exemplified by all the attributes which can win the affections of its citizens and command the respect of the world.

George Washington

1st President • 1789–1797

GEORGE WASHINGTON WAS A PRACTICAL MAN. He may have been the commander in chief of the Continental army and the first president of the United States, but he considered himself foremost a farmer.

Washington believed that by taste, training, and temperament, he was much better suited to agriculture than to politics. He didn't think that he had any particular skill as a statesman. And though it may be difficult to understand today, he believed that the work he did improving farming techniques was as important as any he could do for his country.

Although not much of a visionary, Washington thought that the America of the future would be a great agricultural empire stretching west to the Mississippi River and beyond. He believed in the need for a strong central government to run the business of the country. But, like Thomas Jefferson, he sympathized with the individual farmer who owned his own land. Washington thought that the realities of the nation's geography—its many fertile valleys and the great distances between them—would prevent government from becoming too big and too powerful.

Washington was a naturally modest man, but another reason for his great humility in office was that he considered himself rather simple. It seemed obvious to him that John Adams and Thomas Jefferson were better educated and more intellectual. Of course, Washington was right. Adams and Jefferson were, in many ways, smarter than he was. Yet Washington had other qualities to offer, such as his direct and unyielding will.

Without Washington's leadership, the colonists would never have outlasted Great Britain in their war for independence. Later, Washington was the only American who had enough prestige to make the new national government work. His determination, more than any other man's, made Jefferson's vision of an independent America a reality. "His mind…was slow in operation," Jefferson said, "but sure in conclusion."

The responsibility of being the first president might have intimidated a lesser person. But the practical-minded Washington remained composed and self-confident. During his two terms as president, he gave the country nearly a decade of stability so that it could gradually adjust to its new Constitution. On March 3, 1797, Washington wrote, "To the wearied traveller, who sees a resting-place, and is bending his body to lean thereon, I now compare myself." The next day, he left office and retired to Mount Vernon, where he lived out the remainder of his life "in rural amusement."

• Surveying the Frontier

The Washingtons of Virginia were descended from the Washingtons of Northamptonshire, England. Like their British forebears, the Virginia Washingtons were landowners of the second rank, respectable but not very rich.

George was the eldest child of his father's second marriage. Augustine Washington died when George was eleven. After that, George's half brother Lawrence became his surrogate father. Through Lawrence—who married into the Fairfax family, the wealthiest in Virginia—George was presented with his earliest opportunities.

At sixteen, Washington accompanied George Fairfax on an expedition to survey Lord Thomas Fairfax's vast holdings beyond the Blue Ridge Mountains. He was paid the generous wage of $7.20 per day and taught a profession that appealed to his practical, meticulous nature.

Among the equipment Washington took with him on his surveying trips were this set of fishhooks (left) and compass (right).

In his journal of this trip, the earliest extended piece of writing that we have from his own hand, Washington described his first night in the backwoods: "We got out supper and [were] lighted into a room and I, not being as good a woodsman as the rest of my company, stripped myself very orderly and went in to the bed, as they called it, when to my surprise, I found it to be nothing but a little straw matted together, without sheets or anything else, but only one threadbare blanket, with double its weight of vermin, such as lice, fleas, etc., and I was glad to get up as soon as the light was carried from us. I put on my clothes, and lay as my companions [on the floor]." Apparently, the courteous Washington didn't want to offend the landlord by leaping from the bed in his presence.

• Washington's Hidden Passion

George Washington's marriage to Martha Dandridge Custis was a successful one, both financially (she was rich) and socially (she was an excellent hostess). However, their relationship wasn't, at least at first, a romantic one. In fact, Washington was in love with George Fairfax's wife, Sally.

In a letter he sent to Sally Fairfax shortly after his engagement to Martha, Washington wrote, "The world has no business to know the object of my love, declared in this manner to you, when I want to conceal it." There's no evidence that Martha ever knew of Washington's feelings for Sally, but contemporaries often commented on Washington's apparently bottled-up emotions. After closely studying Washington's face, portrait painter Gilbert Stuart remarked that it was the face of a man with tremendous passion subdued by an iron will.

Although Washington had no children of his own, he did adopt John and Martha Custis, Martha's son and daughter from her previous marriage.

For his time, the six-foot-two-inch, 175-pound Washington was a remarkably large, well-muscled man, and he took great pride in his physique. During the French and Indian War, he wrote of himself, "I have a constitution hardy enough to encounter and undergo the most severe trials and, I flatter myself, the resolution to face what any man durst."

• Revolutionary Service

George Washington didn't join the American Revolution for philosophical reasons. That is, he didn't have a problem with the British monarchy in theory. Instead, he objected to its policies, especially its unwillingness to let American colonists settle the rich farmland in the West.

In June 1775, Washington was serving as a delegate to the Second Continental Congress when John Adams suggested that he be made commander in chief of the new Continental army. Some delegates complained that Washington was too indecisive, but most agreed that he possessed the "magnetic aura of leadership that sways men." This quality proved to be crucial, because Washington's job was less to direct battles than to keep some sort of army in the field. His forces were much too weak to face the British head on, yet if Washington could prolong the war, the British might eventually lose it, which they did.

How did Washington manage this? On the battlefield, he succeeded principally by retreating. He soon became a master of both the tactical withdrawal and the surprise attack. Off the battlefield, he kept the Continental army together, without adequate supplies or arms, by rousing its soldiers to fight for him personally. This approach worked magnificently, and it later became the basis for Washington's enormous postwar personal prestige.

★ ★ ★ ★ ★ ★ ★ ★ ★ ★ ★ ★ ★ ★ ★ ★

• The Farmer President

Left to himself, George Washington would have avoided politics entirely. He preferred, instead, the "domestic felicity" of Mount Vernon, his eight-thousand-acre Virginia estate on the southern bank of the Potomac River. Washington was particularly proud of the work that he did there reforming agricultural practices.

Having learned that Americans were far behind Europeans in growing crops and raising animals, he corresponded with Continental experts and imported new equipment and breeding stock. (One of the first books he had shipped over from England was *A System of Agriculture; or, A Speedy Way to Get Rich*.) With the resources of Mount Vernon at his disposal, he was able to experiment as he pleased, turning over entire fields to new and unusual projects. His personal specialty was the breeding of mules.

Washington at Mount Vernon in 1797, as visualized by nineteenth-century lithographers Currier & Ives.

★ ★ ★ ★ ★ ★ ★ ★ ★ ★ ★ ★ ★ ★ ★

• Martha Washington

GEORGE WASHINGTON MARRIED Martha Dandridge Custis on January 6, 1759. Because eighteenth-century Virginia was relatively small, Washington probably knew Martha from the time she was married to her first husband, Daniel Parke Custis. When Custis died in 1757, he left his entire estate to his wife. This inheritance reputedly made Martha the richest widow in Virginia.

Washington apparently visited Martha twice in March 1758. He left the second time with a promise of marriage (or at least a promise that she would seriously consider the offer). Their union greatly increased Washington's fortune, adding seventeen thousand acres to the five thousand that he already owned and three hundred slaves to his forty-nine. Making wise use of these new assets, Washington prospered as a tobacco planter, land broker, and real estate speculator. He carefully supervised each and every aspect of his business life and soon became one of the richest men in the colony.

Over the years, he and Martha became closer. Throughout the Revolution, she visited him at his field headquarters, providing important moral support despite the hardships of life in those ramshackle military camps. She also displayed, as first lady, a special elegance. In keeping with Washington's own tastes, she acted in a manner that was refined but never excessively ornate or pompous.

MAJOR POLITICAL EVENTS

★ **First Bank of the United States:** One of the most important issues facing the Washington administration was the colonies' Revolutionary War debt. Early in 1790, Treasury Secretary Alexander Hamilton proposed that the federal government assume this debt. By doing so, he argued, the new government could establish its credit with lenders and also bind the states closer together. To pay off the debt, Hamilton wanted to charter a national bank that would manage federal funds and issue uniform paper money. (At the time, English pounds, Russian kopecks, and Mexican pesos were all in circulation.) Fearing the creation of an overly strong central government, Secretary of State Thomas Jefferson opposed the plan, yet he relented when Hamilton agreed to locate the new national capital near Jefferson's native Virginia. In 1791, Congress formally chartered the First Bank of the United States.

★ **Neutrality:** When revolutionary France went to war against England, Americans couldn't decide which side to support. Jefferson, excited by the ideals of the French Revolution, wanted the United States to side with France, its ally during the Revolutionary War. Hamilton urged support for England because of the shared cultural and social values. President Washington was primarily interested in keeping the peace. In April 1793, he issued a proclamation of neutrality warning Americans not to smuggle weapons or commit other acts of partisanship that might draw the United States into the fighting.

About the 1st President

Born: February 22, 1732
Birthplace: Pope's Creek, VA
Died: December 14, 1799
Party: Federalist
Stepchildren: John Parke Custis, Martha Parke Custis

★ **Whiskey Rebellion:** When Congress approved a tax on whiskey in 1791, farmers who made whiskey from their surplus corn were outraged. Corn stored in silos spoiled quickly, but corn whiskey kept for years. (Some country people even used whiskey for money.) The Whiskey Rebellion began in July 1794 when farmers in western Pennsylvania greeted tax collectors with armed opposition, directly challenging the authority of the federal government. In August, Washington mustered a fifteen-thousand-man army to enforce the law. He personally led the troops into Pennsylvania, where a few of the ringleaders were arrested, tried, and finally pardoned. The rebellion never posed a serious military threat, but it gave Washington the opportunity to prove the will of the new national government.

★ ★ ★ ★ ★ ★ ★ ★ ★ ★ ★ ★ ★ ★ ★

During the Washington Administration

1789   *Christopher Colles publishes the first U.S. road maps.*

Dec. 21, 1790   *Samuel Slater begins operating the first successful cotton mill in the United States. The Pawtucket, Rhode Island, mill makes use of British industrial methods.*

May 17, 1792   *Brokers in New York City who have been buying and selling securities sign an agreement formalizing their business. The result is the New York Stock Exchange.*

1792   *The first edition of the* Farmer's Almanac *appears, containing information about life in New England as well as useful facts about the weather.*

Oct. 28, 1793   *Eli Whitney files an application to patent the cotton gin. Whitney's machine speeds up the removal of seeds from cotton by fifty times and makes the planting of cotton much more profitable.*

May 1, 1794   *Shoemakers in Philadelphia form the Federal Society of Journeymen Cordwainers, the first organized trade union in the United States.*

1794   *Work ends on the first major U.S. toll road, the Philadelphia-Lancaster Turnpike. The large profits generated by this hard-surfaced road encourage other companies to invest in road construction.*

1796   *Amelia Simmons publishes the first cookbook to contain recipes for American specialties, including pickled watermelon rind, spruce beer, Indian pudding, johnny-cake, and gingerbread.*

Can anything essential, anything more than mere ornament and decoration, be added to this [government] by robes and diamonds? Can authority be more amiable and respectable when it descends from accidents or institutions established in remote antiquity than when it springs fresh from the hearts and judgments of an honest and enlightened people?

John Adams

2nd President • 1797–1801

JOHN ADAMS WAS SMART, HE KNEW IT, and he couldn't resist letting others know it, too. "Vanity," he wrote in his revealing diary, "is my cardinal vice and cardinal folly." In modern politics, he could never have run for national office. His haughty manner and abrasive personality would be thought much too offensive. But in 1796, he won the first contested national election and became the second president of the United States.

Given how argumentative and overbearing he was, how did Adams prosper, even in eighteenth-century politics? The explanation is simple: The American Revolution was organized by only a few hundred men, and on that small a scale, a single remarkable individual—even a disagreeable one—can make a big difference. Adams's intellect, foresight, and drive were all crucial in convincing the First Continental Congress to resist Great Britain. And without Adams, the Second Continental Congress might not have declared independence as earnestly as it eventually did.

Early on, Adams saw what would be the inevitable outcome of the colonists' demands. Everyone agreed that there could be no government without taxation, for governments needed money. It also made sense that taxation without representation was unfair. Because of the great distances involved, however, colonial representation in London wasn't really a practical solution. Therefore, Adams realized, the colonies must govern themselves. Many patriots knew these facts, yet they closed their minds to the logical conclusion.

During the First Continental Congress in 1774, Adams restrained himself. He worried that the other delegates might pull back if he reminded them too vigorously of what must come: American independence. By the Second Congress, however, events had moved forward so quickly that Adams simply couldn't hold back his passion any longer. Normally a limited public speaker, he became so aroused that he lost all self-consciousness. Thomas Jefferson may have been the one to write the Declaration of Independence, but it was Adams who—almost single-handedly—spurred the delegates to sign it.

Many of his colleagues complained about John Adams's self-righteousness. But in times of crisis, it was an important asset. Often, when delegates were nervous about taking the next step toward independence, Adams would tell them, with great assurance, that he was prepared to take full responsibility for the consequences, whatever they might be. It's unclear what this would have meant if the British had won the war. But Adams's willingness to shoulder blame persuaded many a timid delegate to go along with him. At least he seemed to know what he was doing.

• The Adams Dynasty

During the nineteenth century, John Adams's descendants became one of America's great families. His ancestors, however, were average people. His great-great-grandfather Henry Adams first settled in Braintree, Massachusetts, around 1640, and the next four generations of Adamses were all anonymous small farmers. The greatness clearly began with John.

As a boy, he preferred farm chores to schoolwork, but his parents wanted something better of him. The oldest child, he was given a college education, entering Harvard in 1751 at age sixteen. "I soon perceived a growing curiosity," Adams wrote in his autobiography, "a love of books and a fondness for study, which dissipated all my inclination for sports, and even

for the society of the ladies." Until he was eclipsed by his son John Quincy, John Adams was considered the most learned man in American political life.

Left: The Adams family residence in Braintree (now Quincy), Massachusetts. Below: Some of Adams's personal effects arranged on the desk in his study, including his glasses and the candlesticks that provided his only light while reading.

★ ★ ★ ★ ★ ★ ★ ★ ★ ★ ★ ★ ★ ★ ★ ★ ★ ★ ★

• The Bloody Massacre

In the late 1760s, John Adams, then a lawyer in Boston, began to associate himself with the patriot cause. He was encouraged in this by his famous second cousin, the rabble-rouser Samuel Adams. In 1770, the two Adamses parted company when John agreed to defend the nine British soldiers accused in the Boston Massacre. "Since he was nourished, to a degree, by a sense of persecution," Adams biographer Page Smith has pointed out, "he noted the clamor [against him] with grim pleasure. Self-righteousness, to be fully enjoyed, needs a feeling of isolation, of lonely defiance. The greater the outcry, the more overwhelming the opposition, the greater sense of the righteousness."

Although Adams opposed the presence of British troops in Boston, he believed that these particular soldiers were innocent and in danger of being railroaded to the gallows. Some patriots respected Adams's desire to do what was right in the eyes of the law, but they never expected him to *win*. When Adams did win acquittals for the British captain and six of the eight enlisted men (the other two were branded), he was ostracized, if only temporarily, by his patriot comrades. "Farewell, politics," he wrote in his diary.

Top left: Adams as a middle-aged lawyer. Left: Paul Revere's engraving of The Bloody Massacre, *which showed the mob as an orderly crowd, was a masterful piece of patriot propaganda.*

• Second Fiddle

Nearly forty years old and a bit overweight when the Revolutionary War began, Adams didn't consider soldiering. Instead, after independence was declared, he became a diplomat. In 1778, the Continental Congress sent him to Paris to join Benjamin Franklin, the American minister there. But Franklin and Adams didn't get along very well. Part of the problem was that Adams had become worried that Franklin and Washington were overshadowing him.

"The history of our Revolution will be one continued lie from one end to the other," he told his friend Benjamin Rush. "The essence of the whole will be that Dr. Franklin's electrical rod smote the Earth and out sprang General Washington. That Franklin electrified him with his rod—and thence forward these two conducted all the policy, negotiations, legislations, and war."

For this reason, Adams hated being Washington's vice president. He agreed to play second fiddle to the general only to become president himself.

A Puritan by upbringing and inclination, John Adams blushed at the mention of sex and considered poverty a punishment for transgressions against God.

• "Jefferson Survives!"

Adams and Thomas Jefferson were colleagues and friends during the American Revolution. Sadly, by the time Adams defeated Jefferson for the presidency in 1796, domestic politics had pulled them apart. During a crisis with France, Adams attempted to take Jefferson into his confidence, but Jefferson rebuffed him. The two men rarely spoke from that point on. After losing the election of 1800 to Jefferson, a deeply embittered Adams left Washington before dawn rather than see the sun rise on Jefferson's inauguration.

It took more than a decade, but in 1813—after Jefferson, too, had retired—they renewed their correspondence. Of course, Adams remained prickly: "Your character in history may be easily foreseen," he wrote Jefferson. "Your administration will be quoted by philosophers as a model of profound wisdom; by politicians as weak, superficial, and shortsighted. Mine, like Pope's woman, will have no character at all."

Adams and Jefferson died on the same day: July 4, 1826, the fiftieth anniversary of the signing of the Declaration of Independence. The last words of the ninety-year-old Adams, mumbled with obvious effort, were, "Thomas Jefferson survives." Given that no form of communication faster than a stagecoach existed in 1826, he couldn't have known that Jefferson was already dead.

Adams was sitting in this chair when he died.

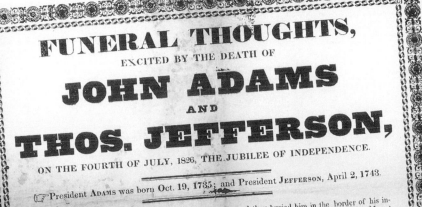

FUNERAL THOUGHTS,
EXCITED BY THE DEATH OF
JOHN ADAMS
AND
THOS. JEFFERSON,
ON THE FOURTH OF JULY, 1826, THE JUBILEE OF INDEPENDENCE.

☞ President ADAMS was born Oct. 19, 1735; and President JEFFERSON, April 2, 1743.

old, and they buried him in the border of his in-

• Abigail Adams

DESPITE CARRYING SOME EXCESS WEIGHT, the young John Adams was, by all accounts, quite popular with—and fond of—girls. Two things kept him out of trouble, though: his growing fascination with his studies and his father's warning that premarital sex automatically caused venereal disease. Perhaps because he kept it in check for so long, his passion was deep and broad. An early flame, Hannah Quincy, remarked that no ordinary woman could return the quantity of love that Adams had to offer. He longed for a wife and family but was cautious. In fact, he proposed only once. The woman was nineteen-year-old Abigail Smith, and they were married on October 25, 1764.

Abigail read more than a lady was supposed to, was considered smarter than a woman ought to be, and spoke out even though the custom of her time called for silence. In a famous March 1776 letter, she asked her husband to "remember the ladies" when making laws for the new nation. "Do not put unlimited power in the hands of husbands," she wrote. "Remember, all men would be tyrants if they could. If particular care and attention is not paid to the ladies, we are determined to foment a rebellion, and will not hold ourselves bound by any laws in which we have no voice or representation."

MAJOR POLITICAL EVENTS

★ **XYZ Affair:** When John Adams took office in 1797, the most pressing item on the presidential agenda was French harassment of U.S. shipping to and from Great Britain. There were even rumors that the French were planning an invasion of North America. An outraged American public wanted war, but Adams knew that the country wasn't yet ready to fight. Instead, heeding Washington's advice to avoid foreign entanglements, he sent three diplomats to French foreign minister Charles Talleyrand. Talleyrand appointed three of his own agents to meet with the Americans. These Frenchmen—later referred to by Adams as X, Y, and Z—promptly asked for a $250,000 bribe. The XYZ affair left Adams indignant but still reluctant to declare war. Rather than fight a naval campaign he couldn't win, he persuaded Congress to suspend trade with France and made arrangements for the British navy to protect transatlantic shipping.

★ **Quasi-War:** Beginning in the spring of 1798, U.S. frigates engaged French warships in an armed struggle over U.S. neutrality. The two-year conflict was known as the Quasi-War because, officially, the two countries were at peace. Adams delayed asking Congress for a formal declaration of war, hoping that the French, busy fighting in Europe, would stop bothering with North America. In September 1800, a second, more successful diplomatic mission to Talleyrand persuaded France to recognize U.S. neutrality in exchange for an increase in U.S. exports to France.

About the 2nd President

Born: October 30, 1735
Birthplace: Braintree, MA
Died: July 4, 1826
Party: Federalist
Children: Abigail, John Quincy, Susanna,
    Charles, Thomas

★ **Alien and Sedition Acts:** During the summer of 1798, when war with France seemed likely, Adams signed the Alien and Sedition Acts. These laws were supposed to protect national security by giving the president special powers to deport dangerous foreigners and suppress dangerous speech. However, in practice the Federalists used the Alien and Sedition Acts not to prosecute spies but to persecute Jefferson's Democratic-Republican party. Democratic-Republican congressman Matthew Lyon of Vermont was sentenced to four months in jail for writing in a personal letter that Adams was selfish and pompous. Another man was fined one hundred dollars for wishing out loud for a cannon wadding to be lodged in the president's backside.

During the Adams Administration

1797	*Philadelphia becomes the first U.S. city to build a centralized water-supply system.*
1798	*Cotton gin inventor Eli Whitney pioneers the use of interchangeable parts. His method for mass producing firearms wins him a large government contract.*
Mar. 29, 1799	*The New York state legislature passes a law that gradually outlaws slavery in the state and frees the slaves there.*
1799	*Philadelphia's Federal Society of Journeymen Cordwainers calls a nine-day strike, the first organized labor action in the United States. The strike ends when the shoemakers win their demand for a pay increase.*
1800	*John Chapman, better known as Johnny Appleseed, collects seeds from cider presses in Pennsylvania, then travels west and plants a series of apple orchards between the Allegheny Mountains and central Ohio.*
1800	*Parson Weems writes* The Life and Memorable Actions of George Washington, *which invents such famous stories as that of young George chopping down his father's cherry tree.*
1800	*William Young becomes the first American to make shoes specifically for the left and right feet. Before Young, all U.S. shoes were straight rather than curved to fit each foot.*
1800	*The 1800 census shows a national population of 5,300,000. This figure includes about 1,000,000 blacks, of whom 90 percent are slaves. Virginia, with 900,000 people, is the most populous state.*

All, too, will bear in mind this sacred principle, that though the will of the majority is in all cases to prevail, that will to be rightful must be reasonable; that the minority possess their equal rights, which equal law must protect, and to violate would be oppression.

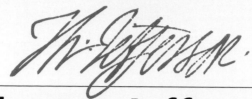

Thomas Jefferson

3rd President • 1801–1809

THOMAS JEFFERSON, THE AUTHOR OF THE DECLARATION of Independence, is remembered today with great reverence. However, during his lifetime, opinions about him were mixed. Jefferson's admirers worshiped his agile mind. In their letters, they often remarked on how struck they were by the breadth of his knowledge and the nobility of his aspirations. But there were just as many people who thought that Jefferson was a fraud, weak and hypocritical. Most presidents can be captured with broad brushstrokes, historian Henry Adams once said, but "Jefferson could be painted only touch by touch, with a fine pencil."

Jefferson's reserved personality made him especially difficult for people to decipher. He was easygoing on the surface, yet acquaintances often got the feeling that he would rather be reading by himself than talking with them. There seemed to be a core to Jefferson that no one, not even his closest friends, could reach. Some people forgave him this detachment; others didn't trust him because of it.

Washington and Adams had been very direct presidents: Once they made up their minds, they dismissed all doubt and acted decisively. Jefferson didn't share this strength. Instead, he often waffled. Friends attributed this wavering to an occasional lack of clarity and focus, which they thought was understandable in a mind as complex as Jefferson's. His political enemies called it shiftiness.

Usually, Jefferson's contradictory nature remained beneath the surface, but sometimes it became painfully obvious. From his earliest days as a public figure, the master of Monticello spoke out against the inhumanity of slavery—though he was, at the same time, one of the largest slave owners in Virginia. Jefferson never gave up his call for emancipation, but later in life, when he actually had some power, he worried that freeing the slaves would crush the southern economy (not to mention his own fragile financial situation). In the end, he decided, with apparently genuine regret, that emancipation would have to be left to the next generation.

Jefferson clearly lived in two worlds: one of ideas, in which he could see remarkably clearly, and one of dollars and cents, in which his vision was murky. His great achievement in the first world was the Declaration of Independence. In the second world, however, the impractical Jefferson sank deeply into debt. At his death, Monticello and everything in it had to be sold off to pay his creditors.

• From Goochland to Williamsburg

Jefferson was born in the foothills of the Blue Ridge Mountains in what is now Albemarle County, Virginia, but was then called Goochland. In 1743, the year of Jefferson's birth, Goochland was on the western frontier, only a hundred miles from the sea but more than a day's horseback ride from civilization in that three-miles-per-hour world.

At seventeen, Jefferson enrolled at the College of William and Mary in Williamsburg, then the colonial capital. Williamsburg was by far the most bustling metropolis Jefferson had ever seen. At well over six feet tall, he was lanky to the point of gangliness. And he was studious to the point of fanaticism: One friend remembered him studying fifteen hours a day.

His professors soon recognized his enormous intellect, and, by their recommendation, he became a regular guest at the governor's dinner table. Bookish and shy, Jefferson found such public occasions difficult, but he was drawn to the elite company and thought the political and philosophical discussions thrilling. By the time he left Williamsburg, he was recognized as one of the best-educated men in Virginia.

This revolving book stand, of Jefferson's own design, allowed him to read up to five books nearly simultaneously.

★ ★ ★ ★ ★ ★ ★ ★ ★ ★ ★ ★

• The Declaration of Independence

Because of his lifelong reluctance to participate in public debate, Jefferson shrank from the rigorous give-and-take of the Second Continental Congress. "During the whole time I sat with him," John Adams recalled, "I never heard him utter three sentences together."

Yet it was Adams who convinced Jefferson to undertake the task of writing a declaration of independence. Benjamin Franklin had refused—as a matter of policy, he said, he didn't write documents subject to the editing of others—and Adams had also declined. "I am obnoxious, suspected and unpopular," he told Jefferson. "You are very much otherwise, [and] you can write ten times better than I can."

Between mid-May and early July, the thirty-three-year-old Jefferson holed up in his rented room on Philadelphia's Market Street. He spent most of his time on other congressional business but left a few days for the declaration. He was quite pleased with his work, though not at all happy with what the other delegates did to it. Afterward, Jefferson sent to friends copies of his unedited draft, inquiring whether or not they agreed that his original text had been better.

Above: The scene at Independence Hall, Philadelphia, as re-created by John Trumbull. Left: One of Jefferson's drafts in his own hand.

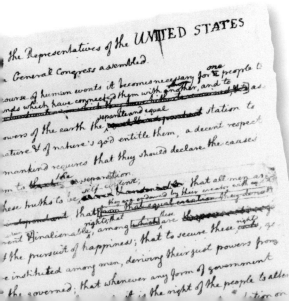

Thomas Jefferson (right) with his chief political rival, Alexander Hamilton (standing), and George Washington.

• Invisible to the Public

Jefferson kept to himself more than any other president. Because he hated appearing in public, he gave only two speeches during his entire presidency—the two inaugural addresses. (And few people heard even these, for Jefferson tended to mumble.)

Instead, he led the American people indirectly. He used intermediaries, such as James Madison and James Monroe, to carry his instructions to Congress and the executive departments. Communicating primarily through letters, Jefferson typically spent ten hours a day at his writing desk while remaining invisible to the public.

On the few occasions when Jefferson did have to interact with strangers, his lack of concern about his public image sometimes got him into trouble. For example, in November 1803, when the new British minister, Anthony Merry, called on the president to present his credentials, Jefferson met him "not merely in undress," Merry wrote indignantly to his superiors, "but actually standing in slippers down at the heels and both pantaloons, coat, and underclothes indicative of utter slovenliness and indifference to appearance."

• A Curious Mind

Throughout his life, Jefferson displayed an eager curiosity for nearly every branch of human knowledge. His favorite scholarly subjects were natural philosophy and mathematics, but he also dabbled expertly in agriculture and, like Washington, believed that improving U.S. practices was very important. In listing his most important achievements, Jefferson included Virginia's Statute of Religious Liberty, the Declaration of Independence, and his importation of olive trees from France.

Even so, no intellectual pursuit thrilled Jefferson so much as architecture. When George Washington organized a contest to design the new president's house in Washington, D.C., Jefferson submitted a design anonymously. (It didn't win.) In retirement, Jefferson founded the University of Virginia and then proceeded to design all the campus buildings. However, his greatest architectural achievement was his estate, Monticello. The house included such unique contrivances as beds that folded up into the walls and a weather vane hooked up to an indoor gauge so that Jefferson could tell the wind direction without having to step outside. For a time after his

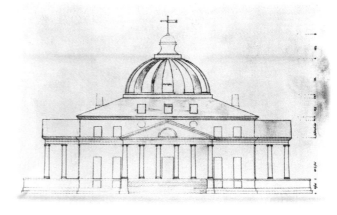

death, Monticello was allowed to decline. But it was eventually purchased by a Jewish family, and they restored it to its glory as a tribute to the man who had made religious freedom the law in Virginia.

Top: Jefferson's design for the president's house. Right: The key to Monticello.

★ ★ ★ ★ ★ ★ ★ ★ ★ ★ ★ ★ ★ ★ ★ ★

• Martha Jefferson

WHEN THOMAS JEFFERSON BECAME president, he had been a widower for nearly twenty years. No known portrait exists of his late wife, Martha, but we know from contemporary accounts that she was pretty, with hazel eyes, auburn hair, and a slim figure. We also know that Jefferson was completely devoted to her. Sadly, her health was poor, and seven pregnancies exhausted her already depleted strength.

After giving birth to a daughter, Lucy Elizabeth, in May 1782, she remained, in Jefferson's words, "dangerously ill." Although bleeding and purging were common treatments at the time, biographer Fawn Brodie notes that "these medical barbarities, at least, seem not to have been employed" because Jefferson distrusted them.

In September 1782, Martha Jefferson died. For three weeks after her funeral, an inconsolable Jefferson refused to leave his room. It has been reported that, as she lay dying, Martha asked the thirty-nine-year-old Jefferson never to remarry. He never did.

Only two of Jefferson's children lived to adulthood. His oldest daughter, Martha (left), whom the family called Patsy, served for a short time as Jefferson's official hostess. The rest of the time, the president honored the wives of cabinet members by asking them to act as hostess on formal state occasions.

MAJOR POLITICAL EVENTS

★ **Barbary Pirates:** The Barbary pirates of North Africa posed the greatest threat to U.S. shipping during the first decade of the nineteenth century. Operating out of Morocco, Algiers, Tunis, and Tripoli, these buccaneers robbed American merchant ships and imprisoned their sailors, often torturing them. At first, the United States paid tribute in exchange for safe passage. In May 1801, however, the pasha of Tripoli declared war, hoping to force a more lucrative deal. In 1805, after a number of setbacks, the U.S. fleet captured Derna, a major Tripolitan port, and forced the pasha to sign a peace treaty ending all tribute payments.

★ **Louisiana Purchase:** During the early 1800s, Jefferson became concerned that France might cut off American access to New Orleans, the port through which most Americans living near the Mississippi River sent and received their goods. Hoping to purchase New Orleans from the French, Jefferson sent James Monroe to Paris in March 1803. Monroe was authorized to spend up to ten million dollars for the port. Instead, Napoleon offered to sell him the entire Louisiana Territory, which included nearly all the land between the Mississippi River and the Rocky Mountains. The price ultimately agreed on was fifteen million dollars, or about three cents per acre. Jefferson's initial impulse was to make Napoleon wait until a constitutional amendment could be passed to give him the necessary authority. Then he sensibly reconsidered and let the wisdom of the purchase be its constitutionality.

About the 3rd President

Born: April 13, 1743
Birthplace: Shadwell, VA
Died: July 4, 1826
Party: Democratic-Republican
Children: Martha, Jane, Mary, Lucy, Lucy

★ **Embargo Act:** In June 1807, the British warship *Leopard* fired on the U.S. frigate *Chesapeake*. Although the public demanded war, Jefferson sought a more reasonable course. He asked for an apology, and when his request was refused, he asked Congress to impose a trade embargo—not merely against Britain, but against all of Europe. Jefferson believed that the withholding of trade would compel both Britain and France, who were still at war, to respect U.S. neutrality. He signed the Embargo Act in December 1807, but it was a disaster. American merchants and shipowners suffered much more than either the British or the French did. On March 1, 1809, three days before leaving office, Jefferson signed the Non-Intercourse Act, which limited the embargo to Britain and France alone.

During the Jefferson Administration

1802 — Boston's board of health orders vaccinations to prevent the spread of smallpox.

1803 — South Carolina approves new slave imports from the West Indies. The rising demand for slave labor has been caused by Eli Whitney's 1793 invention of the cotton gin.

1803 — Eighteen-year-old John James Audubon emigrates from France to the United States. The businesses he starts in Kentucky all fail, but the self-taught naturalist develops a passion for drawing birds.

July 11, 1804 — Aaron Burr shoots Alexander Hamilton in a duel. Burr believes that Hamilton's personal attacks have cost him the vice presidency. Hamilton intentionally fires into the air, but Burr doesn't miss. Hamilton dies the next day.

Nov. 7, 1805 — Meriwether Lewis and William Clark reach the Pacific Ocean. Their expedition had left St. Louis on May 14, 1804.

1806 — Teacher and journalist Noah Webster publishes his Compendious Dictionary of the English Language, *the first dictionary of American English.*

Aug. 1807 — Robert Fulton's Clermont *makes its maiden voyage up the Hudson River from New York City to Albany in just thirty-two hours. The 133-foot-long paddle wheeler is the world's first serviceable steamboat.*

Apr. 6, 1808 — John Jacob Astor founds the American Fur Company to control the fur trade in the region recently explored by Lewis and Clark.

The present situation of the world is indeed without a parallel, and that of our own country full of difficulties. The pressure of these, too, is the more severely felt because they have fallen upon us at a moment when the national prosperity being at a height not before attained, the contrast resulting from the change has been rendered the more striking.

James Madison

4th President • 1809–1817

JAMES MADISON WASN'T A PHYSICALLY IMPRESSIVE PERSON: He stood about five feet four inches tall, weighed just one hundred pounds, had a soft voice, and always seemed young for his age. Typically, he looked sick, weak, and nervous— and on top of that, he was modest and shy, never having mastered the politically useful art of small talk.

When Madison first arrived at the Continental Congress in 1780—its youngest member at twenty-nine—he was assigned to the Maritime Department, a bureaucratic backwater. By year's end, however, he had made his way onto a number of important committees and was being considered for secretary of foreign affairs.

The keys to Madison's success were his sure grasp of complicated issues and his knack for navigating the ins and outs of the lawmaking process. George Washington commanded by physical presence and Thomas Jefferson inspired with words, but Madison simply knew a great deal about what was going on. He was passionate about his goals, particularly American nationhood, but patient and detail oriented as well. These characteristics made him ideally suited to bridge the gap between revolution and stability.

As a delegate to the Constitutional Convention of 1787, Madison argued successfully for the establishment of a strong central government. But he also created a unique system of checks and balances to protect individual rights. The fact that the Constitutional Convention took place behind closed doors appealed to Madison, because he preferred to work behind the scenes.

After personally writing much of the Constitution, Madison took on the equally difficult and delicate task of winning its ratification. Along with Alexander Hamilton and John Jay, he composed *The Federalist Papers* to explain the new government to the people. In essay No. 51, Madison concluded that "ambition must be made to counteract ambition…. It may be a reflection on human nature, that such devices should be necessary to control the abuses of government. But what is government itself, but the greatest of all reflections on human nature? If men were angels, no government would be necessary."

However, Madison's deep faith in limited government worked against him as president. Believing that he had only limited powers, he avoided taking decisive action against the British during the War of 1812. In a certain sense, Madison became a prisoner of his constitutional convictions, and this cost him considerable public support, especially after the British burned Washington.

• Poor Health

Because he had been a fragile child, Madison became obsessed with his health (or lack of it) as a young man and remained obsessed throughout his long life. He suffered from frequent attacks of "bilious fever," which left him bedridden for weeks at a time. He also had occasional seizures that he attributed to epilepsy. It's impossible to say what caused Madison's fevers, but most contemporary historians are certain that his seizures were anxiety attacks.

One of Madison's worst health episodes came during the summer of 1813, when the *Federal Republican* reported that a fever "has made a havoc of his constitution and left him, it is confidently believed, but a few months, perhaps a few days to

Top: A brooch with Madison's portrait and a lock of his hair. Below: The buckles from a pair of his shoes.

live." Madison's Federalist opponents nearly rejoiced at the prospect that the sixty-two-year-old president might die, yet they underestimated his recuperative powers. As one of Madison's close friends had pointed out decades earlier, people of the weakest constitution often outlive those of the strongest, and Madison, in particular, seemed "designed by Providence for extensive usefulness."

• Friendship with Jefferson

James Madison and Thomas Jefferson began their lifelong friendship when Jefferson was governor of Virginia and Madison a member of that state's executive council. In 1812, responding to one of President Madison's many critics, Jefferson wrote, "I have known him from 1779, when he first came into the public councils, and, from three and thirty years trial, I can say conscientiously that I do not know in the world a man of purer integrity, more dispassionate, disinterested, and devoted to genuine Republicanism; nor could I in the whole scope of America and Europe point out an abler head."

Jefferson so treasured this campeachy, or siesta, chair that he gave his friend Madison one just like it. The name comes from the Mexican state Campeche, where the mahogany used to make this style of chair was grown.

Madison served Jefferson long and well, most notably for eight years as his secretary of state. When Jefferson left office, he made it clear that he wished Madison to succeed him. Although Jefferson had often asked Madison for advice before making an important decision, Madison ran the country much more on his own. In fact, only once did he seek Jefferson's counsel: Madison wanted to know how to handle White House architect Benjamin Latrobe and his frequent demands for more money.

The shell of the burned presidential mansion.

• The Capital Is Burned

When Congress declared war on Great Britain in June 1812, the United States wasn't prepared to challenge the world's greatest military power. If this wasn't obvious at the time, it certainly became so in August 1814, when a British invasion force captured and burned Washington, D.C.

The disaster wasn't all Madison's fault. He had warned Secretary of War John Armstrong that he thought the capital's defenses were inadequate, but Armstrong had scoffed at this. Madison had also relied on the command abilities of Gen. William Winder, only to learn too late that Winder was an incompetent leader. Still, to ordinary people, none of this mattered. Madison was the president, and the public blamed him.

A mythology soon arose concerning the burning of Washington on August 24. Stories of Dolley Madison's gallant rescue of several national treasures (including the Declaration of Independence) flattered the first lady. On the other hand, her husband was rumored to have taken flight to Virginia ahead of her. This wasn't true: At the time that his wife left Washington, the sixty-three-year-old president was witnessing the fighting firsthand. In fact, he was so close to the battle that, for a short time, he was even within range of the British guns.

 ★ ★ ★ ★ ★ ★ ★ ★ ★ ★ ★ ★ ★ ★ ★ ★ ★ ★ ★

• A Change of Mind

By late June 1836, it was clear that the eighty-five-year-old former president was finally dying. His doctor offered him stimulants to keep him alive until July 4, so that he might die on the same historic day as Jefferson, Adams, and Monroe—but Madison refused.

On the morning of June 28, Madison appeared for breakfast but couldn't swallow. According to his longtime valet, Paul Jennings, "His niece, Mrs. Willis, said, 'What is the matter, Uncle James?'

"'Nothing more than a change of *mind*, my dear.' His head instantly dropped, and he ceased breathing as quietly as the snuff of a candle goes out."

★ ★ ★ ★ ★ ★ ★ ★ ★ ★ ★ ★ ★ ★ ★ ★ ★ ★ ★ ★

• Dolley Madison

By 1794, Madison was already well known throughout the country as the Father of the Constitution. Certainly, the fashionable widow Dolley Payne Todd of Philadelphia had heard of him. Living only a block from the seat of Congress, she was familiar with its members and even socialized with several of them. But when in the spring of 1794 she learned that Madison wanted to call on her, the twenty-five-year-old Quaker wrote excitedly to her friend Eliza Collins: "Thou must come to me. Aaron Burr says that the great little Madison has asked to be brought to see me this evening."

Most people had presumed that Madison, then forty-three, was a confirmed bachelor; evidently they were wrong. According to one Madison biographer, "The wooing that followed was swift and ardent…. It proved one of those rare marriages that started out with adoration on his part, admiration or more on hers,

and deepened in mutual love throughout their lives."

They were married in September 1794. In a letter to Eliza Collins penned before the ceremony, Dolley wrote, "I give my hand to the man of all others I most admire." She signed the note "Dolley Payne Todd," but then added a postscript: "Evening—Dolley Madison!"

As first lady, Dolley Madison did much to make up for her husband's social inadequacies. In large groups, Madison could be close-mouthed, but the attractively buxom Dolley compensated for this with her own vivaciousness. Although her husband always dressed entirely in black, she wore clothes that were loud with color and often sported feathers as well. According to contemporary reports, Dolley ate heartily, gambled some at cards, and enjoyed the custom of calling on those who had recently called on her. Often she left her card, a poem, or a flower as a souvenir.

MAJOR POLITICAL EVENTS

★ **Tecumseh's Confederacy:** In July 1809, the Shawnee chief Tecumseh began organizing a confederacy of Indian tribes from Florida to the Canadian border. He intended to resist the encroachment of Europeans, who had already seized 100 million acres of Indian land. When the Miami tribe agreed to a treaty with Indiana governor William Henry Harrison transferring another 2.5 million acres, Tecumseh refused to recognize the deal, claiming that the Miami had no right to sell the land. In August 1811, Harrison assembled a thousand-man surveying expedition. He reached the Shawnee camp at Tippecanoe Creek on November 6. Tecumseh was away in the South, per-

suading the Creek tribe to join his confederacy. Harrison's inclination was to attack, but Madison had ordered him to give the Indians a chance to abandon their village. Before dawn the next morning, 650 Indians attacked the governor's camp. Harrison's victory in the battle of Tippecanoe that followed made him a national hero.

★ **War Hawks:** In the congressional elections of 1811, voters replaced nearly half the members of the House with an aggressive group of young politicians anxious for war with Britain. The War Hawks, led by Henry Clay of Kentucky and John Calhoun of South Carolina, complained that Madison's diplomacy wasn't doing enough to stop the continued harassment of U.S. shipping. Many came from the frontier, where people feared attacks by Indians armed with British weapons.

About the 4th President

Born: March 16, 1751
Birthplace: Port Conway, VA
Died: June 28, 1836
Party: Democratic-Republican
Children: None

★ ★ ★ ★ ★ ★ ★ ★ ★ ★ ★ ★ ★ ★

During the Madison Administration

Jan. 10, 1811 — *In New Orleans, state troops crush a slave rebellion that had begun two days earlier on a nearby plantation. Four hundred slaves had killed the plantation owner's son and marched on the city.*

Dec. 16, 1811 — *An earthquake at New Madrid in present-day Missouri rocks the Mississippi Valley—forming new lakes, draining old ones, and making the Mississippi River run backward.*

July 19, 1813 — *Elizabeth Ann Seton founds the Sisters of Charity, the first Roman Catholic order in the United States. When she is canonized in 1975, she becomes the first U.S.-born saint.*

Sep. 14, 1814 — *Lawyer Francis Scott Key, captive aboard a British warship, watches the Royal Navy attack Baltimore. Seeing the U.S. flag still flying over Fort McHenry at dawn, he writes "The Star-Spangled Banner."*

Oct. 21, 1814 — *Congress buys Thomas Jefferson's seven-thousand-volume library for $23,950. The books replace the Library of Congress collection burned by the British.*

Apr. 5, 1815 — *Mount Tambora on the Indonesian island of Sumbawa erupts. The blast kills fifty thousand people, and clouds of volcanic dust affect the world's climate. In the United States, cold weather during 1816 kills crops, and snow falls all summer in New England.*

1815 — *A stagecoach company advertises regular thirty-six-hour trips between Boston and New York City.*

June 11, 1816 — *Baltimore becomes the first U.S. city to charter a gas company to light its streets.*

★ **War of 1812:** In June 1812, worn down by the mounting public pressure, Madison reluctantly asked Congress to declare war on Great Britain. As his justification, Madison cited the ongoing attacks against U.S. vessels and Britain's encouragement of Indian raids along the western and northern frontiers. From the start of the fighting, the war went poorly for the Americans. When Madison called for fifty thousand volunteers, only five thousand enlisted. The New England states, whose economic future depended on lively trade with Britain, opposed the war and refused to allow their militias to participate. The most significant U.S. victories were won by Capt. Oliver Hazard Perry on Lake Erie in September 1813 and by Gen. Andrew Jackson at New Orleans in January 1815. Jackson's victory came two weeks after the Treaty of Ghent formally ended the war.

If we look to the history of other nations, ancient or modern, we find no example of a growth so rapid, so gigantic, of a people so prosperous and happy. In contemplating what we have still to perform, the heart of every citizen must expand with joy when he reflects how near our Government has approached to perfection.

James Monroe

5th President • 1817–1825

JAMES MONROE WAS A TALL, SLENDER MAN of modest appearance. His face was plain, his nose was a little large, and few people considered him handsome. According to Monroe biographer Harry Ammon, "His wide-set eyes were his most striking feature. They reflected a warmth confirmed by his smile." In fact, Monroe's greatest political asset was his personable nature.

Monroe didn't really have any enemies. As the nominee of Jefferson's Democratic-Republican party, he had no trouble beating Federalist Rufus King in the 1816 election. And Monroe won so many admirers during his first term as president that the Federalists didn't bother running anyone against him in 1820. When the electoral college met that year, all but one of the electors, Gov. William Plumer of New Hampshire, voted for Monroe. Most people believed that Plumer voted for John Quincy Adams because he wanted Washington to remain the only president elected unanimously. However, Plumer's son later said that his father simply didn't like Monroe. If this is true, he may have been the only American who didn't.

Of course, Monroe was much less of an intellectual than either his mentor, Jefferson, or his friend Madison. He lacked a dynamic speaking voice, and people often complained that he was barely audible. But he had the patience to think through difficult issues, and this, coupled with his natural caution, enabled him to make wise decisions.

The most widely accepted account of Monroe was that published by lawyer William Wirt in 1803: "Nature has given him a mind neither rapid nor rich, and therefore he cannot shine on a subject which is entirely new to him. But to compensate him for this he is endued with a spirit of restless emulation, a judgment strong and clear, and a habit of application which no difficulties can shake, no labours can tire."

Monroe resented Wirt's suggestion that his mind was slow, but he wasn't a vindictive man. In fact, he was quite the opposite. Although acutely sensitive—Monroe's feelings often were hurt even when no slight was intended—he always overcame his pique and never bore a grudge. In 1817, for example, he named Wirt attorney general.

Jefferson summed up Monroe's best qualities—his innate goodness and sincere concern for the feelings of others—when he commented to Madison in 1787: "Turn his soul wrong side outwards and there is not a speck on it."

Monroe had a rugged constitution that helped him endure the many hardships of life in the Continental army.

• The Revolution Beckons

In June 1774, James Monroe left his home in Westmoreland County, Virginia, and entered the College of William and Mary at Williamsburg. The teaching at William and Mary wasn't particularly distinguished, but the college was located in the colonial capital, which made life there very interesting for a plantation-raised youth such as Monroe.

Although not a bad student, Monroe found it difficult to concentrate once the American Revolution began. In the spring of 1776, unable to wait any longer, he enlisted in the Third Virginia Infantry Regiment. Six months later, the eighteen-year-old lieutenant crossed the Delaware with George Washington. In the subsequent battle of Trenton, Washington's ragtag forces surprised and routed nearly a thousand drunken Hessians on the day after Christmas. Monroe was seriously injured in the fighting but eventually recovered and was promoted to captain for his gallantry. He even returned to duty quickly enough to spend the winter of 1777–78 with Washington, this time at Valley Forge.

After leaving the army, Monroe wisely accepted Virginia governor Thomas Jefferson's offer to prepare himself for a career in politics by reading law under Jefferson's direction. Monroe soon became one of Jefferson's most capable protégés.

• Monsieur Monroe

In 1794, George Washington made Monroe his minister to France. On Monroe's arrival there, he was greeted somewhat coldly by the new revolutionary government, but he worked hard to improve relations. Part of the reason for his success was the gusto with which he and his family adopted the French way of life.

The Monroes learned to speak French so fluently that Monroe himself stopped using an interpreter in 1796. They also bought a great deal of French furniture and even sent their daughter Eliza to a French school. Run by Madame Campan, a former lady-in-waiting to Marie Antoinette, the school was highly regarded by officials of the new French government. (Although these men were revolutionaries, they still wanted their children to have all the elegance of the old monarchy.) However, the finish applied by Madame Campan was as much snobbery as it was polish. Her pupils, including Eliza Monroe, became a little too quick to remind others of their excellent breeding and high stations in life.

Above: Monroe as he appeared in 1794 during his first posting to France. Left: A suit of his formal diplomatic clothes.

An early-nineteenth-century map of the Western Hemisphere.

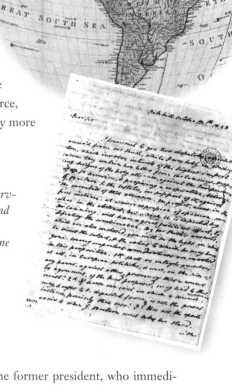

•The Monroe Doctrine

Monroe's secretary of state, John Quincy Adams, had spent nearly half his life in the capitals of Europe. Although Adams generally respected Monroe's abilities, when it came to diplomatic matters, he trusted his own judgment more than the president's. This attitude might have undermined his relationship with a more egocentric boss, but Monroe believed in delegating responsibility and was wise enough to make Adams's shrewd policies his own.

Chief among these policies was the one that later became known as the Monroe Doctrine. On December 2, 1823, as part of his annual message to Congress, President Monroe warned Europe not to meddle in Western Hemisphere affairs. According to the Monroe Doctrine, the United States would act—with force, if necessary—to prevent Europeans from establishing any more colonies in the Americas.

Left: Monroe purchased this Louis XVI desk in 1794 while serving as minister to France. It followed him to various homes and eventually to the White House. On this desk, he signed the Monroe Doctrine. Right: Monroe outlined the proposed doctrine in this October 1823 letter to his mentor, Thomas Jefferson.

★ ★ ★ ★ ★ ★ ★ ★ ★ ★ ★ ★ ★ ★ ★

• The Autobiography

After his retirement from the presidency in 1825, Monroe began work on a book comparing the government of the United States to the governments of other countries, ancient and modern. He gave up the project in 1829, however, after his son-in-law, George Hay, told him, "I think your time could have been better employed. If the framers of our Constitution could have had some work, from a modern standpoint, on the Constitutions of Greece and Rome, it might have been of value to them. I do not think yours is of practical value now." He suggested that Monroe instead write an autobiography.

This idea delighted the former president, who immediately began work on the manuscript. Although the autobiography became the major focus of his last few years, Monroe never completed it.

The sections that do exist reveal very little of their reserved author. Monroe limited his account to the public events in which he participated and added very little that might be called insightful. He even wrote in the third person: "The command then devolved on Lieutenant Monroe, who advanced...at the head of the corps, and was shot down by a musket ball which passed through his breast and shoulder."

Monroe's holster pistols.

★ ★ ★ ★ ★ ★ ★ ★ ★ ★ ★ ★ ★ ★ ★

• Elizabeth Monroe

DURING THE WINTER OF 1786, while attending a session of Congress in New York City, James Monroe fell in love. The object of his affection was Elizabeth Kortright, the daughter of a West Indian merchant who had lost most of his fortune in the Revolution.

Regarded as quite attractive, Elizabeth was well known for her exquisite taste in clothing and accessories. Although her extreme formality made her seem cold in public, in private she became a devoted wife and doting mother. This combination of attitudes was highly desirable during the eighteenth century, when women were expected to focus on home and family, not business and politics.

As first lady, Mrs. Monroe introduced a number of French customs to Washington social life. The most controversial of these concerned the making of social calls. Previous first ladies had always followed the American custom of paying calls on visiting strangers. This had kept them very busy, but some—especially Dolley Madison—had enjoyed the constant socializing.

Elizabeth Monroe, however, had no intention of spending all her time on the social circuit. In fact, the population of Washington had grown so much that making these visits was no longer practical. Instead, she announced that, following the French custom, she would neither make nor return social calls. She did say that she would be at home in the morning to receive visitors, yet when these callers appeared, they were often greeted by Mrs. Monroe's daughter Eliza Hay. Although Elizabeth Monroe's handling of the situation led to much grumbling, Louisa Adams, John Quincy's wife, applauded the new rules and agreed that she could see no reason why Mrs. Monroe (or herself, for that matter) should be "doomed to run after every stranger."

MAJOR POLITICAL EVENTS

★ **American System:** With the War of 1812 over, former War Hawks Henry Clay and John Calhoun proposed a series of ambitious projects designed to improve the nation's infrastructure. The bills that they introduced to Congress for road, bridge, and canal construction were an element of Clay's larger plan, called the American System. Clay argued that internal improvements, combined with protective tariffs and a strong national bank, would help the United States build a stable, self-sufficient economy. President Monroe agreed that the projects were beneficial, but he feared that such extensive public works went well beyond what was permitted by the Constitution.

★ **Missouri Compromise:** The rapid growth of the country, which fueled the prosperity of the Monroe years, also exposed hidden regional tensions over slavery. The balance of power between free and slave states, upon which so much depended, was inherently unstable. Each time new states entered the Union, the balance shifted. Missouri's application for statehood in 1819 made the point well. For more than a year, Congress debated whether or not the federal government could ban slavery in new western states—until Maine's request for statehood in 1820 provided the basis for a compromise. Maine and Missouri were both admitted, Maine as a free state and Missouri as a slave state, thus preserving the balance between slave and free in the Union. In addition, the Missouri Compromise banned slavery in the remainder of the former Louisiana Territory north of latitude 36°30'.

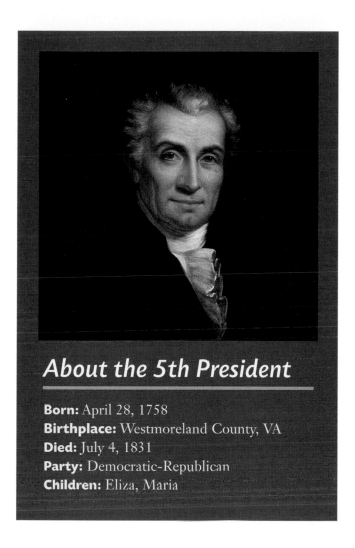

About the 5th President

Born: April 28, 1758
Birthplace: Westmoreland County, VA
Died: July 4, 1831
Party: Democratic-Republican
Children: Eliza, Maria

★ **Supreme Court:** In early 1819, the Supreme Court issued two landmark rulings that significantly limited the power and authority of the states. In February, Chief Justice John Marshall handed down the Court's decision in *Dartmouth College v. Woodward*. This case involved the efforts of the state of New Hampshire to alter the charter of Dartmouth College, originally granted in 1769. Marshall pointed out that Dartmouth's charter was essentially a private contract that a state had no right to change. In the case of *McCulloch v. Maryland*, decided in March, the Court threw out a Maryland state tax on the Second Bank of the United States. The tax was unconstitutional, Marshall explained, because no state can limit the federal government's constitutional powers.

★ ★ ★ ★ ★ ★ ★ ★ ★ ★ ★ ★ ★ ★ ★

During the Monroe Administration

1817	*White opponents of slavery in Virginia organize the American Colonization Society to send free blacks and former slaves to Africa.*
Jan. 5, 1818	*With the voyage of the* James Monroe, *the Black Ball Line begins the first regular transatlantic freight service between the United States and England.*
Apr. 4, 1818	*Congress adopts the familiar stars-and-stripes design for the U.S. flag. To save on cloth, the law limits the number of stripes to thirteen, one for each original colony.*
1820	*Washington Irving publishes* The Sketch Book of Geoffrey Crayon, *which includes "The Legend of Sleepy Hollow" and "Rip Van Winkle."*
1821	*Sequoyah, a half-blood Cherokee, devises an alphabet for the Cherokee language. The system is so simple that most Cherokee quickly learn to read and write.*
1821	*Congress rejects Secretary of State John Quincy Adams's proposal that the United States adopt the new metric system of measurement.*
1823	*James Fenimore Cooper publishes* The Pioneers, *the first of his Leatherstocking Tales. With this novel, he invents a genuinely American genre: the frontier saga.*
Jan. 3, 1825	*Mill owner and social reformer Robert Owen founds New Harmony, Indiana. The town is the first nonreligious utopian community in the United States.*

Less possessed of your confidence in advance than any of my predecessors, I am deeply conscious of the prospect that I shall stand more and oftener in need of your indulgence. Intentions upright and pure, a heart devoted to the welfare of our country, and the unceasing application of all the faculties allotted to me to her service are all the pledges that I can give for the faithful performance of the arduous duties I am to undertake.

J. Q. Adams

John Quincy Adams

6th President • 1825–1829

LIKE HIS FATHER, THE SECOND PRESIDENT, John Quincy Adams kept a detailed series of diaries nearly his entire life. He felt compelled to write in them, not missing a single day between the ages of twenty-nine and forty-nine. "There has perhaps not been another individual of the human race," Adams wrote confidently, "whose daily existence from early childhood to fourscore years has been noted down with his own hand so minutely as mine.

"In his journals, Adams often noted the weaknesses of others, though never to the extent that he recorded his own shortcomings. "I am a man of reserved, cold, austere, and forbidding manners," he wrote with some of his typical exaggeration. But the statement was very nearly true. In the words of one colleague, Adams was "hard as a piece of granite and cold as a lump of ice." His large head, shrill voice, and less-than-pleasant personality didn't make him many friends. Nor did the bouts of vanity, arrogance, and irritability that he had inherited from his father.

In fact, it may seem remarkable that John Quincy Adams ever became president—until one considers his qualifications. Adams's governmental experience, which was unparalleled, included two decades of service as a diplomat in Europe and eight years as secretary of state. He was also widely thought the most learned man in the country; his devotion to public service was rarely challenged, even by his rivals; and his relentless work ethic kept him busy from five in the morning until nearly midnight.

When he became president in 1825, Adams faced a great deal of popular opposition. Because none of the four presidential candidates in 1824 had won the necessary electoral majority, the election had been thrown into the House of Representatives, as required by the Constitution. Andrew Jackson had won the most electoral votes, but Speaker of the House Henry Clay gave his support (and the victory) to Adams. When Adams became president, he made Clay his secretary of state. This led Jackson's supporters to charge that Adams had made a "corrupt bargain" with Clay. The accusation dogged Adams during his entire term.

A modern president would surely have read the polls and offered the Jacksonians some sort of concession to quiet their opposition. However, John Quincy Adams was no democrat. He made decisions not because the people wanted things a certain way, but because he thought that the decisions were right. It didn't matter to him one bit that the nation largely resisted his policies.

• A Precocious Childhood

Born in 1767, John Quincy Adams was the second child (and first son) of John and Abigail Adams. John Adams's brief retirement from public life following his defense of the soldiers charged in the Boston Massacre allowed him to spend a good deal of time with his young son. With this solid beginning, their relationship became close, if not outwardly affectionate.

It pleased John Adams very much that his oldest son was a precocious child. John Quincy was so bright and well mannered that his father took him to Europe on diplomatic missions in 1778 and 1780. Educated in Paris, Amsterdam, and Leyden, as well as by his father, the boy seemed, by his teen years, already a mature adult and was treated that way. In 1781, the fourteen-year-old left school and traveled to St. Petersburg, where he served as private secretary to Francis Dana, the U.S. minister to Russia. John Quincy enjoyed the exposure, and his fluency in several languages served Dana well.

Shortly after John Adams was dispatched to London in 1785, John Quincy returned home and entered Harvard College. After his experiences in Europe, he found American college life rather dull and graduated in just two years.

John Singleton Copley painted this portrait of John Quincy Adams in 1796.

★ ★

• Out to Get the Adamses

Even more than his father, John Quincy Adams was defensive about the Adams family name. Sometimes he was so blinded by his paranoia that he couldn't tell when his political opponents were actually being sincere and reasonable. Instead, all he could see was that they were, once again, out to get the Adamses.

In 1835, he even wrote down a list of names, some belonging to former allies. The thirteen men on this list, he insisted, had devoted themselves to plotting "base and dirty tricks to thwart my progress in life." Fortunately, Adams restricted most of these rantings to his diaries.

Left: A tankard belonging to John Quincy Adams. Above right: The original manuscript of a poem he once composed.

• Regularity

It's difficult to say whether the serious-minded Adams ever *enjoyed* anything, but he certainly took great satisfaction in making his life as regular and precise as possible. As president, he rose at precisely five in the morning (four-fifteen during summer). He then made his own fire, read his Bible, and set out for his morning swim in the Potomac.

Adams preferred to swim in the nude—he thought it more invigorating that way—but this habit had its drawbacks. One day when someone stole his clothes, Adams was forced to stop a passing boy and send him to the White House for a new set. On a far more famous occasion, he was surprised by newspaperwoman Anne Royall, who sat on the president's clothes and refused to get up until he had agreed to grant her an interview. Adams answered her questions while bobbing naked, chin-deep, in the water.

The five-foot-seven-inch, 175-pound Adams typically dressed plainly and without great care.

• The Need to Serve

It has been said that Adamses serve but they don't campaign—nor, apparently, do they win second terms as president. During his 1828 rematch against Jackson, John Quincy Adams refused either to defend himself or to make countercharges, considering both courses beneath his dignity. He kept silent and was soundly beaten. Disgusted, he refused to attend Jackson's inauguration, just as his father had snubbed Jefferson three decades earlier. "The sun of my political life sets in the deepest gloom," he wrote in his diary.

However, being an Adams, he still felt the need to serve. When constituents from his Massachusetts district asked him to run for Congress in 1830, he told them that he would, even though he was well past sixty, on two conditions: He would never publicly solicit their votes and he would not feel bound to follow their wishes. Adams's election to the House that year became one of the great satisfactions of his life.

During his nine postpresidential terms in Congress, Adams suffered two strokes on the House floor. Following the second one on February 21, 1848, he was carried from his desk to the Speaker's Room, where he died two days later. "Where could death have found him," Sen. Thomas Hart Benton asked, "but at the post of duty?"

The desk used by John Quincy Adams in the House of Representatives.

• Louisa Adams

SINCE BOYHOOD, JOHN QUINCY ADAMS had been a lonely sort. As he spent his teenage years in so many foreign lands, that may have been understandable. But as he grew into manhood, it became clear that his loneliness had become part of his character. Sadly, his marriage did little to change things.

While in England on a diplomatic errand, the twenty-nine-year-old Adams met and courted Louisa Catherine Johnson, the daughter of American consul Joshua Johnson and his English-born wife. Adams had consciously set out to find a suitable bride, and when he learned that the Johnsons had three daughters of marriageable age (Louisa was the middle child), he became a regular guest at their home. Often, after dinner, he would grab his hat and leave when the girls began to sing—he disliked most music, especially female singing—but was usually back again the next night for another visit.

Although twenty-two when she married, the only foreign-born first lady later admitted that "in knowledge of the world I was not fifteen." Before Adams, she had never been left alone with a man. When he finally (and awkwardly) revealed his intention to marry her, she found herself being "coaxed into an affection." She later regretted her decision. In fact, while living at the White House, she began but never completed an autobiography in which she condemned her husband (and all the Adams men) for being cold and insensitive to women.

MAJOR POLITICAL EVENTS

★ **Internal Improvements:** President Adams made Clay's American System—a program of protective tariffs, internal improvements, and a strong national bank—the focus of his administration. Although most of his initiatives were blocked by Jacksonians in Congress, Adams was able to spur the construction of several new roads, bridges, and canals. On July 4, 1828, he turned over the first spade of dirt for the Chesapeake & Ohio Canal. The C&O was designed to carry freight across the Allegheny Mountains. Its backers hoped to compete successfully with the Baltimore & Ohio Railroad, but the canal was never completed.

★ **Panama Congress:** In 1826, several newly independent Latin American republics held a congress in Panama. The organizer of the event, Simón Bolívar of Venezuela, wanted to promote friendship in the region and encourage a unified policy toward Spain among its former colonial possessions. When ministers from Mexico and Colombia invited the United States to attend, Adams was delighted. However, opposition among southerners was strong because all of the Latin American republics attending the congress had outlawed slavery. Southern congressmen particularly objected to American ministers negotiating with black and mixed-race foreigners. Allowing white diplomats to treat nonwhites, even foreign nonwhites, with respect would have undermined the principal justification for slavery—that nonwhites were inferior. With the help of northern Jacksonians, who objected to the mission simply because Adams had arranged

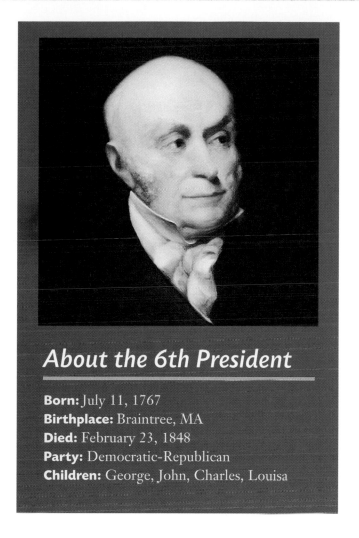

About the 6th President

Born: July 11, 1767
Birthplace: Braintree, MA
Died: February 23, 1848
Party: Democratic-Republican
Children: George, John, Charles, Louisa

it, southerners in Congress were able to delay funding the trip long enough to make attendance impossible.

★ **Tariff of Abominations:** Looking for yet another way to discredit Adams, the Jacksonians in Congress proposed a tariff bill that raised rates across the board, on raw materials as well as on imported goods. Adams's home region of New England had long demanded high tariff rates on imported goods in order to shelter its developing industrial economy, but higher tariffs on raw materials would also increase costs. Because of this, no one expected the bill to pass—its purpose was merely to embarrass the president. However, New England congressmen saw the bill as their only chance for tariff reform, and—to everyone's amazement—they pushed it through. The South, which yearned for cheap imports, called it the Tariff of Abominations.

★ ★ ★ ★ ★ ★ ★ ★ ★ ★ ★ ★ ★ ★ ★ ★

During the Adams Administration

Oct. 26, 1825   *The Erie Canal opens after eight years of construction. The first boat to travel the 363-mile canal is the* Seneca Chief. *Freight rates between Buffalo and New York City drop immediately from one hundred dollars a ton to ten dollars a ton.*

1825   *Six hundred Boston carpenters strike for a ten-hour workday. Their victory encourages the new and growing labor movement.*

May 13, 1826   *Steam-engine pioneer John Stevens demonstrates the first U.S. steam locomotive on a half-mile track on his estate in Hoboken, New Jersey.*

Feb. 1827   *New Orleans holds its first Mardi Gras celebration. The name, which means "fat Tuesday" in French, refers to the practice of using up all the fats in one's house before the beginning of Lent.*

Mar. 16, 1827   *John Brown Russwurm and Samuel E. Cornish begin publishing* Freedom's Journal, *the first black-owned newspaper in the United States.*

1827   *John James Audubon publishes* The Birds of America, *which contains 435 color plates of his paintings along with written descriptions of the birds. When he fails to find a U.S. publisher, Audubon prints the book with a London firm.*

July 4, 1828   *Charles Carroll, the richest American, breaks ground for the Baltimore & Ohio Railroad. Although not the first U.S. railroad to be chartered, the B&O will be the first to begin regular operation.*

Without union our independence and liberty would never have been achieved; without union they never can be maintained.... The loss of liberty, of all good government, of peace, plenty, and happiness, must inevitably follow a dissolution of the Union.

Andrew Jackson

7th President • 1829–1837

ANDREW JACKSON WAS A FIREBRAND. A duelist, an Indian fighter, and a war hero, he was a stalwart friend and relentless enemy. Many people adored him and some hated him; but few Americans could say that they were indifferent to the man.

Jackson's political career has great historic significance. His rise to the presidency marked an important change in the way Americans did their governmental business. His immediate predecessor, John Quincy Adams, was typical of the aristocrats who had been America's revolutionary leaders. These men had been *for*, but not *of*, the people. Few Americans of the time could have imagined having dinner with an Adams, but they could have pictured themselves sharing a jug of home brew with Old Hickory.

Not everyone thought that this was such a good thing. In 1824, Thomas Jefferson warned that Jackson's "passions are terrible. I feel very much alarmed at the prospect of seeing General Jackson president." According to John Quincy Adams, Jackson was "a barbarian who could scarcely spell his own name."

But most American voters were also poor spellers, and they thought Jackson was an excellent fellow. He particularly appealed to frontiersmen, small farmers, factory workers, and other "common" people, who believed that he would faithfully represent their interests against those of the "uncommon" people—the bankers, merchants, and plantation owners.

Jackson's candidacy also came at the right time, just after most states had changed the way they voted for president. In the past, electors had been chosen exclusively by state legislatures. Now every state but Delaware and South Carolina chose its electors by popular vote.

Jackson wasn't a shrewd politician, but a popularity contest was one that he knew how to win. During the War of 1812, he had found himself encamped near Natchez, Mississippi, faced with an order to disband his Tennessee volunteers. The men were eight hundred miles from home, still unpaid, and lacking adequate food and transportation. Suspecting that the order was part of a plan to draft his men into the regular army, Jackson refused to obey it. Instead, he spent his own money on wagons for the sick and wounded and twelve thousand dollars of unauthorized army money on supplies.

During the march back to Tennessee, he gave up all three of his horses to sick men and walked the entire way, handing out food and water. He also supervised personally the widening of roads and construction of bridges. Somewhere along the way, the story goes, one of his soldiers turned to another and remarked of the general, "He's tough, tough as old hickory."

• Hatred for the British

Andrew Jackson was born in a frontier region of South Carolina, the third son of poor Scotch-Irish immigrants. He was the only member of his family to survive the Revolution.

Jackson's fiery personality displayed itself early when, at age thirteen, he joined the Continental army. Captured by the British—he was the only president to have been a prisoner of war—Jackson was ordered to clean an officer's boots. When Jackson refused, the cavalryman drew his saber and slashed the boy's head. The scar, and his hatred of the British, remained with him all his life.

Jackson's formal military career began in 1802, when he was made major general of the Tennessee militia. During the

The artist who created this poor likeness of Jackson must have thought that because the general acted like Napoleon, he must have looked like Napoleon, too.

War of 1812, he earned a reputation as an Indian fighter by defeating the Creeks in a number of important battles. However, his greatest success came at New Orleans, where his undermanned army turned back an invasion force of elite British marines. The battle was fought two weeks after the signing of the Treaty of Ghent, which ended the war. But word hadn't yet reached New Orleans, and many historians agree that had the British won the battle, they would have kept the city.

This detail from an anti-Jackson broadside illustrates an incident in which Jackson stabbed a man with a sword hidden inside his cane.

Andrew Jackson, ca. 1830.

• Dueling

Jackson most likely inherited his combativeness from his mother. "Never sue for assault or slander," she reportedly told him, "settle them cases yourself." Jackson always did so. His preferred method was to thrash his enemies publicly, often caning them into submission. But when his honor was called into question by a "gentleman," Jackson took to the field of honor.

He participated in three duels. The first, a misunderstanding, ended with both parties firing into the air. During the second, Jackson and Tennessee governor John Sevier never stopped cursing each other long enough to fire their weapons.

Jackson's third duel was with Charles Dickinson, a Nashville lawyer who had insulted Jackson's wife. Because Dickinson was a quicker and better shot, Jackson decided to take Dickinson's bullet before returning fire. Fortunately for the skinny Jackson, his loose-fitting clothes confused Dickinson, whose bullet missed Jackson's heart by just an inch. Jackson grimaced but remained upright, took careful aim, and killed Dickinson.

The personal effects shown here include Jackson's spectacles, a miniature portrait of his wife, his George Washington memorial pin, and his pocket watch. The dollar note from the Bank of East Tennessee features the general's portrait.

• Man of the People

Jackson's inauguration on March 4, 1829, vividly demonstrated that his election was a turning point in American history. Certainly, earlier presidents had been devoted to the people, but none had yet been so clearly one of them.

Thousands of ordinary people journeyed to Washington, D.C., to see their hero take his oath of office. Afterward, most of them followed Jackson back to the White House, where they mobbed the mansion, causing a great deal of damage. In their exhilaration, the merrymakers broke dishes, ripped draperies, and trampled on furniture with their muddy boots. Elegant chairs were "profaned by the feet of clodhoppers," one of the invited guests remarked. According to another story, a young Democratic girl was found by her parents jumping up and down on a sofa in the president's private quarters. "Just think, Mama," she said. "This sofa is a millionth part mine!"

Jackson himself felt it necessary to escape the jubilant crowd through a back door. Yet even after he left, the party didn't break up until the White House servants cleverly moved the punch tubs out onto the lawn.

★ ★ ★ ★ ★ ★ ★ ★ ★ ★ ★ ★ ★ ★ ★

• King Andrew

Jackson's political enemies called him King Andrew—and with good reason. More than any president before him, Jackson made vigorous use of his executive power: For example, he vetoed twelve bills, more than all the previous six presidents *combined*. He was also given to quick-tempered remarks: When South Carolina threatened to secede from the Union over high tariffs, Jackson warned, "If one drop of blood be shed…in defiance of the laws of the United States, I will hang the first man of them I can get my hands on to the first tree I can find."

"When Andrew Jackson hated," biographer Robert Remini has observed, "it often became grand passion. He could hate with a Biblical fury and would resort to petty and vindictive acts to nurture his hatred and keep it bright and strong and ferocious. He needed revenge. He always struck back."

★ ★ ★ ★ ★ ★ ★ ★ ★ ★ ★ ★ ★ ★ ★ ★ ★ ★

• Rachel Jackson

AFTER THE REVOLUTIONARY WAR, Andrew Jackson became a lawyer. In 1788, he settled in Tennessee, where he built a successful practice and acquired both land and slaves. While boarding in Nashville with the Donelsons, he met and fell in love with his landlady's daughter. Several years earlier, Rachel Donelson had married a Kentucky man named Lewis Robards, but Robards, given to outrageous fits of jealousy, had accused his young wife of infidelity and sent her away.

When Robards later came to Nashville to collect his wife, she dutifully returned with him. But his jealous rages hadn't subsided, and when Jackson learned of Rachel's unhappiness, he dashed off to Kentucky and rescued her. Robards then took steps to sue for divorce, while Jackson, who mistakenly believed that Robards had already obtained one, "married" Rachel. In fact, Robards had not yet sued for divorce, and Jackson, a lawyer, should have known better.

When Robards learned that Jackson and his wife were living together, he sued successfully for divorce on the grounds of adultery, which mortified Rachel and infuriated Jackson. He and Rachel were married again, this time legally, in 1794. Yet the scandal didn't end there. It became a leading point of character assassination during the 1828 presidential campaign.

Jackson tried to shield his wife, but she eventually learned that her reputation had become the scuttlebutt of the national press. This news, combined with her chronic heart trouble, caused Mrs. Jackson to become seriously ill. She died on December 22, 1828. At her funeral, Jackson wept: "In the presence of this dear saint I can and do forgive my enemies. But those vile wretches [his voice rose] who have slandered her must look to God for mercy!"

MAJOR POLITICAL EVENTS

★ **Nullification Crisis:** After taking office in 1829, Jackson's vice president, John C. Calhoun, quietly orchestrated a relentless campaign against the Tariff of Abominations. Calhoun argued that a state, such as his native South Carolina, could nullify, or refuse to obey, any federal law that harmed its interests. Like most Americans, Jackson hated the 1828 tariff, but as president he felt obligated to enforce it. A crisis developed in November 1832, when the South Carolina legislature approved the Ordinance of Nullification. This state law pronounced the Tariff of Abominations "null, void, and no law" and threatened secession if the tariff continued to be enforced. In December, after rein-forcing the federal garrison in Charleston, Jackson warned South Carolina that federal laws must be obeyed. "Disunion by armed force is treason," he declared. Henry Clay resolved the standoff by shepherding through Congress the Compromise Tariff of 1833, which gradually reduced tariff rates on manufactured goods.

★ **Second Bank of the United States:** After allowing the charter of the first national bank to expire, Congress authorized the creation of a Second Bank of the United States in 1816 as part of Henry Clay's American System. The bank's president, Nicholas Biddle, made money more difficult to borrow, which stabilized the national currency but angered western farmers, whose prosperity depended on easy credit. During the 1832 campaign, Jackson took up the farmers' cause. "The Bank, Mr. Van Buren,

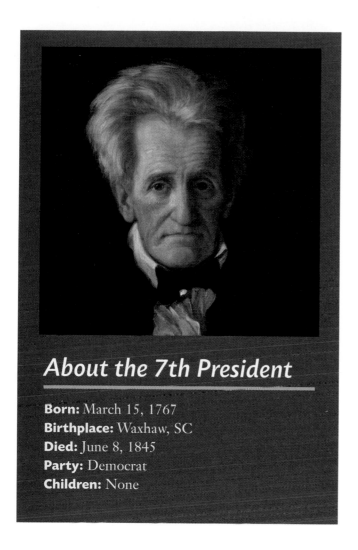

About the 7th President

Born: March 15, 1767
Birthplace: Waxhaw, SC
Died: June 8, 1845
Party: Democrat
Children: None

is trying to kill me," he told his vice-presidential candidate, "but I will kill it." In September 1833, Jackson ordered Treasury Secretary William Duane to "kill" the "monster bank" by shifting federal funds to state banks. When Duane refused, Jackson replaced him with future Supreme Court Justice Roger B. Taney, who carried out the order.

★ **Specie Circular:** After ordering the withdrawal of federal funds from the Second Bank, Jackson began to worry that the availability of easy credit was encouraging too much land speculation. In July 1836, he issued the Specie Circular, which required purchasers of public land to pay for the land with gold or silver coin rather than with paper money. This abrupt reversal of policy bankrupted most speculators and shook the entire economy, causing the financial panic of 1837.

During the Jackson Administration

Oct. 16, 1829
The Tremont House, the first modern U.S. hotel, opens in Boston. Its 170 rooms feature such luxuries as private rooms with door locks and indoor (but shared) toilets.

1829
New York inventor Peter Cooper designs a compact steam-powered locomotive that he calls Tom Thumb. It generates a speed of fifteen miles per hour during its first test.

Apr. 6, 1830
Joseph Smith founds the Church of Jesus Christ of Latter-day Saints and soon publishes The Book of Mormon.

1830
Sylvester Graham begins promoting his whole-wheat Graham cracker. A "nutritional moralist," he encourages people to eat vegetables while avoiding sweets and fats.

Aug. 21, 1831
Virginia slave Nat Turner leads the first and only sustained slave revolt in U.S. history. The rebels kill about sixty whites.

1831
Cyrus H. McCormick makes the first working model of an automatic grain reaper in his father's workshop.

1832
Baltimore merchant Isaac McKim commissions the Ann McKim, the first true clipper ship. Its narrow hull and sharp bow make it the fastest merchant ship on the seas.

Feb. 25, 1836
Samuel Colt patents a six-shot handgun that he calls a "revolver" because the bullets are held in a revolving cylinder.

Mar. 6, 1836
Mexican troops storm the Alamo, an abandoned mission in San Antonio, where 187 besieged Texans have been holding out for twelve days.

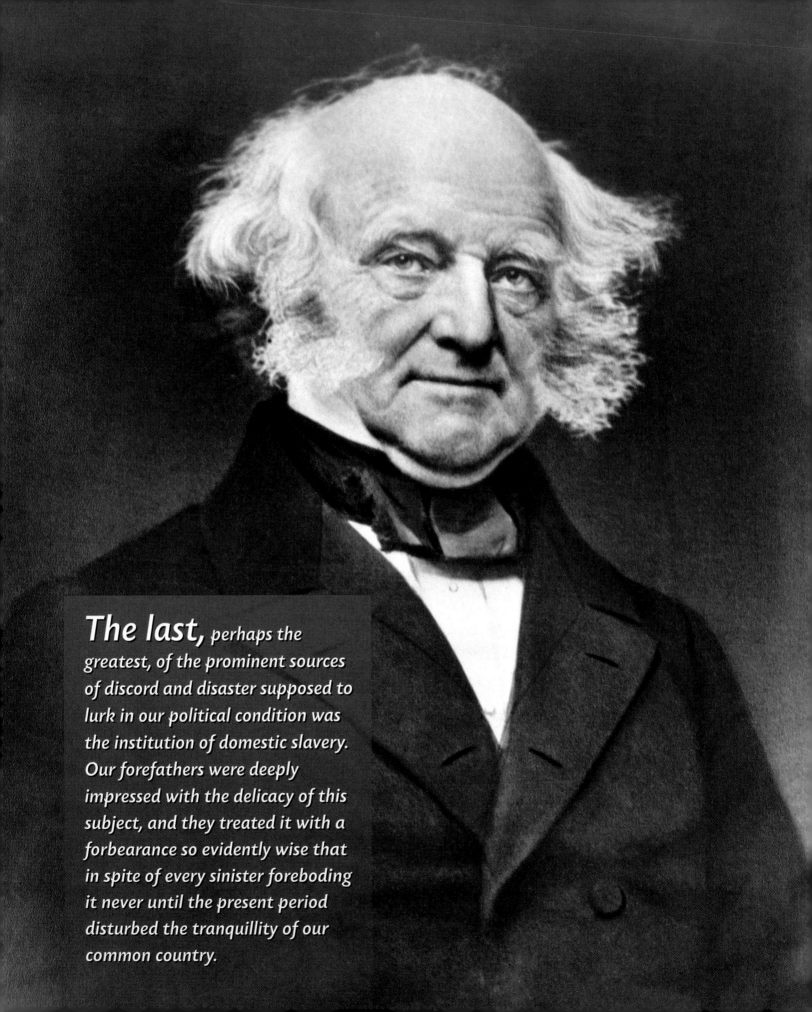

The last, perhaps the greatest, of the prominent sources of discord and disaster supposed to lurk in our political condition was the institution of domestic slavery. Our forefathers were deeply impressed with the delicacy of this subject, and they treated it with a forbearance so evidently wise that in spite of every sinister foreboding it never until the present period disturbed the tranquillity of our common country.

Martin Van Buren

8th President • 1837–1841

MOST PRESIDENTIAL NICKNAMES, being silly campaign devices, are quickly forgotten. (Did anyone really call James Monroe the Last of the Cocked Hats?) But Martin Van Buren actually was known by several nicknames. The most common of these, the Little Magician and the Red Fox of Kinderhook, echoed his reputation as a shrewd politician who wheeled and dealed behind the scenes. Undoubtedly, this was true.

Yet what were Van Buren's goals? What purpose did his manipulations have? These are much more difficult questions, and Van Buren himself rarely let on. As a founding member of the Albany Regency, the political group that ran New York State during the 1820s, Van Buren was the first politician in the country to oppose the jailing of debtors. He also helped rewrite laws that had kept poor people from voting. Later, as his career flourished, Van Buren lost touch with these issues and instead began to focus on party and personal success: He worried now about how the Democrats might please both North and South and about his own chances of winning the presidency.

"Since [Van Buren] never intentionally revealed himself to others," historian Donald B. Cole has written, "anyone studying him must peel off several layers before reaching the inner man."

The outermost layer, the social Van Buren, craved comfort, loved flirting with married women, and rarely passed up an opportunity to gossip with his cronies. "But," Cole continues, "Van Buren's obvious social and political assets masked liabilities. Though certainly not dull, he was not exciting either, for in spite of his flamboyant appearance he was blessed with neither style, presence, nor charisma."

Deep inside, Van Buren was an overwhelmingly cautious man: He flirted with women but never dared have an affair. He used favors to build political capital but never dared gamble with it.

A famous story about Van Buren concerns a senator who once tried to pin him down on a matter of astrophysics. "Matt," the senator said, "it's been rumored that the sun rises in the East. Do you believe it?" "Well, Senator," Van Buren replied, "I understand that's the common acceptance, but as I never get up till after dawn, I really can't say."

One of the most interesting things about this story is that Van Buren included it in his autobiography. Did he really believe that cleverness was more important than conviction? Probably not, deep inside. But one gets the feeling that Van Buren, hungry for popularity, would have done almost anything for a laugh.

The youthful Martin Van Buren.

• Dutch Boy

Martin Van Buren was the first president born an American citizen (the first seven had all been born before the Revolutionary War). His parents were of Dutch ancestry, and the Van Burens usually spoke Dutch at home. A slight Dutch accent stayed with Van Buren all his life, and it reportedly became more pronounced whenever he got excited.

Martin's was the sixth Van Buren generation in the New World. His family, however, hadn't been upwardly mobile. His father, Abraham, was a struggling farmer in New York's Hudson River Valley. When Abraham Van Buren finally realized that farming wouldn't support his family, he converted his farmhouse into a tavern.

Fortunately, the Van Buren tavern in Kinderhook, New York, became a favorite watering hole for politicians on their way to and from the state capital, Albany. Working beside his father in the tavern, Martin met a number of men, including Alexander Hamilton and Aaron Burr, who piqued his interest in politics. He also learned, from living in such close quarters with strangers, the useful art of compromise, for which he later became famous.

★ ★ ★ ★ ★ ★ ★ ★ ★ ★ ★ ★ ★ ★ ★ ★ ★

• What a Dandy

Throughout his political career, but especially as president, Van Buren suffered from his reputation as a dandy. There was some merit to it: He did enjoy the theater and the opera, fine foods and fine wines, flashy coaches and expensive clothing. He liked to wear coats with velvet collars and tight-fitting soft leather gloves.

Davy Crockett, no friend of Van Buren's, once said that the New Yorker was "as opposite to General Jackson as dung is to a diamond…. He struts and swaggers like a crow in the gutter. He is laced up in corsets, such as women in town wear and, if possible, tighter than the best of them. It would be difficult to say, from his personal appearance, whether he was man or woman, but for his large…whiskers."

During the 1840 campaign, a Whig congressman from Pennsylvania complained that Van Buren "luxuriated in sloth and effeminacy" and accused the president of wearing the same perfume as Queen Victoria.

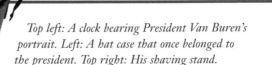

Top left: A clock bearing President Van Buren's portrait. Left: A hat case that once belonged to the president. Top right: His shaving stand.

CAUCUS on the SURPLUS BILL.

A political cartoon from the period of the Jackson administration.

According to some scholars, Van Buren's nickname Old Kinderhook may have been the source for the slang phrase O.K.

• Opposites Attract

The relationship that developed between Andrew Jackson and Martin Van Buren might be proof that opposites do indeed attract. Van Buren first came to Jackson's attention in the late 1820s, when Van Buren was a U.S. senator from New York. They befriended each other, and Van Buren became a key adviser to Jackson during his successful 1828 presidential campaign. Jackson then made Van Buren his secretary of state.

Their bond was strengthened even further during the Peggy Eaton affair. John Eaton, Jackson's secretary of war, was Peggy's second husband. Previously, she had been married to John Timberlake, a civilian navy employee who had spent most of his time at sea. To keep herself busy and supplement her husband's salary, Peggy Timberlake had run a boardinghouse in Washington, D.C., where John Eaton had been one of her regular guests. Soon after John Timberlake's death in 1828, Eaton had married Peggy.

According to widespread gossip, however, Peggy had been having an affair with Eaton while still married to Timberlake. As a result, the wives of most cabinet members considered the new Mrs. Eaton a hussy and refused to socialize with her.

Jackson, on the other hand, remembered that his own wife had been treated in a similar way. He also suspected that the shunning of Peggy Eaton was part of an elaborate political plot against his administration. For these reasons, the president became obsessed with defending Peggy Eaton's honor.

The uproar that the affair caused provided Van Buren with a perfect opportunity to gain ground with the president. He called on Mrs. Eaton as soon as he arrived in Washington and socialized with her openly. As time went on, his behavior so endeared him to Jackson that the president dropped Vice President John Calhoun from the ticket in 1832 (Mrs. Calhoun had left Washington rather than be seen with Peggy) and put Van Buren in his place.

★ ★ ★ ★ ★ ★ ★ ★ ★ ★ ★ ★ ★ ★ ★ ★

• Hannah Van Buren

ALREADY A SUCCESSFUL LAWYER, Martin Van Buren decided at twenty-four that it was time he got married. As was his family's custom, he looked for a bride who shared his Dutch ancestry and chose his childhood sweetheart, Hannah Hoes. Her family had also lived in Kinderhook for many generations, and as one might expect, the Hoeses and the Van Burens were related in several ways. By the closest relationship, Hannah was Martin's first cousin once removed.

The couple had four children, all boys, before Hannah died of tuberculosis in 1819. At the time of her death, when Van Buren was a New York state senator, he wrote of his wife that she was "modest and unassuming" with a "mild" disposition. We know little else about his feelings for her, because he mentioned her rarely in his correspondence and not at all in the nearly eight hundred pages of his autobiography.

Hannah's death left the thirty-six-year-old Van Buren with four sons, ranging from two to eleven, to raise on his own. In the years that followed, he pursued several flirtatious correspondences with eligible women—in the early 1820s, he was rumored to be courting Ellen Randolph, a granddaughter of Thomas Jefferson—but none of these ever became intimate enough to lead to marriage.

When Van Buren moved into the White House in 1837 without a wife or daughter, he had no official hostess. In November 1838, however, that situation was remedied when his oldest son, Abraham, married Angelica Singleton, the daughter of a wealthy South Carolina cotton planter and Dolley Madison's cousin.

MAJOR POLITICAL EVENTS

★ **Panic of 1837:** President Van Buren was inaugurated in March 1837. In May, the United States was hit by its worst economic crisis yet. The financial panic of 1837 dominated Van Buren's term and cost him reelection in 1840. It wasn't his fault. Instead, blame for the crisis truly belonged to Andrew Jackson, whose crusade against the Second Bank had subordinated stable economic policy to Jackson's personal hatred for bank president Nicholas Biddle. When the Specie Circular of 1836 required purchasers of public land to pay in gold or silver, the value of paper money plummeted, causing runaway inflation. The panic formally began on May 10, 1837, when several New York City banks stopped redeeming paper money with gold. Nearly a thousand banks around the country failed, people working on bank-financed construction projects lost their jobs, and hungry people rioted for food in some cities.

★ *Caroline* **Affair:** In late 1837, Canadians seeking an end to British colonial rule attacked Toronto. Losing the battle, the rebels fled to Navy Island in the Niagara River, which separated the United States from Canada. Using the steamship *Caroline*, American sympathizers ferried food, arms, and supplies to the rebels. British colonial authorities ordered loyal Canadian troops to destroy the *Caroline*, which was seized in U.S. waters, set aflame, and sent over Niagara Falls. One American died in the December 29 attack, which Van Buren denounced as "an outrage of a most aggravated character." He sent troops to the

About the 8th President

Born: December 5, 1782
Birthplace: Kinderhook, NY
Died: July 24, 1862
Party: Democrat
Children: Abraham, John, Martin Jr., Smith

★ ★ ★ ★ ★ ★ ★ ★ ★ ★ ★ ★ ★ ★

During the Van Buren Administration

1837   *Illinois blacksmith John Deere makes the first steel plow out of a circular saw blade. Deere's invention greatly improves farming in the Midwest, where prairie soils tend to stick to cast-iron blades.*

1837   *Nathaniel Hawthorne publishes* Twice-Told Tales, *his first collection of short stories issued under his own name.*

Apr. 8-23, 1838   The Great Western *makes the first regular transatlantic steamship voyage. It takes fifteen days, half the time required by a normal sailing ship.*

1838   *Samuel F. B. Morse creates a dot-and-dash system for communicating via the telegraph.*

July 1839   *Fifty-three slaves being shipped between Cuban ports mutiny aboard the Spanish ship* Amistad. *They kill all but two of the ship's crew and order the survivors to guide the ship to Africa. Instead, the Spaniards sail toward the United States, where the slaves are arrested.*

1839   *Mississippi becomes the first state to grant property rights to married women.*

1839   *Charles Goodyear accidentally drops rubber mixed with sulfur onto a hot stove, thus discovering the process of vulcanization. Vulcanized rubber is tougher and less sticky than raw rubber.*

1839   *Magazine editor Edgar Allan Poe publishes* Tales of the Grotesque and Arabesque. *This collection of short stories with supernatural themes includes "The Fall of the House of Usher."*

border yet resisted calls for war. Relations with Britain remained strained for the next five years.

★ **Independent Treasury Act:** Being a Jacksonian Democrat, Van Buren wasn't about to propose a new national bank. However, he couldn't ignore the fact that federal funds had been lost when state banks failed during the panic of 1837. These losses persuaded him that the federal government needed its own secure depositories. Van Buren's solution was the Independent Treasury Act of 1840, which established a system of regional subtreasuries. When the Whigs came to power in 1841, they repealed the independent treasury system but failed to charter a new national bank. When control of Congress passed back to the Democrats after the 1844 election, the subtreasuries were reestablished.

Our citizens must be content with the exercise of the powers with which the Constitution clothes them. The attempt of those of one State to control the domestic institutions of another can only result in feelings of distrust and jealousy, the certain harbingers of disunion, violence, and civil war, and the ultimate destruction of our free institutions.

William Henry Harrison

9th President • 1841

DURING THE 1830s, Henry Clay, Daniel Webster, and other political enemies of Andrew Jackson formed a new party. The Whigs loosely followed Clay's probusiness policies, but what really held them together was their hatred of Jackson and the Democrats. This made picking a presidential candidate tricky, because the wrong one could break up the fragile Whig coalition.

In December 1839, when the Whigs nominated William Henry Harrison for president, the sixty-six-year-old former general was enjoying his retirement in North Bend, Ohio, earning some extra money as a court clerk. Although Harrison had been one of three Whig candidates in 1836, he was by no means a party leader. In fact, Harrison's career as a politician (not to mention as a general) had been mediocre.

The Whigs picked him because he was considered a war hero and seemed to be cooperative. (Harrison's nickname, Tippecanoe, referred to his "great" victory over the Shawnee at Tippecanoe Creek.) Even more important, unlike Clay and Webster, Harrison had no well-known views that might make him controversial.

It was made clear to Harrison that he should keep quiet during the campaign. He was also told that, if he was elected, he should take his directions in Washington from Clay and Webster. If Harrison had any objections to this plan, he never voiced them.

The 1840 campaign—famous for the slogan "Tippecanoe and Tyler, Too"—was particularly frivolous. As one Jacksonian newspaper complained, "We could meet the Whigs on the field of argument and beat them without effort. But when they lay down the weapons of argument and attack us with musical notes, what can we do?" For the first time, mindless campaign souvenirs, including songbooks, were everywhere.

Harrison's campaign hoopla might have been less effective, however, if the panic of 1837 hadn't caused such a deep and ongoing depression. The hard times had made Martin Van Buren very unpopular and just about handed the White House to the Whigs. All that the party asked of Harrison was that he follow orders and stay alive.

The new president was thought by the people who knew him to be considerate, genial, and benevolent. In fact, his personal charm had been his strength all along. However, he could be too generous and often promised things he couldn't deliver. During the 1840 campaign, for example, he promised cabinet appointments two and three times over. As a result, after his election he was mobbed by people seeking government jobs. What little time he had in office he spent fending them off.

• An Aristocrat Joins the Army

The youngest of seven children, William Henry Harrison didn't grow up in a log cabin, as his campaign handlers later boasted. Actually, he spent his childhood in a three-story brick mansion on his family's large Virginia estate. He was tutored privately until age fourteen, when he left home to become a premedical student.

In the spring of 1791, he moved to Philadelphia to begin medical school at the University of Pennsylvania. But just as he arrived, he received news that his father, a signer of the Declaration of Independence, had died. At first, Harrison obeyed his father's instructions to continue his medical education. Yet that fall, when his money ran out, he was forced to abandon his studies. Not wanting to live out his life as an impoverished aristocrat, Harrison joined the army and headed west.

Harrison's most famous military victory came against the Shawnee at Tippecanoe Creek in 1811. During this battle, Harrison's thousand-man army managed to fight off an Indian force of about six hundred men.

★ ★

• Humanitarian

On several occasions, Harrison's campaign biography points out the general's wonderful humanitarian qualities. One of the incidents described, an alleged assassination attempt just before the battle of Tippecanoe, involves a "negro" who

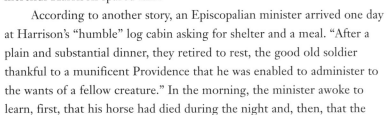

was arrested while "lurking near the Governor's marquee." After the battle, a drumhead court-martial sentenced the man to death, though the merciful Harrison spared him.

According to another story, an Episcopalian minister arrived one day at Harrison's "humble" log cabin asking for shelter and a meal. "After a plain and substantial dinner, they retired to rest, the good old soldier thankful to a munificent Providence that he was enabled to administer to the wants of a fellow creature." In the morning, the minister awoke to learn, first, that his horse had died during the night and, then, that the devout general had graciously provided him with a new one. The minister initially refused to accept the gift, but "he who giveth to the poor lendeth to the Lord," said Harrison before sending the man on his way.

These stories are no doubt exaggerations, yet Harrison was a bit of a humanitarian. As governor of Indiana between 1800 and 1812, he was considered fair and compassionate in his treatment of Indians. And in 1811, he even won a slander suit against a man who had accused him of cheating some local tribesmen.

• Log Cabins and Hard Cider

During the 1840 campaign, thinking the statement was an insult to Harrison, a Democratic newspaper in Baltimore wrote, "Give him a barrel of hard cider and a pension of two thousand a year, and, our word for it, he will sit the remainder of his days in his log cabin…and study moral philosophy." This sarcastic remark was meant to call attention to Harrison's lack of intellectual depth. Instead, it spawned the enormously successful "log cabin and hard cider" campaign.

The Democrats, of course, tried to fight back, calling Harrison General Mum because he rarely spoke out on public issues. In fact, Harrison was the first presidential candidate to make campaign speeches, but these were mostly fluff, and he never mentioned any subjects that might be controversial. "Probably most Americans knew that the log-cabin campaign was humbug," one historian has noted. "But they *liked* humbug."

As one Washington pundit remarked, the only mandate won by the Whigs in the 1840 campaign was to tear down the Capitol and build a log cabin in its place.

• Death in Office

In general, President-elect Harrison did as he was told. The only trouble he made came just before his March 4 inauguration, when he refused to deliver the speech that Webster had written for him. He insisted on reading his own speech, an inflated oration that Webster had spent many hours editing down to its final length of one hour and forty minutes. Even so, it remains the longest inaugural address in American history.

Harrison was sixty-eight years old the day he delivered that speech, and he was tired from all the hubbub surrounding the inauguration. Sometime during the ceremonies, he came down with a cold. Then, a week or two later, before he had fully recovered, he was caught outside during an unexpected rainstorm and drenched. On March 27, he came down with pneumonia, suffering a relapse on April 3. The next day, he died, "taken away thus providentially," John Quincy Adams said, "from the evil to come."

Top left: The 1841 inaugural parade. Right: Harrison's doctors couldn't prevent him from becoming the first president to die in office.

★ ★ ★ ★ ★ ★ ★ ★ ★ ★ ★ ★ ★ ★ ★ ★ ★ ★ ★

• Anna Harrison

IN THE SPRING OF 1795—while on a military errand to Lexington, Kentucky—Lt. William Henry Harrison met Anna Symmes. The daughter of a prosperous Ohio farmer, Anna was in Lexington visiting some relatives when she encountered her future husband. Unfortunately, Harrison didn't have much time. He had to get back to his commander, Gen. Anthony Wayne, who was negotiating an important treaty with the Indians. Work on the treaty ended up lasting most of the summer.

As soon as it was over, Harrison rushed off to North Bend, Ohio, where he presented himself at the home of Judge John Cleves Symmes and asked for Anna's hand in marriage. Having heard several unflattering (and most likely untrue) rumors about Harrison, the judge refused and ordered Harrison to stay away from his daughter. But the twenty-two-year-old lieutenant ignored Symmes's wishes and met Anna secretly. When the judge rode off to Cincinnati on a business trip in early November, the couple were married in his absence.

During the 1840 campaign, visitors to the Harrison household commented often on Mrs. Harrison's pleasant appearance. According to one guest, Anna Harrison was among "the handsomest old ladies I ever saw…a perfect beauty and such a *good* person." This same observer also remarked that Mrs. Harrison appeared to rule her husband, but even if she did, she couldn't keep him out of politics. "I wish," she said after hearing the presidential election results, "that my husband's friends had left him where he is, happy and contented in retirement."

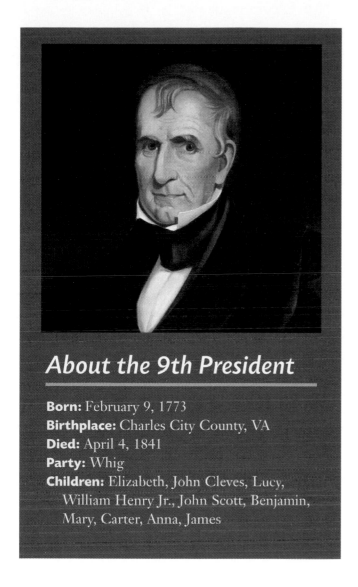

About the 9th President

Born: February 9, 1773
Birthplace: Charles City County, VA
Died: April 4, 1841
Party: Whig
Children: Elizabeth, John Cleves, Lucy, William Henry Jr., John Scott, Benjamin, Mary, Carter, Anna, James

A bootjack owned and used by William Henry Harrison. The general would stand on the bootjack with one foot directly behind the other. Then he would put the heel of his front foot inside the bootjack's V-shaped notch. This notch held the boot in place while Harrison pulled his foot up and out of it.

During the Harrison Administration

★ ★ ★ ★ ★ ★ ★ ★ ★ ★ ★ ★ ★ ★ ★

Mar. 9, 1841   *The Supreme Court rules in the case of the July 1839* Amistad *mutiny that the mutineers can return to Africa because they were enslaved illegally. Although President Van Buren had wanted the mutineers deported to Spain, former president John Quincy Adams had defended the men and made sure that they had received a fair trial.*

Apr. 1, 1841   *Transcendentalist leader George Ripley and twenty of his followers move to Brook Farm in West Roxbury, Massachusetts, near Boston. The utopian community that they form becomes an influential experiment in communal living. The experiment ends six years later when a fire destroys the farm's newly completed (and badly needed) central hall. Unable to recover financially, Brook Farm disbands in 1847.*

Apr. 1841   *Edgar Allan Poe publishes "The Murders in the Rue Morgue," the first detective story, in* Graham's Magazine. *Poe's amateur investigator, C. Auguste Dupin, uses analysis (rather than guesswork) to reveal the identity of the murderer. Poe considered the story one of his best.*

1841   *Swiss immigrant John Sutter builds a fort at the junction of the Sacramento and American Rivers in California. Having obtained the permission of the Mexican governor, Sutter plans to establish the colony of Nueva Helvetia, or New Switzerland.*

1841   *Harvard professor Henry Wadsworth Longfellow publishes* Ballads and Other Poems, *which includes "The Wreck of the Hesperus." Longfellow's poems are among the most popular of the nineteenth century.*

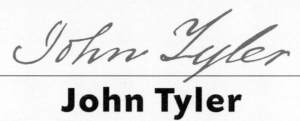

John Tyler

10th President • 1841–1845

WHEN CHARLES DICKENS VISITED the White House in March 1842, he remarked that President John Tyler, then in his early fifties, "looked somewhat worn and anxious, and well he might, being at war with everybody."

No one, especially not the Whigs who had picked him, expected Tyler to have become president. When the former Virginia governor was nominated for vice president in December 1839, he was a convenient southern slave owner who could balance the Whig ticket. Then William Henry Harrison died and everybody's plans were upset—including those of Tyler, who had expected a quiet four years.

Unlike Harrison, Tyler had no intention of simply rubber-stamping the work of the Whig leaders in Congress. This became abundantly clear when he began vetoing their legislation. The Whigs, of course, were furious, though there was little that they could do. They tried to undermine Tyler's authority by claiming that he had lied about his views during the 1840 campaign, but this didn't work. No one had even bothered to ask Tyler his views on the Whig platform for two reasons: The first was that no one had cared what Tyler had thought; the second was that there had been no Whig platform.

As president, Tyler demonstrated a remarkable amount of poise and determination. The news of Harrison's death produced immediate chaos. No president had ever died in office, so no one knew what to do. But Tyler handled the crisis with swift and sure decision making. Most important, he claimed from the start all the powers of the presidency. When the Whigs realized that he wouldn't be playing along, they began calling Tyler His Accidency and insisted that he was only the "acting president." However, Tyler never gave in to these power grabs, and his firmness set an important precedent that served later vice presidents well.

The warfare between Tyler and his former party lasted his entire term. Perhaps the pettiest attack came when Congress refused to appropriate money for the upkeep of the White House. As a result, Tyler was forced to pay these costs out of his own limited resources. Even so, he became one of the most gracious and sociable presidents, making a great many political enemies but apparently no personal ones.

As Dickens described him, "The expression of [Tyler's] face was mild and pleasant, and his manner was remarkably unaffected, gentlemanly, and agreeable. I thought that, in his whole carriage and demeanour, he became his station singularly well."

• Tyler, Too

At dawn on April 5, 1840, Vice President John Tyler slept peacefully in the bedroom of his Williamsburg, Virginia, home. After the inauguration of Harrison in early March, Tyler had returned to Williamsburg, where he looked forward to spending much of the next four years. His Whig colleagues had made it clear to him that his position as vice president would be essentially honorary. As far as running the country was concerned, his involvement would be neither required nor tolerated. In fact, when President Harrison fell ill, no one even bothered to send word to Williamsburg.

The White House as it appeared during the Tyler administration.

That April morning, Tyler was awakened by several loud knocks at his front door. Going downstairs to see who had disturbed his sleep, the vice president found two messengers from the capital. One was Daniel Webster's son Fletcher, who told him that President Harrison was dead.

After making rapid preparations, a shocked Tyler left Williamsburg by seven o'clock that morning, arriving in Washington several hours before dawn the following day. That it took him just twenty-one hours to cover 230 miles by horse, boat, and rail was a remarkable record for speed in 1840.

★ ★

• "My Course of Life"

In 1842, in a letter to a friend, Tyler described his daily routine: "My course of life is to rise with the sun, and work from that time until three o'clock. The order of despatching business pretty much is, first, all diplomatic matters; second, all matters connected with the action of Congress; third, matters of general concern falling under the executive control; then the reception of visitors, and despatch of private petitions. I dine at three-and-a-half o'clock, and in the evening my employments are miscellaneous—directions to secretaries and endorsements of numerous papers. I take some short time for exercise, and after candlelight again receive visitors, apart from all business, until ten at night, when I retire to bed. Such is the life led by an American President. What say you?—would you exchange the peace and quiet of your homestead for such an office?"

Left: One way that Tyler forced his opponents to show him some respect was by returning unopened all mail addressed "Acting President Tyler." Above: The parlor at Tyler's Sherwood Forest estate.

• A Patron of Science and the Arts

Among the ways in which Tyler followed the example of his hero, Thomas Jefferson, was his support for science and the arts. As president, he sent writers Washington Irving and John Howard Payne on diplomatic missions: Irving became Tyler's minister to Spain and Payne the U.S. consul in Tunis.

Even more significantly, Tyler encouraged artist Samuel F. B. Morse in his efforts to make the telegraph a practical form of communication. He helped Morse win thirty thousand dollars in congressional funding for an experimental line between Washington and Baltimore. And when the connection between these cities was completed on May 24, 1844, Tyler's greetings from the Capitol to Chief Justice Roger Taney in Baltimore was one of the first messages sent.

A sketch of Tyler drawn (not very well) by Samuel F. B. Morse.

• A Man without a Party

Literally a man without a party, Tyler considered launching an independent campaign for president in 1844. He gave up the idea when he realized that running would only undermine the campaign of Democrat James Polk and probably elect Henry Clay instead. Tyler thus abandoned his personal ambition for the accomplishment of a larger goal—the annexation of Texas, which Polk also supported.

Although he didn't run for president, Tyler hadn't yet reached the end of his political career. For a time he enjoyed the calm of his twelve-hundred-acre plantation outside Richmond, but as the Civil War approached, he rallied to the cause of the South. After presiding over a last-ditch peace conference in Washington in February 1861, Tyler decided that Virginia must secede, and quickly. In November 1861, he kept intact his record of never having lost a race for public office when he won election to the Confederate House of Representatives, but he died the following January before taking his seat.

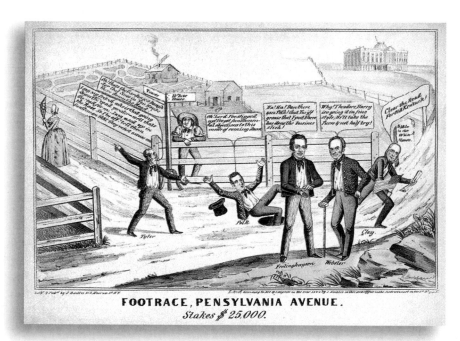

FOOTRACE, PENSYLVANIA AVENUE.
Stakes $ 25,000.

This political cartoon from the 1844 campaign shows Tyler quitting the race to follow Julia Gardiner, whom he married that year, down the road to Texas.

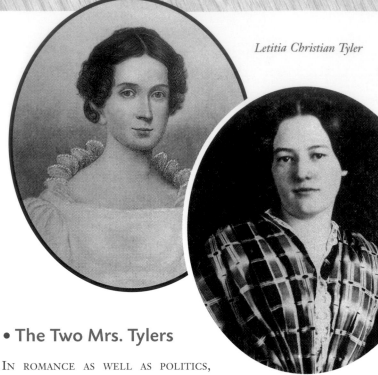

Letitia Christian Tyler

Julia Gardiner Tyler

• The Two Mrs. Tylers

IN ROMANCE AS WELL AS POLITICS, John Tyler was proud and chivalrous. He once declared, "The very moment a man can say to himself, 'If I die tomorrow, my wife will be independent,' he is fully authorized to obey the impulse of affection." Apparently this sense of financial independence came to Tyler sometime before his twenty-third birthday, because on that day he married Letitia Christian.

Often described as quiet and introverted, Letitia belonged to a wealthy and politically prominent family, which made the match advantageous for Tyler. However, the young couple were also in love, and they remained so throughout twenty-nine years of marriage. A stroke in 1839 left Letitia a semi-invalid, but her health remained stable until early 1842, when she became seriously ill. She died that September, during her husband's second year as president.

A sincerely distraught Tyler mourned her death, though he was also determined to remarry. The object of his affection was twenty-three-year-old Julia Gardiner, the daughter of socially prominent New Yorkers. Because the fifty-three-year-old Tyler courted her discreetly, very little is known about their early relationship.

We do know that Julia thought Tyler oldish but attractive, and that her mother raised no objections when Tyler asked for her hand (although she did wonder whether Tyler had enough money to satisfy Julia's expensive tastes). The marriage—which took place in New York on June 26, 1844—was kept secret until the newlyweds returned to Washington. A short while later, Mrs. Gardiner wrote a note to her daughter reproving her for touching the president too much in public. She told Julia that the caresses were interfering with Tyler's duties.

MAJOR POLITICAL EVENTS

★ **Webster-Ashburton Treaty:** In September 1841, after President Tyler vetoed two separate national bank bills, his entire cabinet resigned in protest—with one exception. Secretary of State Daniel Webster stayed on, not out of respect for Tyler but because he was in the midst of important negotiations with England. The treaty that he finally concluded with Lord Ashburton in August 1842 settled a long-standing border dispute with Canada. The Webster-Ashburton Treaty fixed the U.S.-Canadian border from the Atlantic Ocean all the way to the Rocky Mountains. It did, however, leave ownership of the Oregon Territory unresolved.

★ **Gag Rule:** In 1836, in order to avoid the controversial issue of slavery, Congress had imposed a gag rule that banned discussion of antislavery petitions on the floor of the House. Although it was sponsored by southerners, northern congressmen went along with the rule, either because they believed that Congress had no right to interfere with slavery or because the avoidance of controversy made political sense. From the start, John Quincy Adams attacked the gag rule as an unconstitutional denial of the right to petition the government. To prove his point, the former president, now serving as a congressman from Massachusetts, spent many hours reading abolitionist petitions into the official record. As public opinion in the North turned against slavery, more and more northern congressmen began to side with him. In December 1844, after more than eight years, Adams won his fight, and the gag rule was repealed.

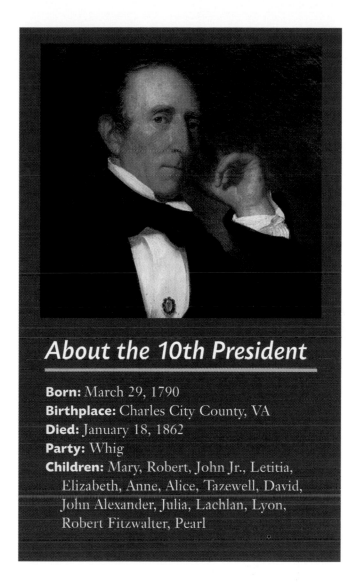

About the 10th President

Born: March 29, 1790
Birthplace: Charles City County, VA
Died: January 18, 1862
Party: Whig
Children: Mary, Robert, John Jr., Letitia,
Elizabeth, Anne, Alice, Tazewell, David,
John Alexander, Julia, Lachlan, Lyon,
Robert Fitzwalter, Pearl

★ **Annexation of Texas:** The question of whether or not to annex the Republic of Texas had been facing Congress since the Van Buren administration. Sam Houston's defeat of the Mexican army at San Jacinto in April 1836 had won Texas its independence from Mexico. However, Van Buren feared that admitting Texas as a slave state would disrupt the balance of power achieved by the Missouri Compromise of 1820. In 1843, when frustrated Texans began discussing the possibility of remaining independent under British protection, Tyler began secret negotiations. These produced a treaty of annexation in early 1844. Although the Senate rejected Tyler's treaty in April 1844, the election of James K. Polk in November made it clear that the public wanted territorial expansion. Three days before leaving office, Tyler signed a joint resolution of Congress admitting Texas to the Union.

★ ★ ★ ★ ★ ★ ★ ★ ★ ★ ★ ★ ★

During the Tyler Administration

Nov. 1841
After a two-thousand-mile journey, 130 settlers reach the Oregon Territory. They represent the first wagon train of immigrants to arrive there.

Mar. 3, 1842
Massachusetts passes a law limiting the length of time that children can work each day. Children under twelve are allowed to work only ten hours each day.

Mar. 30, 1842
Georgia doctor Crawford Long pioneers the use of ether as an anesthetic when he gives some to a patient during a neck operation.

1842
P. T. Barnum buys the American Museum in New York City and imports the most sensational attractions he can find. Exhibits include a mermaid (fake) as well as Siamese twins Chang and Eng.

Jan. 1843
In a speech before the Massachusetts legislature, Boston schoolteacher Dorothea Dix condemns the state's harsh treatment of mental patients. Her report leads to important reforms.

June 27, 1844
A mob murders Mormon founder Joseph Smith and his brother in Carthage, Illinois. The brothers were in jail for smashing the offices of a rival Mormon newspaper.

1844
The New York Hotel becomes the first U.S. establishment to offer private baths. Meanwhile, the Irving Hotel, also in New York City, introduces the bridal suite.

1845
Runaway slave Frederick Douglass publishes his autobiography, Narrative of the Life of Frederick Douglass.

It is confidently believed that our system may be safely extended to the utmost bounds of our territorial limits, and that as it shall be extended the bonds of our Union, so far from being weakened, will become stronger.

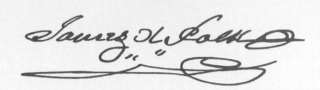

James K. Polk

11th President • 1845–1849

JAMES K. POLK HAD A LUST FOR LAND, without which he would never have become president. In 1844, the map of United States looked very different than it does today: Texas was an independent republic, Mexico owned California, and the United States still had to share the Oregon Territory with Great Britain. Polk didn't like what he saw. He believed that the United States should control—in fact, was *destined* to control—all North America from the Rio Grande north to Russian Alaska.

Later, supporters of westward expansion called this policy "manifest destiny"—*manifest*, because it was so obvious. Polk summed it up during the 1844 campaign with the slogan "Fifty-four Forty or Fight!" That slogan referred to the Democrats' demand for all of Oregon to latitude 54°40' (the southern border of Alaska).

The Whigs went with "Who Is James K. Polk?" A poor slogan, perhaps, though a reasonable question. With the exception of some politicians in Washington and some voters in Tennessee, few people had ever heard of him. That was mostly because Polk hadn't done much, but also because he had a rather boring personality.

A former congressman from Tennessee, Polk was Speaker of the House from 1835 until 1839, when he resigned to become governor of Tennessee. However, those credentials aren't nearly as impressive as they sound. He owed the speakership to his mentor, Andrew Jackson, and he served only one term as governor before being voted out in 1841. He lost again in 1843 and was nominated for the presidency only because the Democrats needed a compromise candidate.

And yet Polk turned out to be a highly skilled and important president. As a result of the Mexican War (which he provoked), he annexed California and nearly the entire Southwest. A treaty with Great Britain also added about half of Oregon—not all that he had wanted, but not bad.

In a recent survey conducted by Arthur M. Schlesinger Jr., a panel of leading historians ranked Polk as a "near great" president, just behind Jackson and just ahead of Theodore Roosevelt. The qualities that made Polk so "near great" were honesty (up to a point), shrewdness, hard work, and—most of all—a desire to represent the will of the majority. Polk may not even have had any personal views. Instead, he believed that it was the president's job to do what the country wanted. "If he had ever tried to control or dominate the people," one historian noted, "his colorlessness would have been fatal, but as a mirror he was adequate to his task."

• Young Hickory

Andrew Jackson knew just about everything that went on in Tennessee politics, and Polk's victory in the congressional elections of 1825 caught his eye. Jackson had been a friend of Polk's father. And as he was childless, the general often took a paternal interest in younger politicians who shared his views.

In fact, Polk became so closely associated with Old Hickory that some of his congressional colleagues began calling him Young Hickory. Of course, this nickname was

something of a joke—Jackson's boisterous personality had little in common with Polk's tepid one.

During the early 1830s, Polk led the fight in Congress to abolish the national bank, which Jackson hated. As a reward, Jackson used his influence to make Polk Speaker of the House. So far, Polk has been the only former Speaker to become president.

James Polk's inkwell, made from volcanic ash.

★ ★

This daguerreotype of the Polks was taken at the White House about 1847.

• The Hardest-Working Man in America

Historians generally agree that Polk was a man without personal magnetism. He had no intimate friends (with the possible exception of his wife), seemed stiff to people, and looked, in the words of one biographer, "as insignificant as he had always hitherto been." Sam Houston once said of the sober Polk that he "drank too much water."

Because he didn't think much of socializing, Polk naturally took his job very seriously. He felt that he "could not lose half a day just to go and dine," so he left the purely social aspects of the presidency to his wife, Sarah, one of the most popular and vivacious first ladies. During his entire four-year term—and early on Polk made it clear that he would serve only one—the president was away from Washington for a grand total of only six weeks. In his diary, he called himself "the hardest-working man" in America.

Long White House reception lines were a particular annoyance to him, so he invented a special handshaking technique to cope with them: "When I saw a strong man approaching, I generally took advantage of him by being a little quicker than he was and seizing him by the tip of his fingers, giving him a hearty shake, and thus preventing him from getting a full grip upon me."

Sarah Polk carried this gift from her husband on inauguration day. It's a fan decorated with the portraits of all the presidents, including Polk himself.

• Dark Horse

Polk was the first "dark horse" presidential candidate. Originally a horse-racing term, a dark horse is a little-known contender that performs surprisingly well. In politics, the phrase refers to a candidate who is nominated unexpectedly, usually as a compromise between two factions.

Former president Martin Van Buren arrived at the 1844 Democratic convention with enough votes to win the nomination, yet he lost crucial support when he indiscreetly remarked that he opposed the annexation of Texas. He still had a majority of the votes, but not the two-thirds he needed to win the nomination. After eight fruitless ballots, the convention turned to Polk (who had been the leading contender for vice president) because of his popular expansionist views.

• The Mexican War

There's no doubt that Polk would have started the Mexican War even if the Mexicans hadn't provided him with a convenient excuse. On May 9, 1846, Polk prepared a message asking Congress for a declaration of war because Mexico was unwilling to sell California. That evening, however, he received news that Mexican soldiers had crossed the Rio Grande and attacked U.S. soldiers. Polk rewrote the message.

However, he didn't give the location of the raid. This was because the border of Texas had for the last century been the Nueces River, which was north of the Rio Grande. According to the Mexicans (and many Whig congressmen), the United States had no claim whatsoever to the land between the Nueces and the Rio Grande where the fighting had taken place.

Polk (shown here with his cabinet) personally planned the overall strategy for the war and supervised its details all the way down to the purchase of mules.

Rep. Abraham Lincoln of Illinois demanded to know the exact "spot" where the Americans had been attacked, believing the territory to be clearly part of Mexico. Lincoln later said that Polk's explanation was "the half insane mumbling of a fever-dream" in "a bewildered, confounded, and miserably perplexed man." In the end, the armies of Zachary Taylor and Winfield Scott won a rather easy victory, which forced Mexico to cede not only California but also land that became the states of New Mexico and Arizona.

★ ★ ★ ★ ★ ★ ★ ★ ★ ★ ★ ★ ★ ★ ★ ★

• Sarah Polk

SARAH CHILDRESS, THE DAUGHTER OF a prosperous Tennessee farmer, had all the social charm that Polk himself lacked. She was a serious woman, well educated for her time, and Polk trusted her completely. She was intimately familiar with his political affairs, and, to ease the burden of his office, she even became his personal secretary during their White House years. Yet Sarah Polk also knew how to have a good time.

A devout Presbyterian, Mrs. Polk had particular views about what was proper and what was not. Card playing, dancing, and alcohol were forbidden in the White House during the Polk administration. And on Sundays, so was music. The rest of the time, however, Sarah Polk reveled in the pomp of her position and was known throughout the capital as a delightful conversationalist.

In 1848, during her last year as first lady, gaslight came to the White House. Congress had commissioned a gas plant for the Capitol and then had lines run down Pennsylvania Avenue to service the White House. Most of the formal rooms in the White House were fitted with burners. However, Mrs. Polk, because she preferred candlelight, refused to let the workers convert the chandelier in the Blue Room. She was teased for this, but on the night of the first gaslit state reception, all the gas burners went out around nine o'clock. Apparently, no one had thought to ask the gas plant to stay open late. So the White House went dark—except for the spot beneath the Blue Room chandelier in which Sarah Polk stood, bathed in candlelight.

MAJOR POLITICAL EVENTS

★ **Oregon Treaty:** When President Polk took office in 1845, the southern border of Russian Alaska was 54°40' north latitude. The northern border of Spanish California was 42° north latitude, or the forty-second parallel. Between these two borderlines, from the Rocky Mountains to the Pacific Ocean, lay the territory of Oregon. Although Polk liked to pretend otherwise, both Britain and the United States had justifiable claims to this land. At first, Polk refused to negotiate with the British. However, as violent confrontation with Mexico became more likely, he compromised rather than risk having to fight wars on two fronts. Under the terms of the Oregon Treaty signed by Polk in June 1846, land south of the forty-ninth parallel became U.S. territory and land north of that line became part of British Canada.

★ **Wilmot Proviso:** In August 1846, Pennsylvania congressman David Wilmot, a Democrat opposed to Polk's prosouthern policies, introduced a controversial amendment to a Mexican War spending bill. The Wilmot Proviso proposed a ban on slavery in all territory acquired from Mexico as a result of the war, whether by force or by treaty. With the help of the Whigs, the amendment passed in the House. Although the Senate, as expected, rejected the proviso in February 1847, Wilmot continued to attach his amendment to other bills in order to promote further debate about the expansion of slavery into new U.S. territories.

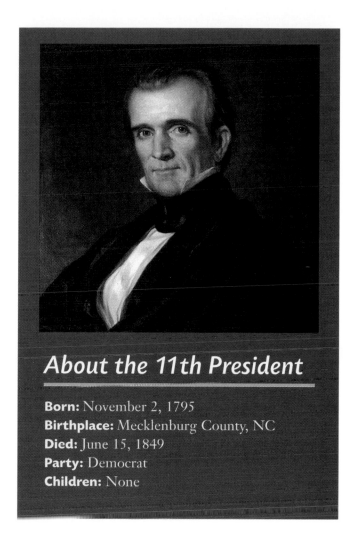

About the 11th President

Born: November 2, 1795
Birthplace: Mecklenburg County, NC
Died: June 15, 1849
Party: Democrat
Children: None

★ **Treaty of Guadalupe Hidalgo:** The Mexican War ended in February 1848 with the signing of the Treaty of Guadalupe Hidalgo. The terms of this treaty, dictated by the victorious Americans, included the transfer of more than five hundred thousand square miles of Mexican territory to the United States. In return, Mexico received fifteen million dollars cash, forgiveness of three million dollars in debt to U.S. citizens, and a promise that Mexican citizens living on the ceded land would be allowed to remain there. The Mexican Cession, the nation's largest land acquisition since the Louisiana Purchase, included territory that would later be incorporated into the states of California, Nevada, Arizona, New Mexico, Colorado, and Utah.

★ ★ ★ ★ ★ ★ ★ ★ ★ ★ ★ ★ ★ ★

During the Polk Administration

Sep. 1845	*While helping to found the amateur Knickerbocker Base Ball Club, Alexander Cartwright establishes the modern rules of baseball.*
Sep. 10, 1846	*Elias Howe receives the first patent for a sewing machine.*
Dec. 1846	*Eighty-seven immigrants led by George and Jacob Donner become stranded in the Sierra Nevada when snow blocks their path to California. Some members of the Donner Party eat human flesh to survive.*
May 1, 1847	*Joseph Henry becomes the first secretary of the Smithsonian Institution, funded by the estate of James Smithson "for the increase and diffusion of knowledge."*
Jan. 24, 1848	*While building a sawmill for John Sutter about forty miles from Sacramento, James Marshall discovers gold. Prospectors soon overrun Sutter's land.*
Mar. 29, 1848	*John Jacob Astor, the richest man in America, dies at age eighty-four. He leaves behind an estate worth twenty million dollars, earned in the fur trade and New York City real estate.*
July 19, 1848	*Three hundred women and forty men attend the Seneca Falls Convention in New York to discuss the cause of women's rights.*
Jan. 23, 1849	*Elizabeth Blackwell becomes the first female doctor in the United States.*
Feb. 28, 1849	*The first gold seekers arrive in San Francisco from the East aboard the California.*

I this day renew the declarations I have heretofore made and proclaim my fixed determination to maintain to the extent of my ability the Government in its original purity and to adopt as the basis of my public policy those great republican doctrines which constitute the strength of our national existence.

Zachary Taylor

12th President • 1849–1850

O N FIRST MEETING ZACHARY TAYLOR, most people misread him. A young lieutenant delivering a message to General Taylor during the Mexican War battle of Resaca de la Palma was shocked to find his commanding officer dressed like a "Vermont farmer." Taylor wore a loose coat, a big straw sombrero, and a pair of enlisted man's trousers that were much too short for him.

Taylor's forty-year military career was filled with many such stories of newly transferred officers mistaking him for a laborer. The good-hearted Taylor usually played along with the gag, and later in life, as a political candidate and president, he would sometimes tease visitors by acting the part of a country bumpkin. But he was no fool, and—unlike William Henry Harrison, another general turned president—he was no political puppet.

Although Taylor had no formal education (and no desire to have one), he kept his eyes wide open and was completely his own man. Straightforward and stubborn, simple and kind, he was an honest frontiersman with a contempt for political tricksters and "their obvious forms of nonsense." Taylor was consigned to remote outposts throughout his military career and thus was a Washington outsider (and proud of it). Until he ran for president, he had never bothered to vote.

Taylor had always considered himself, like Andrew Jackson, a man of the people. That's why, when offered the presidency, he took it. The job made sense to him: A man of the people *should* be leading the people.

Although his most important political asset was his status as a war hero, he knew that he needed a political party behind him, so he declared himself "a Whig, but not an ultra-Whig." This gave the Whig party regulars the excuse they needed to adopt him. It didn't matter that few of them knew Taylor's mind. In fact, ignorance of his intentions was considered a plus, for ideas, if Taylor had any, could be controversial.

The first phase of the Whig plan succeeded brilliantly: Taylor was elected. But then the alliance began to fall apart. Like so many junior officers before them, the Whigs had misread the general. Southerners had simply assumed that because Taylor was a slave owner, he would support slavery.

They were wrong. As president, Taylor surprised almost everyone by opposing the extension of slavery into the new territories acquired from Mexico. The reason was that Taylor's nationalism had long since eclipsed his regional pride. Fortunately for the South, he died in office before learning enough about politics to exercise his will.

• Old Rough and Ready

Taylor's four-decade military career began in 1808, when he was twenty-four years old. At that time, the army represented one of the few opportunities for a young man of modest means to earn both money and social status. (Taylor's parents weren't wealthy enough to set him up as a banker, and he lacked the mental discipline necessary to become a lawyer.)

Like most officers in the pre–Civil War army, Taylor had a generally uneventful career. Before the Mexican War, he saw action only four times, none particularly memorable. But that all changed in 1846, when President Polk ordered him to advance into the disputed area between the Nueces River and the Rio Grande, a move provoking the Mexican War.

Victories at Palo Alto, Resaca de la Palma, and Monterrey made Taylor a national hero, much to Polk's chagrin. Having heard rumors that Taylor might be Whiggish, the president, a Democrat, took steps to promote a rival general,

During the Second Seminole War, Taylor was nicknamed Old Rough and Ready by troops who appreciated his willingness to share the hardness of life in the field.

Winfield Scott. Polk ordered Scott to attack Mexico City and used this as an excuse to transfer troops from Taylor's command. The ploy backfired, however, when Taylor's depleted army, outnumbered four to one, nevertheless won the battle of Buena Vista. This February 1847 victory against such difficult odds made the general even *more* of a hero.

Just how much credit Taylor deserved for these victories remains open to debate. His son-in-law, future Confederate president Jefferson Davis, made it a point to praise Taylor's strategic cleverness as often as he could. But the opinions of others, although they knew Taylor not as well, suggest that Davis exaggerated.

"I thought well of him as a General but never for a moment regarded him as a great one," Polk's secretary of war, William L. Marcy, wrote. "His knowledge of military affairs beyond the details in which his life had been spent was very limited…. But he was attentive to the duties of his command and brought a common sense judgment to bear on all subjects to the extent of his information. He was brave to a degree which commands admiration and remarkably firm in his purposes."

Above left: Taylor's eagle-claw pipe. Left: A campaign flask.

Nathaniel Currier's depiction of Taylor at the battle of Resaca de la Palma, printed about 1846. Somehow, Currier seems to have missed the sombrero.

GRAND, NATIONAL, WHIG BANNER.

• Postage Due

When the Whig convention in Philadelphia nominated Zachary Taylor for president on June 9, 1848, the news flashed over telegraph lines as far south as Memphis. There a side-wheeler appropriately named the *General Taylor* was waiting to carry the news to Cypress Grove, Taylor's Baton Rouge plantation. By all accounts, the general took the news rather mildly. Shortly afterward, Whig party chairman John M. Morehead sent a formal notification to Taylor by mail. Morehead became concerned, though, when Taylor (who had also been considering an independent campaign) failed to reply.

It turned out that the letter never reached Taylor because it had been sent collect, or postage due. During the mid–nineteenth century, it was a common practice to send mail without stamps, in which case the recipient would pay the postage. Taylor, however, had begun receiving so many postage-due letters from admirers around the country that he had told his local post office to stop delivering them. Morehead's postage-due letter sat in the Baton Rouge dead letter office for nearly six weeks before it was rescued and acknowledged by Taylor.

★ ★ ★ ★ ★ ★ ★ ★ ★ ★ ★ ★

• "I Shall Be a Dead Man"

On July 4, 1850—a sunny, hot, and humid day—President Taylor attended a long ceremony at the unfinished Washington Monument, then went for a walk along the Potomac. He returned to the White House about four o'clock, his usual dinner hour, and had some iced water and chilled milk along with a bowl of cherries and possibly some other fruit. All were foods and liquids that residents of Washington had recently been warned not to eat because of an ongoing cholera epidemic.

Taylor spent an uncomfortable night, and the next day his symptoms worsened. On Saturday, July 6, an army doctor examined the president, diagnosed a form of cholera, and prescribed opium, which produced an immediate improvement. On Sunday, however, Taylor began to sink again. On Monday he predicted that "in two days I shall be a dead man," and late on Tuesday night he died.

In 1991, a historian who suspected that Taylor had been poisoned persuaded the president's family to have his remains exhumed. Samples of hair and fingernail tissue were taken, but forensic tests found no evidence of foul play.

Because the first lady didn't have the strength to endure formal state dinners and long receiving lines, she turned over the duties of White House hostess to her twenty-five-year-old daughter, Mrs. Betty Taylor Bliss (pictured above).

★ ★ ★ ★ ★ ★ ★ ★ ★ ★ ★ ★ ★ ★ ★ ★

• Peggy Taylor

LIKE HER HUSBAND, WHO WAS DEVOTED TO HER, Peggy Taylor had no intellectual pretensions. However, she was an extraordinarily capable woman and an outstanding frontier wife. In her prime, she was described as stately and slender, but no authentic portrait of her survives.

The former Margaret Mackall Smith married Lt. Zachary Taylor on June 21, 1810, at the home of the bride's sister near Louisville, Kentucky. (The couple had met while Peggy was visiting her sister and Taylor was home on leave.) Thereafter and throughout his military career, Peggy Taylor shared her husband's lonely and sometimes dangerous frontier life. She learned quickly to make do with what little the army provided in the way of domestic conveniences.

A dedicated Episcopalian, Mrs. Taylor prayed regularly for her husband's safe return from battle. In later years, she was rumored to be something of a recluse. According to one story, she had promised God that she would give up the pleasures of society if He would, in turn, deliver her husband from harm.

This story is colorful but almost certainly untrue. The actual cause of Mrs. Taylor's social withdrawal was her poor health. Six pregnancies and years of difficult circumstances had drained her considerably. As a result, during her years in the White House, she rarely left the family quarters on the second floor. Yet she was hardly a recluse. She attended informal dinners and entertained as best she could in her room. One political wife called Mrs. Taylor's quarters the "bright and pretty" retreat of the best female society in Washington.

MAJOR POLITICAL EVENTS

★ **California Statehood:** In November 1849, voters in California approved a constitution that banned slavery. Soon afterward, California's territorial government applied to Congress for statehood. To the surprise of many, President Taylor supported the admission of California as a free state. Nevertheless, statehood was blocked by southern congressmen for the same reason that northerners had resisted the admission of Missouri in 1819: Making California the thirty-first state would upset the balance between slave and free states in the Senate. Moreover, southern slave owners viewed any limitation on slavery as a dangerous precedent. In South Carolina, where

there hadn't been discussions of secession since the nullification crisis of 1832–33, talk of leaving the Union was renewed.

★ **Clayton-Bulwer Treaty:** Soon after the California gold rush began, the United States funded construction of a railroad across Panama that greatly reduced travel times between the Atlantic and the Pacific. Taking a train across the narrow Isthmus of Panama (rather than sailing around South America) saved passengers several months. Mistakenly believing that a canal would soon be built across Central America, the United States and Britain agreed in the Clayton-Bulwer Treaty of April 1850 that neither would seek exclusive control of a canal across either Nicaragua or Panama. After the Spanish-American War of 1898, however, the United States became much less interested in sharing control with other nations, including Britain.

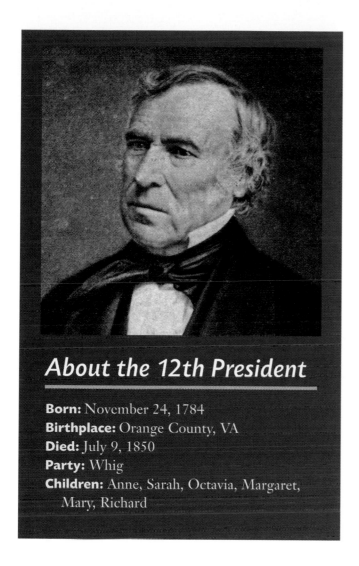

About the 12th President

Born: November 24, 1784
Birthplace: Orange County, VA
Died: July 9, 1850
Party: Whig
Children: Anne, Sarah, Octavia, Margaret, Mary, Richard

★ **Compromise of 1850:** With the gold rush shifting large numbers of Americans from the East to the West Coast, statehood for California became a pressing matter. To avoid another bloodbath in the Senate—and perhaps a bloody civil war as well—Henry Clay proposed in January 1850 a compromise designed to satisfy both northern and southern concerns. Its key points included the admission of California as a free state, the abolition of slavery within the District of Columbia, and the passage of the Fugitive Slave Act, which would require northerners to return escaped slaves to their southern masters. In addition, the question of whether or not slavery would be permitted in the territories of the Mexican Cession would be left for each territorial government to decide. While he lived, Taylor opposed the Compromise of 1850 and promised to veto any bill that might result in the spread of slavery.

During the Taylor Administration

May 1849
Henry David Thoreau publishes "Civil Disobedience" in a collection entitled Aesthetic Papers. *The essay explains why Thoreau refuses to pay taxes: He doesn't believe that his money should support government policies that he opposes.*

July 1849
Maryland slave Harriet Tubman escapes to the North along the Underground Railroad. She soon becomes one of its most active "conductors."

July 1849
Gail Borden gives a supply of his latest invention, the meat biscuit, to friends heading west to California. The recent tragedy of the Donner Party has prompted Borden to develop a long-lasting food item, but the meat biscuit doesn't catch on.

1849
Walter Hunt invents the safety pin as a means of paying off a man to whom he owes some money.

1850
Mathew Brady's book A Gallery of Illustrious Americans *features engravings of photographs he has made of famous people, including Andrew Jackson, John James Audubon, and Henry Clay.*

1850
Levi Strauss sails to San Francisco, where he plans to get rich selling dry goods to miners. He brings with him a supply of canvas for tents and wagon covers, but he finds that the miners need clothing, so he uses the canvas to make durable pants called jeans.

1850
According to the 1850 census, the United States has twenty-three million people. Forty-five percent of them live west of the Allegheny Mountains.

Millard Fillmore

13th President • 1850–1853

ALTHOUGH TODAY HE'S THE "FORGOTTEN" PRESIDENT, known mostly for being so obscure, Millard Fillmore was once something of a national figure. Before becoming Zachary Taylor's vice president, he had been chairman of the important House Ways and Means Committee, which controlled tariff rates, and a serious contender for the 1844 vice-presidential nomination.

Despite these accomplishments, contemporaries considered Fillmore a faceless party man with few opinions of his own. Most historians today have even less respect for him. "If he had opinions," according to one, "nobody cared."

Fillmore was put on the Whig ticket in 1848 principally because he was so dull. He was nominated to appease the supporters of Taylor's chief rival, Henry Clay, and most convention delegates went along because none thought that the wishy-washy New Yorker would cost them any votes. Fillmore had never met Taylor—and didn't meet him until after the election. (Apparently no one thought that such a meeting was worth the general's time.)

The great crisis of the Taylor administration involved the land acquired during the Mexican War: Would slavery be permitted in these new territories? The South renewed its threat to secede. Meanwhile, Henry Clay proposed a five-part compromise that would allow the residents of each territory to choose for themselves. To placate the South, Clay also included the Fugitive Slave Act, which forced northerners to return all escaped slaves.

Taylor opposed the compromise, believing that the threat of force would eventually muffle the South. But whatever influence he had on the debate raging in the Senate was lost when he died. Fillmore, who didn't share Taylor's view, supported the compromise and used the powers of his new office—patronage, lobbying, even flattery—to promote its passage. His efforts, however, were obscured by the actions of others, notably the much more prominent senators Clay and Daniel Webster.

Most historians believe that the only significant part Fillmore played in the drama was to sign the bills that made up the Compromise of 1850. "Fillmore would have been a nonentity in any company, or at any period in history," reports one nineteenth-century expert, "but in Washington during the crisis of 1850 he was so overshadowed as to be indiscernible."

In fact, Fillmore was considered so friendly and agreeable to the will of Congress that many southern Whigs supported him for president in 1852. However, most party leaders objected to his nomination. They pointed out, correctly, that the Whigs had elected only two presidential candidates and both had been generals. In the end, Fillmore was passed over for Gen. Winfield Scott.

• The Young Lawyer

Millard Fillmore's father was a dirt-poor farmer. Duped by a land salesman, Nathaniel Fillmore had moved his family from Vermont to northwestern New York, only to find out that his new land title was faulty. The elder Fillmore was forced off the land and had to lease another property, resigning his family to a life of tenant farming.

Like his father, Millard was a hard worker, but he deeply resented having to waste himself on manual labor. He learned to read a little using his father's "library"—a Bible, a hymnal, and an almanac—but he turned nineteen before he read a history of the United States or even saw a map of the country.

Fillmore's big break came when his father persuaded Walter Wood, a local judge with a thriving legal practice (based on land title litigation), to take on Millard as a clerk. By his own account, Fillmore exchanged cowhide boots for a pair of shoes, donned a homespun suit, and began wearing starched white collars. He even bought a cane.

This wood engraving, from the 1848 campaign biography of Taylor and Fillmore, shows young Millard beside Judge Wood.

★ ★

• A Secondhand President

Soon after Fillmore became president, a story began to circulate around the Capitol. Fillmore, thinking that he needed a new carriage, had gone with White House servant Edward Moran to inspect one that could be had for a bargain.

"This is all very well, Edward," Fillmore said after looking the vehicle over, "but how would it do for the president of the United States to ride around in a secondhand carriage?" "But, sure," Moran allegedly replied, "your excellency is only a second-hand president!"

Fillmore was also mocked because of his manner. In public, he spoke slowly and tended to use common household words in short, direct sentences. This style gave the impression of good-natured, simple sincerity, but it didn't suggest a great deal of intelligence. During the nineteenth century, crowds expected something different from great orators—elegant language and ornate, even florid figures of speech, neither of which suited the plain-speaking Fillmore.

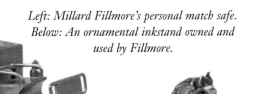

Left: Millard Fillmore's personal match safe. Below: An ornamental inkstand owned and used by Fillmore.

A popular cabinet card image of Fillmore.

• Mission to Japan

For more than two hundred years, Japan had kept her ports closed to foreign ships and treated ship-wrecked sailors as criminals. In the meantime, trade with China had blossomed, and so had steamship travel. It became crucial for the United States to establish coaling stations on the Pacific Rim.

Six months after Fillmore took office, Commodore Matthew C. Perry wrote to the secretary of the navy, urging that an expedition be sent to Japan. Perry had no interest in going himself, but Fillmore became so infatuated with the idea that he persuaded Perry to command the mission. Quickly, the president and Perry became close friends: Perry became a familiar guest at the White House, and Fillmore traveled monthly to Annapolis to lunch with the commodore aboard his flagship. Together they plotted the expansion of American prestige abroad, certainly Fillmore's most lasting achievement.

Fillmore took special care in preparing a grand November 1852 send-off for Perry—he knew that somebody else would be occupying the White House when the commodore returned. In the end, the result of Perry's mission was a profitable new trade agreement with the Japanese that President James Buchanan signed in 1860 on the eve of the Civil War.

After Perry's visit to Japan, local artists recorded the event in woodblock prints such as this one, picturing Perry's warship in Yedo Bay.

• An Oxford Degree

Early in 1855, Fillmore quietly informed the leaders of the secretive anti-immigrant American party, commonly called the Know-Nothings, that he would accept their nomination for president in 1856. Fillmore believed that the party's attacks on foreigners might be the only way left to bind North and South together. Having made his decision, the former president then left for Europe while matters developed on their own.

His first stop was England, and while in Oxford, he was offered an honorary degree. Realizing that the citation would be in Latin, Fillmore modestly declined. "I had not the advantage of a classical edu-

This political cartoon shows Fillmore during his ill-advised 1856 campaign for president.

cation," he said, "and no man should, in my judgment, accept a degree he cannot read." Fillmore must have been thinking then of the jokes still being made about the time Andrew Jackson accepted an honorary degree at Harvard. On that occasion, Jackson concluded his prepared remarks by shouting the only Latin phrases he knew: *"E pluribus unum! Sine qua non! Quid pro quo! Ne plus ultra!"*

★ ★ ★ ★ ★ ★ ★ ★ ★ ★ ★ ★ ★ ★

• Abigail Fillmore

AS A TEENAGER, MILLARD FILLMORE worked as an apprentice in a cloth-dressing mill. In his spare time, he began to educate himself, first by purchasing a share in a circulating library and then by attending a local academy. It was at this academy in New Hope, New York, that the nineteen-year-old Fillmore met his future wife, Abigail Powers, then twenty-one.

Abigail was both a child of privilege and the sister of a local judge, which made her social status nearly royal compared to Fillmore's. But their mutual affection made this difference small. Throughout the winter of 1819–20, they kept company together and fell in love, though Millard refused to consider marriage until he had secured a place for himself in the world. Abigail had to wait nearly six years while Fillmore built his career as a lawyer. During this time, she rarely saw him, but somehow their relationship survived. They were finally married on February 5, 1826.

An avid reader, First Lady Abigail Fillmore was appalled to learn that the White House had no permanent library of its own. She remedied this immediately by ordering bookcases built into the curved walls of the oval room on the second floor. In the fall of 1852, Congress rewarded her initiative with two thousand dollars for the purchase of books to fill those shelves.

Sadly, Mrs. Fillmore died less than a month after leaving the White House. She came down with a bad cold while attending Franklin Pierce's inauguration. The cold developed into a fever and then pneumonia.

MAJOR POLITICAL EVENTS

★ **Fugitive Slave Act:** The principal enticement that Henry Clay offered the South in the Compromise of 1850 was the Fugitive Slave Act. This law gave southerners the right to pursue runaway slaves into the North. (Previously, slaves that had successfully escaped to the North were allowed to remain there.) Abolitionists were particularly outraged by the provision that allowed slave owners to carry away blacks accused of being runaway slaves without a trial or any other legal proceeding. Antislavery newspapers reported many cases of free northern blacks being kidnapped into slavery, sometimes by mistake and sometimes by unscrupulous slave hunters. In February 1851, a mob in Boston broke into a local jail and freed an escaped slave before he could be returned to the South.

★ **Railroad Land Grants:** In September 1850, Congress made the first land grant to a railroad, the Illinois Central. The land straddled the railroad's right-of-way between Cairo and Galena. It was understood that the Illinois Central would sell the land in order to pay for track construction. During the next half century, the U.S. government used land grants more and more often to encourage construction of railroads in sparsely populated regions such as the Great Plains and the Southwest. In July 1862, the Pacific Railway Act made extensive land grants to the Union Pacific and Central Pacific Railroads, which built the first transcontinental rail line. By the 1870s, these railroads and others had been granted millions of acres of land in the West.

About the 13th President

Born: January 7, 1800
Birthplace: Cayuga County, NY
Died: March 8, 1874
Party: Whig
Children: Millard, Mary

★ **Know-Nothings:** The American, or Know-Nothing, party developed as the public political arm of a secret organization, the Order of the Star-Spangled Banner, apparently founded in New York City in 1849. Its adherents were called Know-Nothings because whenever members of the party were asked about its organization, they invariably replied, "I know nothing." The American party was anti-immigrant in general and anti-Catholic in particular, attracting most of its support from white Anglo-Saxon Protestants in the urban East and Midwest. The Know-Nothing cause represented one of the first "third party" movements in American history. Fillmore, its one and only presidential candidate, carried the state of Maryland in the 1856 election.

★ ★ ★ ★ ★ ★ ★ ★ ★ ★ ★ ★ ★ ★ ★

During the Fillmore Administration

May 29, 1851
Sojourner Truth delivers her famous "Ain't I a Woman" speech at the second Women's Rights Convention in Akron, Ohio.

June 2, 1851
Maine passes the first statewide temperance law. It bans the sale and manufacture of alcoholic beverages.

July 4, 1851
Workers begin laying track for the Pacific Railroad, the first railroad west of the Mississippi River.

Aug. 31, 1851
The clipper ship Flying Cloud sets a speed record sailing from New York City to San Francisco in eighty-nine days, twenty-one hours.

Nov. 1851
Herman Melville publishes Moby-Dick, which sells very few copies during the author's lifetime.

1851
Emanuel Leutze paints Washington Crossing the Delaware. Like the German-born Leutze's other historical paintings, the work isn't accurate, yet it profoundly influences the way Americans view their history.

1851
Florida doctor John Gorrie receives the first U.S. patent for mechanical refrigeration.

Mar. 1852
Harriet Beecher Stowe publishes Uncle Tom's Cabin. Her novel about plantation life raises the nation's consciousness about slavery.

1852
Elisha Otis builds the first safety elevator. It includes a clamping mechanism that stops the elevator platform from falling even if the lift ropes break.

I believe that involuntary servitude, as it exists in different States of this Confederacy, is recognized by the Constitution. I believe that it stands like any other admitted right, and that the States where it exists are entitled to efficient remedies to enforce the constitutional provisions.

Franklin Pierce

14th President • 1853–1857

LIKE POLK, FRANKLIN PIERCE WAS A DARK-HORSE candidate nominated by a deadlocked Democratic convention. After forty-eight ballots, the southerners who ran the party finally realized that there might be advantages to having a northerner as figurehead. They settled on Pierce, a New England country lawyer and former congressman, because he seemed to be a realist. That is, he knew that the southerners were calling the shots.

Pierce happened to be handsome and personally charming, but his merits as a candidate were beside the point. In 1852, the old Whig party was literally dying: Both Henry Clay and Daniel Webster passed away that year. Any Democratic candidate would have won.

The image of Pierce that has survived his unsuccessful presidency is that of a vain, showy, pliant man. Historian Allan Nevins called him "one of the quickest, most gracefully attractive, and withal weakest, of the men who have held his high office." He's best known for bending to the will of southern congressmen, who persuaded him to use the presidency to promote slavery in the new territory of Kansas. Pierce defended his actions by citing the Constitution, which explicitly permitted slavery. But this defense didn't wash—not with northerners at the time and not with historians afterward.

While it may not be possible to defend Pierce's policies, they can be explained. At forty-eight, the youngest president yet elected, Pierce was a man of outward ease. Yet inside there was great conflict. From his robust father, he inherited a sound and healthy body, but his troubled mother passed on to him worry and doubt. From an early age, these two sides of Pierce warred against each other.

Before 1853, when his only son died and his wife's grief devastated their marriage, Pierce had been able to succeed despite his fears and melancholy. In fact, he had never lost a race for public office. And were it not for these personal tragedies, he might have risen to the challenge of the presidency. His weakened condition, however, made him more inclined to seek approval from the southern leaders of his party than to act independently against them.

The political climate of the 1850s encouraged daring and ruthlessness, though Pierce could muster neither. Although he didn't personally approve of slavery, he went along with it. His rationalization was that slavery was an evil whose dimensions were known and limited. On the other hand, if he were to push for abolition (or even the limitation of slavery to the South), who knew what the result would be? Certainly it would be bloody. His friend writer Nathaniel Hawthorne called Pierce a "statesman of practical sagacity," for he chose the reality of Union over the vague promise of emancipation.

• Pierce, by Hawthorne

Traveling by stage back to Bowdoin College in Maine for his sophomore year, Pierce fell in with three freshmen who boarded the same coach. One of them was Nathaniel Hawthorne, a shy, peculiar fellow with a faraway air who became Pierce's lifelong friend. During his political career, Pierce often used his influence to arrange patronage jobs for Hawthorne that might supplement his friend's meager earnings as a writer. When Pierce won the 1852 Democratic nomination, Hawthorne naturally offered his services as a campaign biographer. The time they spent together preparing the biography deepened their friendship greatly.

"I have come seriously to the conclusion that he has in him many of the chief elements of a great ruler," Hawthorne wrote to a mutual Bowdoin classmate soon after completing his *Life of Franklin Pierce*. "His talents are administrative, he

Top: Pierce as a senior at Bowdoin. Right: Hawthorne's campaign biography.

has a subtle faculty of making affairs roll onward according to his will, and of influencing their course without showing any trace of his action. There are scores of men in the country that seem brighter than he is, but [he] has the directing mind, and will move them about like pawns on a chess-board…. He is deep, deep, deep."

After the election, Pierce rewarded Hawthorne with the consulship to Liverpool. This diplomatic post paid Hawthorne much more than he had ever earned from his books, and the frugal Hawthorne saved enough money to stabilize his finances for the rest of his life.

★ ★ ★ ★ ★ ★ ★ ★ ★

• The Fainting General

Franklin Pierce revered his father, who had fought with great distinction in the Revolutionary War. In May 1846, when the Mexican War was declared, Pierce was back home in New Hampshire, having given up his Senate seat and returned to private life at the insistence of his wife. Of course, she didn't want him to go to Mexico, though he felt the call and wanted to respond as his father had.

Pierce enlisted as a private for appearance's sake but was soon made a brigadier general of volunteers. He saw his first action in August 1847 at Contreras, where poorly aimed but quite noisy artillery fire caused his horse to jump. This pressed Pierce's groin fiercely against the high pommel of his saddle, causing temporary (but nevertheless excruciating) pain. The general passed out. Six years later, the Whigs unearthed this story, accusing Pierce of "fainting" under fire.

The equipment of a general. Left: Pierce's sword, for battle. Below: His carpetbag, for clothes.

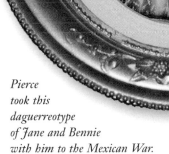

Pierce took this daguerreotype of Jane and Bennie with him to the Mexican War.

• Bennie

One of the great disappointments of Pierce's life was that he was never able to share his ambitions with his wife or his son.

After the 1852 convention, eleven-year-old Bennie wrote to his mother, "Edward brought the news from Boston that Father is a candidate for the Presidency. I hope he won't be elected for I should not like to be at Washington and I know you would not either."

Bennie never did see Washington. In early January 1853, he was riding with his parents on a train when an accident caused their car to roll down an embankment. The president-elect and his wife were hardly injured, but their only son was mangled to death before their eyes. Mrs. Pierce never recovered from this trauma; she secluded herself upstairs at the White House and spent nearly two years writing maudlin letters to her dead son.

Pierce himself was also deeply affected. The death of his beloved Bennie became the most important fact of his life, weakening his self-confidence and unsettling his thoughts at a time when he most needed peace of mind and self-control. "Pierce's great justification for assuming the burdens of the presidency [against his wife's wishes] had been the thought of building a heritage which might aid Bennie's advance in life," wrote Pierce biographer Roy Franklin Nichols. "Now this great station was no longer a half-compensated responsibility, but an impending horror."

• Frankly Hilarious

Even good friends such as Hawthorne wouldn't have described Frank Pierce as a sturdy man. He was often in poor health and suffered prolonged fits of depression. His melancholy moods rarely had much to do with particular events, however. They seemed to reflect a battle that he was constantly waging with himself over whether or not he deserved his success.

On a more superficial level, Pierce's reputation for frailty was reinforced by the fact that he couldn't hold his liquor. Washington has long been a heavy-drinking town, and Pierce, who desperately wanted to be liked, couldn't quite resist the prevailing social custom. Soon enough, he would be in a "hilarious state," according to one Pierce biographer, while his companions "were hardly conscious of having taken anything."

During 1852, the Whigs exaggerated as much as possible Pierce's personal weaknesses—standard practice for a nineteenth-century political campaign.

★ ★ ★ ★ ★ ★ ★ ★ ★ ★ ★ ★ ★ ★

• Jane Pierce

JANE MEANS APPLETON GREW UP in Amherst, New Hampshire, at the mansion of her widowed mother's wealthy family. The house was ruled by a matriarchy led by her grandmother, the formidable Madame Means. There's no record of how Jane and Pierce met or what persuaded Pierce to give up his early conviction that he was destined to go through life alone. But Jane's sister had recently married one of Pierce's former instructors at Bowdoin, and this man probably introduced them. Their wedding on November 19, 1834, was a small affair. Jane wore a traveling dress, and after the service, the couple left for Washington, where Pierce held a seat in the House of Representatives.

The word most often used to describe Jane was *delicate*. Apparently, she was petite, shy with strangers, and somewhat frail. Her health was poor because of tuberculosis, though there was nothing flimsy about her mind. She had been raised as a New England aristocrat, and her will was strong. At the time of his marriage, the twenty-nine-year-old Frank was buoyant and sociable. These qualities may have attracted the melancholy Jane at first, but eventually they began to grate on her. Although she must have had some affection for him, she hated public life and regularly implored him to give up politics.

From the beginning, Pierce made her welfare the centerpiece of his attention—out of devotion, if not love. When her health took a turn for the worse in 1842, Pierce agreed to resign his Senate seat and return to New Hampshire. When President Polk offered him the post of attorney general in 1845, he refused. But he couldn't refuse the 1852 presidential nomination, and his wife perhaps never forgave him that.

MAJOR POLITICAL EVENTS

★ **Gadsden Purchase:** In May 1853, President Pierce sent U.S. minister James Gadsden to Mexico to negotiate the purchase of an important parcel of land south of the Gila River. Surveys had shown that the ideal route for a transcontinental railroad between the South and the Pacific coast passed through this region. In December, Gadsden agreed to pay ten million dollars for thirty thousand square miles of territory. The Gadsden Purchase, which later became southern New Mexico and southern Arizona, marked the end of U.S. continental expansion and enabled mapmakers to draw an outline of the continental United States that has remained unchanged ever since.

★ **Kansas-Nebraska Act:** In early 1854, Illinois senator Stephen Douglas made a deal with his southern colleagues to ensure that the first transcontinental railroad would pass through the Midwest. In exchange for southern support on the railroad issue, Douglas proposed a bill that allowed new states to decide for themselves whether or not to allow slavery. Douglas's doctrine, called "popular sovereignty," became the theoretical basis for the Kansas-Nebraska Act of May 1854, which overturned the Missouri Compromise because it allowed for the possibility of slavery north of the previous 36°30' line. The immediate result was a bloody struggle in Kansas between abolitionist Jayhawkers and mercenary Border Ruffians from the slave state of Missouri. When these groups drafted and approved rival territorial constitutions, Pierce placed the power of the presidency firmly behind the proslavery faction.

About the 14th President

Born: November 23, 1804
Birthplace: Hillsborough, NH
Died: October 8, 1869
Party: Democrat
Children: Franklin Jr., Frank Robert, Benjamin

★ **Ostend Manifesto:** In October 1854, at the request of Secretary of State William L. Marcy, U.S. ministers James Buchanan (Great Britain), John Mason (France), and Pierre Soulé (Spain) met in Ostend, Belgium, to discuss Pierce's plan to buy Cuba from the Spanish government, which owned the island. In their secret report, known as the Ostend Manifesto, the three diplomats recommended that Spain be offered up to $120 million for Cuba. If the Spanish refused to sell, the report continued, then Cuba should be taken by force. In March 1855, the Ostend Manifesto was leaked to the press. Its suggestion that Pierce might be willing to fight a war over Cuba caused an uproar among northerners, who suspected that Pierce's interest in Cuba was its slaves. The commotion forced Pierce and Marcy to renounce their plans.

During the Pierce Administration

May 1853	*Continuing his work on concentrated foods, Gail Borden files a patent application for condensed milk. This evaporated and sweetened milk lasts longer than untreated milk.*
1854	*Henry David Thoreau publishes* Walden; or, Life in the Woods, *an account of two years that the author spent living by himself near Walden Pond in eastern Massachusetts.*
1855	*Engraver Frank Leslie begins publishing* Frank Leslie's Illustrated Newspaper, *America's first weekly newsmagazine.*
1855	*Eight hundred members of the Community of True Inspiration found the Amana Colony in Iowa. Unlike other utopian communities, this one prospers, lasting until the 1930s.*
1855	*Walt Whitman pays to publish* Leaves of Grass, *the first collection of his radical, free-spirited poetry.*
1855	*The first edition of John Bartlett's* Familiar Quotations *appears.*
May 22, 1856	*Rep. Preston Brooks of South Carolina attacks Sen. Charles Sumner of Massachusetts on the Senate floor. Brooks beats Sumner unconscious because Sumner denounced his uncle, Sen. Andrew Butler, for defending slavery.*
1856	*Edward Clark of I. M. Singer & Company introduces the first installment plan, which allows customers to spread out payments.*
1856	*Margarethe Schurz opens the first U.S. kindergarten in Watertown, Wisconsin.*

Let every Union-loving man exert his best influence to suppress this agitation [against slavery], which since the recent legislation of Congress is without any legitimate object.

James Buchanan
15th President • 1857–1861

DURING THE FALL OF 1855, JAMES BUCHANAN was living in London, serving as U.S. minister to Great Britain, when he learned that one of his nieces had died. Another niece living with him, Harriet Lane, was grief stricken at the news. She remained in her room for weeks and even thought about joining a convent.

To help Harriet through this difficult time, Buchanan passed on to her the core of his own personal philosophy: Heartrending tragedies are the common lot of humanity, he said. Man's duty on earth is to submit to God's will with humble resignation. "In all calamitous events," he told her, "we ought to say, emphatically, 'Thy will be done.'"

This philosophy of passivism might explain why, as president, Buchanan did so little to prevent the Civil War. Of course, such a war had become inevitable. However, Buchanan's aloofness during the greatest crisis in his nation's history remains a glaring failure. Perhaps he didn't take action because he believed that God would provide.

Some historians have tried to explain Buchanan's reluctance in a different way: by pointing to his long-standing belief in the constitutional system of checks and balances. Buchanan did worry that a president who took too much power onto himself might threaten the stability of the government. But surely he realized that soon there might not be any government left.

Whatever the reason for his behavior, Buchanan was certainly a woeful president. The proof of this statement is the record of the man who succeeded him. Had Buchanan been even half the leader that Lincoln was, the course of American history would surely have been changed.

In retrospect, the South's attempt to spread slavery to Kansas was arrogant madness. It had no hope of success and just gave the new Republican party a moral cause for which to fight. Buchanan might have made himself useful by pointing this out to his southern associates, but the president, according one Buchanan biographer, "wasn't a man to influence or instruct those about him."

Buchanan's apparent weakness as president was made all the more pitiful by the fact that personally he was a highly decent man. Without any fanfare, he bought slaves in Washington, D.C., and set them free in Pennsylvania. He also conducted himself with the highest degree of dignity and scrupulously avoided any conflict of interest between his political and his financial affairs. Sadly, there was one conflict of interest that he never did resolve: the one between his political career and the immorality of slavery.

• "Happiness Has Fled Me Forever"

In 1818, when he was twenty-seven years old, James Buchanan of Lancaster, Pennsylvania, fell in love. The girl was Ann Coleman, a black-haired, willowy beauty who happened to be the daughter of one of the richest men in the country. She was a bit emotionally unstable—quiet and introspective one moment, giddy and wild the next—but Buchanan didn't seem to mind. The following summer, they became engaged.

Ann's parents, however, objected to the relationship and finally persuaded her in December 1819 to break it off. When she did, she became very depressed. Hoping that a change of scenery might lift her spirits, her parents suggested a trip to nearby

Buchanan's strength as a lawyer wasn't his intelligence—he wasn't particularly bright—but his painstaking preparation.

Philadelphia. Ann died there five days later. The attending physician, a Dr. Chapman, said that hers was the first case in his experience of "hysteria" causing death.

Buchanan, who had hoped for a reconciliation, was devastated. "I may sustain the shock of her death," he wrote Ann's parents, "but I feel that happiness has fled from me forever." Once married, he had planned to focus on his law practice. But now he surrendered to the many requests that he run for Congress, hoping that politics would distract him from his grief.

★ ★

• The Court Dress Affair

In 1853, President Pierce made Buchanan his minister to Great Britain. About the same time, Secretary of State William L. Marcy issued an order requiring U.S. diplomats to perform all their duties "in the simple dress of an American citizen." At the court of Queen Victoria, however, simple dress simply wouldn't do.

Protocol chief Sir Edward Cust informed Buchanan that he wouldn't be presented at court in everyday attire. Such dress showed a lack of respect for the monarchy, and, Cust pointed out, Buchanan would probably be mistaken for a servant. Eventually, Buchanan and Cust agreed to a compromise: Buchanan would wear his regular clothes adorned with a plain black-handled sword. The sword would show respect for the queen and set Buchanan apart from the servants.

This anti-Buchanan cartoon from the 1856 campaign also raises, figuratively, the subject of Buchanan's dress. In this case, it's the candidate's old Federalist "coat" with Democratic "patches." Buchanan was, in fact, a Federalist before joining the Democratic party in 1828.

Top: Buchanan
greeting the Japanese
delegation. Right:
The president's
Japanese dictionary.

• The Japanese Have Arrived!

During the spring of 1860, the Democratic party was literally breaking up. On April 30, southern delegates walked out of the national convention in Charleston, South Carolina, over the issue of slavery in the territories. Buchanan had a great deal of work to do before the northern Democrats reconvened six weeks later in Baltimore, but he was distracted by an incredible uproar in the capital: The Japanese had arrived.

In May, a large delegation of Japanese came to Washington to sign the first commercial treaty ever negotiated with this mysterious empire. The Japanese—especially their translator, Tommy, who spoke not English but Dutch—caused a sensation with their exotic dress and manners. "They are really a curiosity," White House hostess Harriet Lane observed of her colorfully costumed guests. "All the women seem to run daft about them."

• Intoxicating Drink

Buchanan was well known as a connoisseur of spirits, as much for his taste as for his capacity. During his temporary retirement from politics between the Polk and the Pierce administrations, he purchased Wheatland, a country estate outside Lancaster, and began filling its vaulted cellar with many fine vintages of wine. Still, Buchanan remained more a drinker than a collector. "The Madeira and sherry that he has consumed," his friend John Forney wrote, "would fill more than one old cellar, and the rye whiskey that he has 'punished' would make Jacob Baer's heart glad."

Baer was a local distiller who produced a whiskey brand called Old J. B., and Buchanan kept so much of it on hand that some guests at Wheatland thought the whiskey's initials were Buchanan's rather than Baer's. When Buchanan's supply ran low, he often used his Sunday drive to church as an excuse to stop by Baer's distillery for another ten-gallon cask.

At dinner parties, Buchanan would often start with a stiff cognac, drink two or three bottles of heavy wine, and then

Buchanan with his cabinet in 1859.

finish the meal with a few glasses of rye. "And then the effect of it!" Forney marveled. "There was no head ache, no faltering steps, no flushed cheek. Oh, no! All was as cool, as calm and as cautious and watchful as in the beginning."

★ ★ ★ ★ ★ ★ ★ ★ ★ ★ ★ ★ ★ ★ ★ ★ ★

• Harriet Lane

BUCHANAN WAS THE ONLY PRESIDENT to remain a bachelor his entire life. During his years in the White House, his niece Harriet Lane served as his official hostess. Harriet had been placed in her uncle's care during the early 1840s after the death of her parents. She was only about thirteen at the time.

Grateful for Buchanan's generosity, Harriet was devoted to him, but she also began to find life in the White House somewhat claustrophobic. Whether by design or by innocent error, Buchanan often opened Harriet's mail. He usually wrote on such letters, "Opened by mistake. I know not whether it contains aught of love or treason." But Harriet wasn't satisfied.

In order to consult privately with her close friend Sophie Plitt, who lived in Philadelphia, Harriet needed a more secure system of communication. The one that she devised made use of a locked brass-bound kettle, in which the White House received regular butter shipments from Philadelphia. Harriet borrowed the White House steward's key and made a copy, which she sent to her friend. During the last year of the Buchanan administration, Harriet and Sophie sent letters back and forth "via the kettle," as they wrote on the envelopes.

MAJOR POLITICAL EVENTS

★ **Dred Scott Case:** Two days after President Buchanan's inauguration in March 1857, the Supreme Court ruled in the *Dred Scott* case. The Court declared that Scott, a slave, had no standing to sue for his freedom because he was property and not legally a person. This decision confirmed Buchanan's view, expressed in his inaugural address, that ownership of slaves was a constitutional right. In fact, few Americans favored ending slavery where it already existed. Following this logic, the Court ruled that the Missouri Compromise was unconstitutional because Congress had no power to deny citizens of new states the same right that slave owners in other states enjoyed.

★ **Kansas Statehood:** As Pierce had, Buchanan used his influence to support the proslavery faction in Kansas. In October 1857, proslavery delegates meeting in Lecompton drafted a new territorial constitution that protected the rights of slave owners and barred free blacks from entering the territory. In a December vote boycotted by Kansas Free Staters, the new constitution was approved. Two months later, Buchanan asked Congress to admit Kansas as a slave state under the Lecompton Constitution. The Senate went along, but the House refused. Another vote was held in Kansas in August 1858. This time, with Free Staters participating, the proslavery Lecompton Constitution was defeated by a wide margin. Kansas was finally admitted as a free state in January 1861, but not until six slave states had seceded from the Union to form the Confederate States of America.

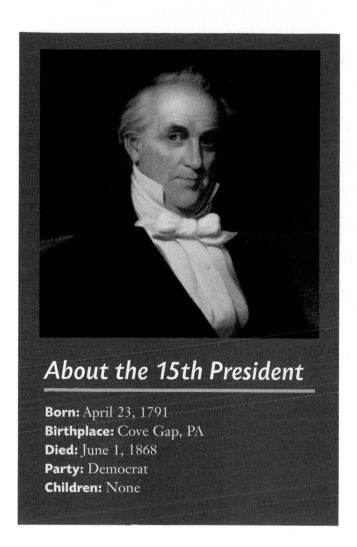

About the 15th President

Born: April 23, 1791
Birthplace: Cove Gap, PA
Died: June 1, 1868
Party: Democrat
Children: None

★ **Harpers Ferry Raid:** Antislavery fanatic John Brown believed that God had sent him to Kansas to destroy slavery there. After Border Ruffians sacked the abolitionist stronghold of Lawrence in May 1856, Brown and his sons retaliated by killing five proslavery settlers in the Pottawatomie Creek Massacre. Brown then escaped to the East, where he organized an attack on the federal arsenal at Harpers Ferry, Virginia. He intended to use the weapons stored there to arm a slave revolt. On October 16, 1859, Brown and twenty-one zealous followers managed to capture the lightly guarded arsenal, but they were discovered by the townspeople of Harpers Ferry, who kept them pinned down until a company of marines led by Col. Robert E. Lee arrived two days later. The marines stormed the arsenal and captured Brown. He was tried for treason and hanged on December 2.

During the Buchanan Administration

1857	*In New York City, Frederick Law Olmsted and Calvert Vaux win a competition to design Central Park.*
1857	*Printer Nathaniel Currier and his bookkeeper, James Merritt Ives, begin making Currier & Ives prints. The prints feature historical events, sentimental scenes, and landscapes.*
Aug. 16, 1858	*Queen Victoria of England sends President Buchanan the first transatlantic telegraph message.*
Sep. 16, 1858	*Owner John Butterfield rides aboard the first overland mail stage to leave St. Louis for San Francisco. The trip takes twenty-five days. A one-way fare is two hundred dollars.*
June 1859	*On land in the Utah Territory owned by Henry Comstock, prospectors make the first major U.S. silver strike.*
Aug. 28, 1859	*Edwin L. Drake strikes oil in Titusville, Pennsylvania, beginning the U.S. commercial oil industry.*
Sep. 1, 1859	*The Pullman sleeper becomes an instant success during its first run on the Chicago & Alton Railroad.*
Apr. 3, 1860	*The first Pony Express rider leaves St. Joseph, Missouri, for Sacramento. The Pony Express's horse-and-rider relay system carries mail across the Rockies in just ten days.*
1860	*Oliver F. Winchester's Volcanic Repeating Arms Company makes the first Winchester repeating rifle.*

With malice toward none, with charity for all, with firmness in the right as God gives us to see the right, let us strive on to finish the work we are in, to bind up the nation's wounds, to care for him who shall have borne the battle and for his widow and his orphan, to do all which may achieve and cherish a just and lasting peace among ourselves and with all nations.

Abraham Lincoln

16th President • 1861–1865

B Y NATURE, ABRAHAM LINCOLN was passive and modest. In 1864, when a fellow Kentuckian asked him why he had abandoned his inaugural pledge not to interfere with slavery, Lincoln explained that events had forced him to change his mind: As the Civil War dragged on and the mustering of black troops became a military necessity, he was left with no choice but to free the slaves.

Lincoln had similar feelings about the war itself, which he believed had also been forced on him. The South had started the fighting, Lincoln was quick to point out. His decision to resist with force was merely a response to the Fort Sumter attack. "In telling this tale I attempt no compliment of my own sagacity," Lincoln wrote. "I claim not to have controlled events, but to confess plainly that events have controlled me."

This comment reflected Lincoln's deep belief in predestination. The rest of the country knew that his leadership abilities, pragmatism, and shrewd political sense were indispensable to the Union cause, but Lincoln often discounted the role that he played.

"From his earliest days," wrote biographer David Herbert Donald, "Lincoln had a sense that his destiny was controlled by some larger force, some Higher Power." The president wasn't religious in any formal sense—he didn't belong to any church—but he did like to quote these favorite lines from *Hamlet:* "There's a divinity that shapes our ends/Roughhew them how we will."

Lincoln's fatalistic attitude didn't stop him from working very hard to change the world. However, it did cushion the impact of the numerous setbacks that he experienced as a lawyer, a politician, and especially a commander in chief. Lincoln's ambition was great: It carried him from a frontier log cabin to the presidency. But such ambition rarely succeeds without great failures. How many recall, for instance, that the famous Lincoln-Douglas debates between Lincoln and Stephen Douglas were part of an 1858 Senate race that Lincoln *lost*?

The mounting Civil War death toll weighed heavily on the president. Late at night, he would struggle with his own responsibility for the slaughter. To comfort himself, he read the Bible, and this reinforced his idea that a divine will was somehow at work, an idea that permitted him to sleep.

"The purposes of the Almighty are perfect, and must prevail, though we erring mortals may fail to accurately perceive them," Lincoln wrote in 1864. "Surely He intends some great good to follow this mighty convulsion, which no mortal could make, and no mortal could stay."

Top: This daguerreotype, taken about 1846, is the earliest known photograph of Lincoln. Right: Lincoln's hands, from a casting made during his lifetime.

• Appearances Can Be Deceiving

"He was not a pretty man by any means," Lincoln's law partner, William Herndon, wrote, "nor was he an ugly one." Lincoln stood six feet four inches tall but looked even taller because he was so thin. He's often pictured as grave and unsmiling, but that was largely the doing of photographers, who required him to hold the same expression for several seconds. The daguerreotypes of Lincoln, therefore, don't capture his well-developed sense of humor, which he usually expressed through comical, folksy anecdotes. The images also don't capture Lincoln's speaking voice, which was high with a strong frontier accent. He regularly pronounced *get* as *git* and *there* as *thar*.

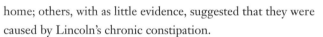

• Bouts of Depression

Lincoln was often seized by deeply melancholy moods. Some biographers have traced these depressions to the death of his mother when he was nine. Although Lincoln wrote a great deal about himself, this was a wound too sensitive to touch. The closest he came was a letter that he wrote years later to a bereaved child: "In this sad world of ours, sorrow comes to all; and, to the young, it comes with bitterest agony, because it takes them unawares…. I have had experience enough to know what I say."

His marriage in 1842 moderated his mood swings, but William Herndon noted that Lincoln still would sit for hours sometimes, staring silently into space. Herndon attributed these spells to unhappiness at home; others, with as little evidence, suggested that they were caused by Lincoln's chronic constipation.

His worst attacks came during the Civil War. "Doesn't it seem strange to you that I should be here?" he asked a visiting congressman. "Doesn't it strike you as queer that I, who couldn't cut the head off of a chicken, and who was sick at the sight of blood, should be cast into the middle of a great war, with blood flowing all about me?"

When nothing he did seemed to speed a Union victory, he wrote, "I am almost ready to say…that God wills this contest, and wills that it shall not end yet."

Lincoln debriefs Union general George B. McClellan.

Tad with his father in the White House.

• Parenting

The Lincolns had three sons who survived to boyhood: Robert, Willie, and Tad. Robert's clearest childhood memory of his father was of Lincoln packing his saddlebags before riding out on the court circuit. But the death of Lincoln's own father in 1851 changed his attitude toward parenting, and he became much more of an active father.

One of the earliest changes was that he began babysitting the younger boys (the neighborhood ladies called him "henpecked"). Lincoln liked to wheel his sons around in a little wagon with one hand while reading a book held in the other. However, at times he became so engrossed in his reading that he didn't notice when one of the boys fell out of the wagon.

★ ★ ★ ★ ★ ★ ★ ★ ★ ★ ★

• Assassination at Ford's Theatre

April 14, 1865, began as a remarkably cheerful day for Lincoln. After breakfast, he heard details of Lee's surrender from his son Robert, just returned from Grant's army. That afternoon, he took a break from his duties for a carriage ride with his wife and told her, "I consider *this day* the war has come to an end."

In the evening, the Lincolns had planned to attend a performance of the comedy *Our American Cousin* at Ford's Theatre. Mary complained of a headache and suggested that they stay home, but Lincoln pointed out that his appearance had already been announced in the afternoon newspapers and many tickets had been sold on that basis.

Lincoln's regular bodyguard, away on a mission, had explicitly asked the president not to visit the theater. Secretary of War Edwin M. Stanton had also warned Lincoln about mingling with crowds. But Lincoln went anyway, arriving at eight-thirty. The play had already begun, but the orchestra leader interrupted the actors and played "Hail to the Chief" while the audience cheered.

One of the most predictable applause lines in the play came during the second scene of the third act, when the leading man reacts to a haughty woman's complaint about his manners: "Don't know the manners of good society, eh? Well, I guess I know enough to turn you inside out, old gal—you sockdologizing old man-trap!" The laughter almost covered the sound of the gunshot in the president's box.

* * * * * * * * * * * * * * * * * * * * *

• Mary Lincoln

ACCORDING TO ONE MEMBER OF his social circle in Springfield, Illinois, "Lincoln could not hold a lengthy conversation with a lady" because he was "not sufficiently educated and intelligent in the female line." Having grown up on the frontier, where women generally kept to themselves, Lincoln had heard a lot of rough talk about sex but not gained much experience of it.

When he met Mary Todd, however, his lack of social grace didn't seem to matter—she was gracious enough for both of them. Lincoln first met Mary in 1839 at a dance, where he told her that he wanted to dance with her "in the worst way." Mary laughed. At that time, she was just turning twenty-one, and marriage was on her mind. Lincoln, then a rising lawyer, seemed to be a suitable prospect. After a hesitant courtship, they were married on November 4, 1842.

For the next several years, the Lincolns had a pleasant, peaceful marriage. However, Mary's family had a history of mental illness, and she eventually began to exhibit signs of emotional instability. For example, she developed a terrible temper. Neighbors of the Lincolns often spoke of the tongue-lashings she gave maids, workmen, street vendors, and even her husband. According to one story, she chased Lincoln out of the house and down the street waving a butcher's knife in her hand—or perhaps it was a broomstick.

Every spring, she had to endure excruciatingly painful headaches—possibly the result of an allergy, but certainly upsetting. She also suffered from terrible menstrual cramps and several severe phobias. She was especially terrified of lightning storms, dogs, and robbers. Once she flew into a panic when an umbrella salesman knocked on her door.

Lincoln was able to calm her while he was alive, but after his death, Mary's mental health deteriorated quickly. She hallucinated and imagined people plotting to kill her. Her son Robert was forced to have her committed in 1875, but she improved and the following year was declared competent once again to handle her own affairs.

MAJOR POLITICAL EVENTS

★ **Civil War:** The Civil War began at 4:30 A.M. on April 12, 1861, when Confederate batteries opened fire on Fort Sumter in Charleston Harbor. The first battle between Confederate and Union armies came three months later at Bull Run, where the Confederates repulsed a Union advance into Virginia. President Lincoln responded by signing the first military draft law and placing George B. McClellan in command of the Army of the Potomac. An extremely cautious general, McClellan devised the 1862 Peninsular Campaign to capture the Confederate capital of Richmond, Virginia, but he overestimated the opposition and never pressed his advantage. In September 1862, Confederate general Robert E. Lee marched north into Maryland. At the battle of Antietam, the bloodiest of the war, Lee and McClellan fought to a standstill, after which Lee retreated. Following Antietam, Lincoln dismissed McClellan as commander in chief of the Union's main army and replaced him with Ambrose Burnside (who lost at Fredericksburg), then Joseph Hooker (who lost at Chancellorsville), and finally George Meade (who won at Gettysburg). Meanwhile, in March 1864, Lincoln turned over command of all Union forces to Gen. Ulysses S. Grant, whose bloody victories in the West had persuaded the president that he had the aggressiveness necessary to win the war. During the fall of 1864, Union general William Tecumseh Sherman burned Atlanta and completed his famous March to the Sea, which destroyed the southern economy and thus the South's ability to make war. In early 1865, Sherman's army turned north to join

About the 16th President

Born: February 12, 1809
Birthplace: Hardin County, KY
Died: April 15, 1865
Party: Republican
Children: Robert, Edward, William,
Thomas (Tad)

★ ★ ★ ★ ★ ★ ★ ★ ★ ★ ★ ★ ★ ★

During the Lincoln Administration

Oct. 24, 1861   *Western Union completes the first transcontinental telegraph line. The new service costs six dollars for ten words and puts the Pony Express out of business.*

Dec. 1861   *Julia Ward Howe writes the "Battle Hymn of the Republic" after visiting Washington, D.C., a gloomy place since the Confederate victory at Bull Run.*

Mar. 9, 1862   *The ironclad Union* Monitor *and Confederate* Merrimack *meet in battle, beginning a new era in naval warfare.*

Jan. 26, 1863   *The governor of Massachusetts forms the first official Negro regiment, the Fifty-fourth Massachusetts Volunteer Infantry.*

Mar. 3, 1863   *Congress passes the nation's first conscription law, requiring men between the ages of twenty and forty-five to register for army service.*

July 13, 1863   *Four days of draft riots begin in New York City. Irish-American workers, fearing that freed slaves will compete with them for jobs, lynch blacks and burn their neighborhoods.*

Oct. 3, 1863   *President Lincoln declares Thanksgiving Day an official national holiday.*

1863   *John D. Rockefeller invests in the oil business. He builds a refinery outside Cleveland, Ohio, taking advantage of nearby oil fields in Pennsylvania.*

Jan. 13, 1864   *Songwriter Stephen Foster dies in the charity ward of Bellevue Hospital in New York City. His last song, "Beautiful Dreamer," was written just days before.*

Grant for an attack on Richmond, which fell on April 3. Six days later, Lee surrendered.

★ **Emancipation Proclamation:** In late August 1862, Lincoln responded to an editorial calling for emancipation of all slaves by restating his policy that the end of slavery wasn't his chief war aim. "My paramount object," Lincoln wrote, "is to save the Union…. If I could save the Union without freeing any slave I would do it." A month later, however, Lincoln reversed this policy. Using the narrow Union victory at Antietam as an excuse, he issued the Emancipation Proclamation, warning all states in rebellion that he would free their slaves unless they returned to the Union by January 1, 1863. The proclamation had little effect in the South, where it was ignored, but in the North it helped morale by turning the war into a moral crusade.

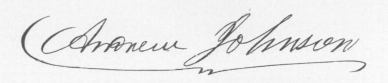

Andrew Johnson

17th President • 1865–1869

FROM THE TIME OF HIS ADOLESCENCE, Andrew Johnson was galled by the way that rich and influential power brokers held sway over common folk. He particularly despised the South's plantation aristocracy, even though he was from Tennessee. As a senator during the late 1850s, he championed the Homestead Bill, which would have given working people a chance to own their own farms. Southerners quashed this proposal because the small midwestern farms that the bill created would have been worked by free (not slave) labor.

In 1861, when it came time to choose between the Union and the Confederacy, Johnson didn't have to think very long. He was not an abolitionist—in fact, he owned several slaves—yet he hated the plantation owners more than he loved the South. In his mind, the only way poor southern whites could prosper was through the destruction of the plantation economy. The enemy of the South wasn't the North, he insisted, but the wealthy. Also, in his own stubborn way, Johnson thought the Constitution was even more sacred than the Bible.

When Abraham Lincoln ran for a second term in 1864, the Civil War still appeared endless. Lincoln speculated that it might last another three years. If this were so, Democrat George B. McClellan, the former Union general fired by Lincoln, might well win the November election.

To attract Democratic votes, Lincoln chose as his running mate Andrew Johnson, the only southern senator to remain loyal to the Union after his state seceded. The choice was good politics, but Lincoln must have also seen in Johnson's character something that attracted him.

Like Lincoln, Johnson had been raised in poverty. They were both self-made men whose will and determination had carried them through tumultuous periods in their careers. However, the similarity ended there. While Lincoln emerged from his experiences with a broad understanding of people and their motivations, Johnson grew to manhood with a prickly pride and a chip on his shoulder. He was as tough as Lincoln but lacked Lincoln's great capacity for sympathy. As one contemporary said, Johnson's face offered "no genial sunlight."

As president, Johnson meant well, but his stubbornness sabotaged his efforts to make the best of a difficult situation. When it became clear that Congress would fight him over Reconstruction, he decided to take his case to the people. During the 1866 congressional campaign, he toured the East and Midwest. The trip started well but ended badly, with Johnson frequently losing his temper and responding to hecklers with inappropriate language. Newspapers reported that he was either "touched with insanity" or "stimulated with drink," and things went downhill from there.

• A Tailor's Apprentice

Andrew Johnson's father worked as a handyman at an inn in Raleigh, North Carolina; his mother worked at the inn as a barmaid. Both were poor whites in the South, which meant that they had little chance of bettering themselves.

When Johnson was three years old, his father died while saving two wealthy men from drowning. His mother, penniless with two small children, became almost an object of charity. She made a little money as a weaver, but it was barely enough to keep her family alive. When the boys were old enough—in Johnson's case, fourteen—she apprenticed them to the town tailor, James J. Selby.

Tradesmen often hired people to read to the boys as they worked, and Selby was no exception.

A man named Dr. Hill often read to Selby's apprentices from a collection of great orations. Johnson was illiterate (he never attended a single day of school), so Dr. Hill's reading was his first exposure to learning. It excited him. In fact, his desire to learn more became so apparent that Dr. Hill gave him the book of orations as a present. Poring over this book at night, Andrew Johnson slowly taught himself to read.

Far left: Johnson's tailoring shears.
Left: His iron (also called a goose)
and a coat he made.

★ ★ ★ ★ ★ ★ ★ ★ ★ ★ ★ ★ ★ ★ ★

• Shoot First

Johnson's combativeness was most obvious during his political campaigns. His race for reelection as governor of Tennessee in 1855 was particularly memorable.

Having heard rumors that he might be shot, Johnson appeared on the stump the next day with a pistol. "I have been informed that part of the business to be transacted on the present occasion is the assassination of the individual who now has the honor of addressing you," Johnson began. "I beg respectfully to propose that this be the first business in order. If any man has come here today for the business indicated, I do not say to him, let him speak, but let him *shoot*."

Johnson stepped back, flung open his coat, and stood there, waiting. After a moment's silence, he relaxed and continued, "Gentlemen, it appears that I have been misinformed. I will now proceed to address you on the subject that has called us together."

• He Ain't No Drunkard

Johnson's strength as a politician was that he identified with the common man, being one himself. However, his manners did leave something to be desired. In Tennessee, which still embraced its frontier heritage, Johnson's lack of grace mattered little, but in Washington, D.C., it produced a great deal of unkind talk.

Johnson didn't help himself any when he showed up at his 1865 vice-presidential inauguration apparently drunk. Ill with a fever, Johnson had a drink of whiskey before taking his oath, hoping that it would fortify him. Instead, it nearly knocked him out. During his speech, he spoke disjointedly and slurred some words, and people could smell the alcohol on his breath. Lincoln tried to quash the stories of Johnson's intoxication: He admitted, "He made a bad slip the other day, but I have known Andy a great many years, and he ain't no drunkard." But Lincoln didn't have much time to build up his vice president's reputation—five weeks later Lincoln was dead.

Johnson's final party, or levee, at the White House in March 1869.

• Impeachment

Johnson's relatively lenient plan for Reconstruction was much like the one Lincoln had proposed. However, Johnson was no Lincoln, and the Radical Republicans who ran Congress had no intention of negotiating with him. The new president was politically isolated, had little personal stature, and wasn't even a Republican. (Johnson had been a Democrat before the war.)

In one of many moves to strip Johnson of his power, Congress passed the Tenure of Office Act, forcing the president to seek the Senate's permission before replacing one of his cabinet members. Never one to back down from a dare, Johnson fired Secretary of War Edwin M. Stanton, a Lincoln holdover who had refused to carry out Johnson's orders. On February 24, 1868, the House used the dismissal of Stanton as an excuse to impeach the president.

Johnson's trial in the Senate lasted two months. He wanted to attend the hearings personally, but cooler heads prevailed. This was fortunate, because when some of his accusers suggested that he might have played a part in Lincoln's assassination, Johnson would likely have hit someone.

The seven Radical Republicans who managed Johnson's impeachment trial.

On May 16, the roll was called with fifteen hundred spectators jamming the Senate galleries. The final vote remained in doubt until near the end, when a young Kansas senator named Edmund Ross sacrificed his political future by voting not guilty. Johnson was saved by this single vote.

★ ★ ★ ★ ★ ★ ★ ★ ★ ★ ★ ★ ★ ★ ★ ★

• Eliza Johnson

AFTER TWO YEARS AS AN APPRENTICE to tailor James J. Selby, Andrew Johnson ran away. One account suggests that Selby insulted him, another that he had "rocked" an old lady's house and feared she would have him arrested. In any case, he rambled about, finally settling in Greenville, Tennessee, where he opened his own tailor's shop at age eighteen. Two months later, he married sixteen-year-old Eliza McCardle. According to a local legend, they met on Johnson's first day in town and took an instant liking to each other.

The couple lived in the back room of the shop, where Johnson's education began in earnest. Although he could read simple words and spell a few, he couldn't write. Eliza remedied this during the short time each day when he wasn't busy with needle and thread. Over the next ten years, she taught him how to read more effectively, how to write a legible letter, and how to spell fairly well. (Of course, spelling was not a widely respected art at this time. As Andrew Jackson told his secretary when the secretary pointed out that Jackson had misspelled his own name, "It is a man of small imagination who cannot spell his name more than one way.")

After giving birth to her fifth child at age forty-one, Eliza became seriously ill with a form of tuberculosis. The disease left her a semi-invalid for the rest of her life. As first lady, she was usually too weak to leave her room, so her two daughters, Martha and Mary, acted as White House hostesses.

MAJOR POLITICAL EVENTS

★ **Reconstruction:** During the summer of 1865, President Johnson formulated a simple and lenient plan for the readmission of southern states into the Union. Under the direction of temporary federal governors, the former Confederate states would draft new constitutions that abolished slavery and renounced secession. When Congress met again in December 1865, the states that had met Johnson's conditions sent delegations. (Georgia's included Confederate vice president Alexander H. Stephens.) However, the Radical Republicans who ran Congress refused to seat the former rebels. During the remainder of Johnson's term, the Radical Republicans passed a series of laws (over the president's veto) that imposed harsh penalties on the South while championing the political and civil rights of former slaves. These laws included the Civil Rights Act of 1866, which overturned the repressive southern Black Codes, and the First Reconstruction Act of 1867, which divided the former Confederacy into five districts, each ruled by a federal military governor.

★ **Constitutional Amendments:** In the aftermath of the Civil War, Congress passed three amendments to the Constitution: The Thirteenth Amendment, ratified in December 1865, abolished slavery in the United States. The Fourteenth Amendment, proposed in June 1866, made elements of the recent Civil Rights Act a permanent part of the Constitution. Johnson advised the southern states to withhold ratification of this amendment, but

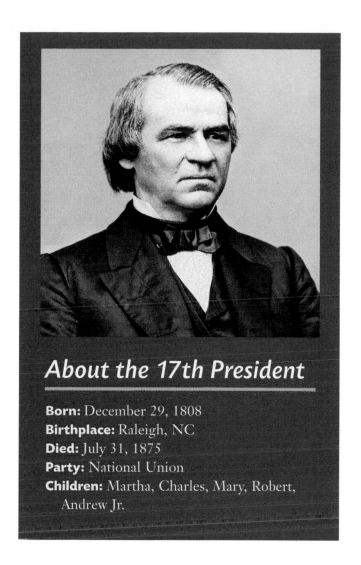

About the 17th President

Born: December 29, 1808
Birthplace: Raleigh, NC
Died: July 31, 1875
Party: National Union
Children: Martha, Charles, Mary, Robert, Andrew Jr.

Congress responded by making ratification a precondition for readmission to the Union. In February 1869, Congress sent to the states the Fifteenth Amendment, which prohibited states from denying the vote to any citizen "on account of race, color, or previous condition of servitude."

★ **Seward's Folly:** In March 1867, Secretary of State William H. Seward agreed to pay $7.2 million, or about 2¢ an acre, for the Russian colony of Alaska. Its five hundred thousand square miles were nicknamed Seward's Folly by those who questioned the wisdom of buying such a "large lump of ice." The Senate ratified the purchase on April 9. Although Alaska was known to be rich in furs and fish, its vast interior seemed useless until the discovery of gold there near the end of the nineteenth century.

During the Johnson Administration

May 5, 1865 *Thieves commit the first train robbery in the United States. They derail an Ohio & Mississippi Railroad train, then hold up passengers and loot the freight car.*

Dec. 24, 1865 *Former Confederate soldiers in Pulaski, Tennessee, organize the Ku Klux Klan. The organization begins as a social club for Confederate veterans but soon becomes a focus for violent resistance to Reconstruction.*

Dec. 25, 1865 *Chicago's Union Stockyards receives its first shipment of livestock. Nine railroads organized and built the stockyards to create a center for meatpacking in the Midwest.*

1865 *Philadelphia hatmaker John B. Stetson creates the first Stetson hat, which features a wide brim and a high crown.*

July 30, 1866 *Rioters kill forty-eight blacks in a New Orleans race riot that erupts after Louisiana gives black men the right to vote.*

Jan. 1867 *Horatio Alger publishes the first installment of* Ragged Dick *in* Student and Schoolmate *magazine. The novel is the first of Alger's many rags-to-riches stories.*

1867 *Brooklyn Excelsiors pitcher William A. "Candy" Cummings throws baseball's first curveball in a game against Harvard.*

Jan. 16, 1868 *Fish merchant William Davis patents a refrigerated railroad car designed to carry meat and fish. The cars have side tanks for cracked ice but work only in winter.*

June 23, 1868 *Christopher Sholes obtains a patent for the first practical typewriter.*

I have taken this oath without mental reservation and with the determination to do to the best of my ability all that is required of me. The responsibilities of the position I feel, but accept them without fear.

Ulysses S. Grant

18th President • 1869–1877

DURING THE WORST FIGHTING of the Civil War, when hundreds of thousands of lives were being lost, Lincoln's advisers urged him to get rid of Gen. Ulysses S. Grant. In one month, Grant's 118,000-man army had lost nearly 55,000. But Lincoln refused. "I cannot spare this man," Lincoln said. "He fights."

Grant's personality, however, didn't match his tough public image. He was a highly sensitive man: squeamish, shy, and soft spoken. He always bathed in a closed tent, for example, so that others wouldn't see him naked. According to Grant biographer W. E. Woodward, "There was a broad streak of the feminine in his personality. He was almost half-woman, but this strain was buried in the depths of his soul…and he was probably not aware of it himself."

When Grant was elected president in 1869, the numerous dishonest elements in Congress held their collective breath. None of them knew what to expect from the general. He had been elected because he was a war hero, and no one knew his political opinions or even whether he had any.

Once they had a chance to observe Grant in office, however, unscrupulous politicians all over Washington relaxed. Grant was the perfect patsy: Because he was himself an honest man, he stubbornly refused to believe anything bad about his colleagues, no matter how strong the evidence against them. And he had no plans for the country but seemed merely to enjoy being president. "It was clear," observed one historian, "that they had only to keep him from making too great a fool of himself, to re-elect him indefinitely and the spoils were theirs."

There was simply no precedent for the scandals of the Grant administration. First, "robber barons" Jay Gould and Jim Fisk bribed Grant's brother-in-law to help them corner the gold market. "The worst scandals of the eighteenth century," Henry Adams wrote, "were relatively harmless by the side of this, which smirched…all the great active forces of society in one dirty cesspool of vulgar corruption." That was nothing, however, compared to the scandals that followed, which ruined a number of leading congressmen and Grant's first vice president.

"To retain such innocence in the Washington of Grant's days was an almost pathological eccentricity," one Grant biographer has noted. Yet Grant was that innocent. Except for his Civil War glory days, he had failed at just about everything he tried, from farming to real estate to running a country store. And he failed at being president, too: Few honest men could have been worse presidents than Grant.

• A Colossal Sick Joke

As commander of the Union forces, Gen. Ulysses S. Grant taught the country that war was annihilation and that the winning side would be the one with more men available for dying. Unlike the other Union generals, Grant understood how elementary war was, a point that he made in his memoirs: To make war is simply to kill. His strategy from the outset was to kill as many southerners as possible, because nothing short of annihilation would end the rebellion. Meanwhile, "in his throw-away lines—in his throw-away life," Grant biographer William S. McFeely wrote, he "kept trying to get people to see the colossal sick joke."

Although he knew that this was the only way to end the war, the responsibility of sending so many men to their deaths sickened the general. He suffered regularly from severe headaches and couldn't bear the sight of blood. He refused, for example, to eat any meat unless it was cooked dry, for even the hint of blood in the meat juices made him queasy.

Left: Grant in 1864. Right: The general's cigar case. During the Civil War, he often smoked twenty cigars a day.

• Horses

President Grant worked only about four hours per day. He didn't cross over from the White House family quarters to his second-floor office until late in the morning, usually around ten o'clock. Then he worked for two hours before going downstairs for his midday meal. After about an hour, he returned to his office, where he greeted visitors, spending five to fifteen minutes with each of them. At three o'clock, he promptly left his office and went down to the White House stables, where he spent the remainder of the afternoon with his horses.

From the time of his youth, Grant had been obsessed with horses, and he got along with them remarkably well. (For Grant, it was probably easier to get along with horses than with people.) At West Point, he was the best horseman in his class, and during his army career he always rode large, difficult mounts that commanded respect.

To relax, President Grant liked to drive himself around Washington in a gig—a light two-wheeled, one-horse carriage. One day, he was stopped for speeding on M Street by a policeman who didn't recognize him. Grant paid the twenty-dollar fine and wrote a commendation for the officer.

The corruption pervading Grant's administration was often linked by political cartoonists to his alleged alcoholism.

• Was Grant a Drunkard?

During Grant's lifetime and after, it was considered common knowledge that he was an alcoholic. Certainly he liked to drink, but the charge isn't quite fair.

There are three recorded cases of Grant being drunk while in the military. According to a friend, "Whenever he was idle and depressed, this appetite came upon him." The first (and worst) episode took place during the winter of 1853–54, when he was stationed at Fort Humboldt, California. Grant was alone and had nothing to do, so he drank. The colonel in command of the fort finally forced him to resign his commission because of his drunken behavior.

The second and third incidents came in 1863. Both times Grant sobered up quickly and returned, refreshed, to the activities of war. But his reputation as an alcoholic dogged him. The Democrats sang campaign ditties about his drunkenness, and in Washington whenever he did anything awkward—which was often (and normal) for Grant—people simply assumed that he was drunk.

It wasn't until after he left office that Grant actually made a fool of himself. During a round-the-world trip, he visited India and spent one of many uninspiring evenings as the guest of the British viceroy. That night, Lord Lytton recalled, Grant "got as drunk as a fiddle…. He fumbled Mrs. A., kissed the shrieking Miss B.—pinched the plump Mrs. C. black and blue—and ran at Miss D. with intent to ravish her." Finally, the former president was subdued by six sailors who "relieved India of his distinguished presence."

★ ★ ★ ★ ★ ★ ★ ★ ★ ★ ★

• Memoirs

As more than one historian has noted, Grant's adult life can be summarized as twenty years of failure, followed by four years of greatness, followed by twenty more years of failure. After his presidency, Grant went into business with his son and financier Ferdinand Ward. Sadly, like so many other Grant associates, Ward was a scoundrel, and he spent three years fleecing the brokerage house and its investors of more than sixteen million dollars.

When the firm of Grant & Ward declared bankruptcy in 1884, Grant was left personally bankrupt as well. To help Grant out, showman P. T. Barnum offered him one hundred thousand dollars for the right to display his Civil War memorabilia. The general declined and instead began writing his memoirs, having been assured by Mark Twain that such a book would sell well. Although Grant was dying, he worked tirelessly so that he might leave something behind for his family. He finished the book on July 1, 1885. Three weeks later, he was dead. Grant's memoirs ultimately earned nearly half a million dollars in royalties.

Grant, near death, completes his memoirs.

★ ★ ★ ★ ★ ★ ★ ★ ★ ★   ★ ★ ★ ★ ★ ★ ★ ★ ★ ★

• Julia Grant

AFTER LEAVING WEST POINT IN 1843, Grant was assigned—along with his roommate, Frederick Dent—to an infantry post outside St. Louis. Because the young lieutenants had plenty of time on their hands, they often visited White Haven, the Dents' nearby plantation. There Grant became acquainted with Dent's sister Julia, whose self-image was thoroughly that of a southern belle.

In her own memoirs, Julia recalled her idyllic girlhood, especially the fun she had fishing: "Oh! what happiness to see the nibble, to feel the pull, and to see the plunge of the cork; then the little quivering, shining creature was landed high on the bank." Careful to reestablish her femininity, Julia then noted that a slave or a brother was always on hand to remove the fish from the pole.

Even at seventeen, when she met Grant, Julia wasn't an attractive girl. She had a plain face, a stumpy figure, and a problem with her right eye that made it move up and down involuntarily. Yet Grant fell in love. And when he learned that his regiment was being transferred to Louisiana, he proposed.

During the course of their four-year engagement—it spanned the entire Mexican War—Grant and Julia saw each other only once. But they kept their relationship lively through correspondence that apparently included its share of sexual innuendo. Not long after Grant's return from Mexico in 1848, they were married.

As first lady, Mrs. Grant entertained on the lavish scale befitting a daughter of the Old South. Her greatest social triumph was the wedding of her daughter, Nellie, held at the White House in May 1874. There were white flowers everywhere, even atop the great pyramidal wedding cake, and the menu featured soft-shell crab on toast, followed by lamb, beef, wild duck, and chicken. As late as 1902, the year that Julia Grant died, the wedding was still being written about as one of the most brilliant ever given in the United States.

MAJOR POLITICAL EVENTS

★ **Force Acts:** When Grant became president, laws passed by the Radical Republicans in Congress had given federal troops control of nearly every aspect of southern life. These laws were later supplemented by a series of Force Acts that were intended to protect the rights granted to blacks by the Fourteenth and Fifteenth Amendments. The first and second Force Acts of 1870 and 1871 protected black voting rights and gave the federal government the power to control elections in cities with more than twenty thousand people. The Ku Klux Klan Act of 1871, the third Force Act, authorized the president to use military force against terrorist organizations such as the Klan. In October 1871, Grant used this law to declare martial law in South Carolina, where Klan violence against blacks had become epidemic. The last of the Force Acts, the Civil Rights Act of 1875, outlawed racial discrimination in public places such as hotels and restaurants but contained no means of enforcement. It was eventually declared unconstitutional by the Supreme Court in October 1883.

★ **Scandals:** After the failed attempt to corner the gold market in 1869, the next major scandal to beset the Grant administration involved the Crédit Mobilier, a construction company set up by the directors of the Union Pacific Railroad. The purpose of this subsidiary company was to steal some of the federal loan and subsidy money that paid for most of the transcontinental track work. In 1872, the *New York Sun* revealed that bribes had been paid to

About the 18th President

Born: April 27, 1822
Birthplace: Point Pleasant, OH
Died: July 23, 1885
Party: Republican
Children: Frederick, Ulysses Jr., Ellen, Jesse

During the Grant Administration

May 10, 1869 — The Central Pacific and Union Pacific Railroads join tracks at Promontory Point, Utah, forming the first transcontinental line. Owners Leland Stanford and Thomas Durant use a golden spike to mark the spot.

Nov. 6, 1869 — Rutgers beats Princeton, 6–4, in the first college football game.

Dec. 10, 1869 — The territory of Wyoming grants women the right to vote.

Oct. 8, 1871 — The great Chicago fire rages for twenty-four hours, burning four square miles and killing 300 people. Of Chicago's 334,000 residents, nearly 100,000 are left homeless.

1871 — James McNeill Whistler paints Arrangement in Grey and Black, No. 1: Portrait of the Artist's Mother, otherwise known as Whistler's Mother.

July 21, 1872 — The James Gang, led by brothers Frank and Jesse James, robs its first train after six years of targeting banks and stagecoaches.

Nov. 18, 1874 — Meeting at a church in Cleveland, Ohio, women from seventeen states form the Woman's Christian Temperance Union, dedicated to ending the sale of liquor in the United States.

Mar. 10, 1876 — Using his telephone, patented three days earlier, Alexander Graham Bell speaks the first sentence transmitted by voice over wire.

June 22, 1876 — Sioux and Cheyenne warriors massacre Seventh Cavalry commander George Armstrong Custer and most of his regiment on the banks of the Little Bighorn River.

top government officials, including Vice President Schuyler Colfax, to stop an investigation of Crédit Mobilier. Two years later, Treasury Secretary William A. Richardson was forced to resign in disgrace after the revelation of a secret deal he had made with a tax collector allowing that man to keep half the money he collected. In May 1875, Richardson's replacement, Benjamin Bristow, exposed the Whiskey Ring, a group of midwestern distillers and Internal Revenue Service officials who had conspired to steal millions of dollars in liquor taxes. Finally, in March 1876, Congress voted to impeach Secretary of War William W. Belknap after a trader accused him of demanding twelve thousand dollars in exchange for control of the Indian trading post at Fort Sill in Oklahoma. An investigation of Belknap's Indian Ring found that the secretary had already taken twenty-five thousand dollars in bribes.

The president of the United States of necessity owes his election to office to the suffrage and zealous labors of a political party, the members of which cherish with ardor and regard as of essential importance the principles of their party organization; but he should strive to be always mindful of the fact that he serves his party best who serves the country best.

Rutherford B. Hayes

19th President • 1877–1881

A S ONE BIOGRAPHER DESCRIBED RUTHERFORD B. HAYES, the nineteenth president "shone…in a modest way—not sparkling, not brilliant, but pleasing, satisfying." He was a friendly, easygoing man who was genuinely interested in other people's thoughts and problems. When he traveled, he always sat in the smoking car so that he could strike up conversations with other passengers on the train.

In 1876, the Republican party had real problems. Eight years of Grant administration scandals had left them poised to lose the presidency for the first time since 1856. To highlight the corruption issue, the Democrats nominated Samuel J. Tilden, the nationally famous reformer who had exposed New York City's notorious Tweed Ring.

The Republicans needed a reform candidate of their own, someone who was fair, honest, and above reproach. Hayes was an obvious choice. A good Christian, a Civil War veteran, and a three-term governor of Ohio, Hayes was about as benevolent a man as the Republicans could find in 1870s politics. Like Jimmy Carter a century later, Hayes sincerely wanted to help people of all kinds, though his presidency didn't turn out as he had planned.

The trouble began immediately. Although the candidates were clean, the 1876 election was the dirtiest in history. In fact, the Republicans stole it. Tilden won the popular vote and led Hayes in the electoral college, 184 to 165, with 20 votes in dispute. If Tilden had received just one of these votes, he would have won. But a special commission (with a Republican majority) voted them all to Hayes. In exchange for the presidency, Hayes promised the Democrats that he would remove all federal troops from the South, thus ending the era of Reconstruction that followed the Civil War.

At the time, Hayes was praised as a "statesman of reunion," and Mark Twain predicted that his presidency, in "its quiet & unostentatious but real & substantial greatness, would steadily rise into higher & higher prominence." Twain was wrong. Instead, even Hayes's friends began to criticize him for not doing enough to clean things up. Hayes countered that he needed time and patience.

Historians disagree about Hayes. His defenders point out that he made all his political appointments based on merit, not party affiliation. Others counter that Hayes failed to pass his number-one priority: a civil service reform bill. His defenders praise him for extracting from southern Democrats a promise to respect black political rights after the removal of federal troops. His detractors note the hollowness of this promise. The argument goes on and on, but perhaps it can be settled in this way: If Hayes wasn't a good president, he was surely a good man.

Hayes at Harvard Law School, 1845.

• "If Ever I Am a Public Man"

Even though Rutherford Hayes's father died nearly three months before he was born, his maternal uncle Sardis Birchard made sure that "Rud" never lacked for anything. He was sent to a college preparatory school in Middletown, Connecticut; returned to his home state of Ohio to attend Kenyon College; and then spent the remainder of his academic career at the Harvard Law School.

Between his sophomore and junior years at Kenyon, the cloyingly earnest Hayes wrote in his diary: "I am determined from henceforth to use what means I have to acquire a character distinguished for energy, firmness, and perseverance.... It is another intention of mine, that after I have commenced in life, whatever may be my ability or station, to preserve a reputation for honesty and benevolence; and if ever I am a public man, I will never do anything inconsistent with the character of a true friend and good citizen."

★ ★

• South Mountain

Hayes served with the Twenty-third Ohio Volunteers from June 1861 until June 1865, rising during the course of the Civil War from a major to a brevet major general. He was wounded six times and had his horse shot out from under him on four occasions.

His worst injury came in September 1862 at the battle of South Mountain, one of the preludes to Antietam. As Hayes's regiment scaled the mountain under heavy fire, he felt a stunning blow to his arm. A musket ball had hit him just above the elbow, fracturing a bone and leaving a gaping hole.

Becoming weak and faint, he lay down about twenty feet behind the regiment's skirmish line. Musket balls passed near his face, kicking up dirt and stones all around him. Then a shift in the line caused his men to fall back—leaving him stranded, barely conscious, between his own troops and the enemy.

"I never enjoyed any business or mode of life as much as I do this," Hayes wrote his wife in August 1861, before he had seen any real action. "I really feel badly when I think of several of my intimate friends who are compelled to stay at home."

Lying there during a lull in the fighting, weakened by loss of blood, Hayes faced the fact that he might die. He thought of his wife and family and was comforted by three letters he had received from his son Sardis that morning. He also had a "considerable talk" with a Confederate soldier lying wounded nearby, to whom he gave a message for his wife, Lucy.

After his rescue and recovery, the unflappable Hayes recalled his surprise at how "right jolly and friendly" this southerner had been. He said that their exchange, which he had thought might be his last on earth, "was by no means an unpleasant experience."

• The Good Life

More than most presidential couples, the Grants had lived the "good life" of their era, which had been quite good indeed. Under Julia Grant's direction, the Gilded Age White House had been particularly flamboyant. However, the financial panic of 1873 had put a damper on things, and by the time that the Hayeses moved into 1600 Pennsylvania Avenue in 1877, the nation had sobered up.

The Hayeses were the richest people to occupy the White House during the nineteenth century, but they didn't live extravagantly. *Their* idea of the good life was devotion to decency and public service. The president and first lady both felt that their family life should be a model for the country, so

The first family and guests sing hymns at the White House. Interior Secretary Carl Schurz is playing the piano. Vice President William Wheeler stands with his hand on Hayes's chair. At the back of the room, Treasury Secretary John Sherman shares a hymnal with Hayes's daughter, Fanny.

they attended church regularly, went to bed early, and banned liquor from White House events. Lucy Hayes also made it a point to get rid of the billiard table that President Grant had purchased, because the game was commonly associated with drinking and gambling.

The harmonious Hayes family at table.

• New Technology

Although generally reserved, President Hayes could be captivated by a new piece of technology. This was his attitude: If it works, buy it. During his first year in office, Hayes heard late one night that Thomas Edison was in town. Disregarding the time (it was already past eleven) and the fact that Mrs. Hayes was asleep, the president invited Edison over to the White House that very evening to demonstrate his new phonograph. The commotion awakened Mrs. Hayes shortly after midnight; even so, Edison didn't leave until after three o'clock.

The first new device that Hayes purchased to make his White House office more efficient was a telephone. In May 1879, he had one installed in the telegraph room. The device worked well, but it was so new, and there were so few others in Washington, that he had almost no one to call.

The following year, Hayes bought an early typewriter for his staff. Soon enough, presidential correspondence began appearing in ragged lines of type rather than the familiar fancy penmanship of his clerks.

★ ★ ★ ★ ★ ★ ★ ★ ★ ★ ★ ★ ★ ★ ★ ★ ★ ★

• Lucy Hayes

WHEN IT CAME TO MARRIAGE, Rud Hayes was a procrastinator. A popular beau, he fell in love with a number of women during his early twenties but sooner or later dropped all of them. In 1847, when he was twenty-four, he met Lucy Webb, the daughter of a family friend. Although Hayes thought her much too young to marry (she was just turning sixteen), he remarked in his diary that she was a "bright, sunny-hearted" girl. Three years later, when their paths crossed again after Lucy had graduated from college, she made a much deeper impression on him.

He described her with abundant admiration in his diary: "Her low sweet voice is very winning, her soft rich eye not often equaled; a heart as true as steel…. Intellect, she has, too, a quick sprightly one…. It is no use doubting or rolling it over in my thoughts. By George! I am in love with her!" Hayes proposed in June 1851, and they sealed their engagement with their first kiss.

Unlike most Victorian women, the young Mrs. Hayes had definite political views. Early on, she sensitized her husband to the inhumanity of slavery and persuaded him to join the new anti-slavery Republican party. Later, she became a crusader against alcohol.

When Hayes became president, Lucy and her friends in the National Women's Christian Temperance Union began to pressure him to make the White House dry. They argued that such a move would reinforce his call for greater Christian morality in public affairs. Hayes drank, but he knew Lucy's mind and agreed to ban liquor from presidential functions.

Hayes's well-publicized decision made Lucy more of a celebrity than any first lady since Dolley Madison. She was nicknamed Lemonade Lucy and became the idol of temperance people all over the country. Many women's rights activists also praised her lavishly for taking such a strong stand on a public issue.

MAJOR POLITICAL EVENTS

★ **Civil Service Reform:** Since the introduction of the "spoils system" during the administration of Andrew Jackson, civil service jobs had become the currency of political loyalty. Believing that government jobs shouldn't be handed out as political rewards, President Hayes issued in June 1877 an executive order that barred civil servants from taking part in political activities. (In July 1878, he fired future president Chester Arthur from his job in the New York Customhouse for disobeying this order.) Hayes also encouraged the efforts of Interior Secretary Carl Schurz to develop exams for hiring and promotion, yet he was unable to persuade Congress to act on large-scale reforms.

★ **Great Uprising:** On July 14, 1877, the Baltimore & Ohio Railroad announced a 10 percent pay cut, its second major pay cut since the financial panic of 1873 started a national depression. The Great Uprising began two days later when B&O workers in West Virginia staged a spontaneous strike. As news of the B&O strike spread, sympathetic workers took over entire towns and shut down most U.S. railroad service. When fighting broke out between the striking workers in West Virginia and state militiamen, Hayes sent federal troops to protect railroad property. Meanwhile, the center of the labor revolt shifted to Pittsburgh, where ironworkers had walked out in support of railroad workers. Militiamen called in from Philadelphia fired into a crowd on July 20, killing several people. On the same day, Maryland militiamen killed nine strikers in Baltimore. Putting the government firmly on the side of big business, Hayes used

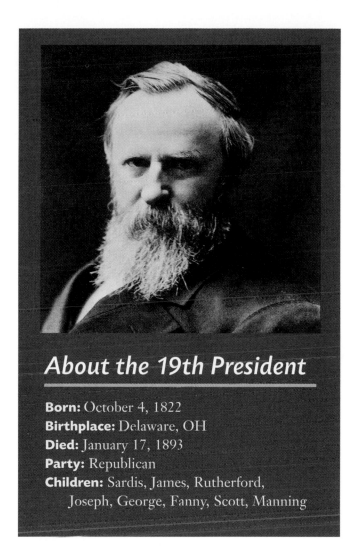

About the 19th President

Born: October 4, 1822
Birthplace: Delaware, OH
Died: January 17, 1893
Party: Republican
Children: Sardis, James, Rutherford,
Joseph, George, Fanny, Scott, Manning

During the Hayes Administration

May 6, 1877 — Tired of the relentless army pursuit, Crazy Horse gives himself up in exchange for the promise of a Sioux reservation in Montana. Four months later, during a parley, an army private spears Crazy Horse in the belly with a bayonet, killing him.

Dec. 6, 1877 — Thomas Edison recites "Mary Had a Little Lamb" into his new invention, the phonograph, which reproduces his voice.

Feb. 18, 1878 — The Lincoln County War between rival ranchers in New Mexico begins with a dispute over government beef contracts.

Feb. 15, 1879 — President Hayes signs a bill that allows women lawyers to argue cases before the Supreme Court.

Feb. 22, 1879 — Frank W. Woolworth opens the Great Five Cent Store in Utica, New York. It fails, but Woolworth soon opens a more successful "five-and-ten" store in Pennsylvania.

Oct. 1879 — Thomas Edison finally discovers a filament material that will make his incandescent lightbulb work: charred cotton thread. Later, he settles on bamboo filaments.

Nov. 4, 1879 — Saloon owner James J. Ritty patents the cash register, which he calls the Incorruptible Cashier.

1879 — Paper bag manufacturer Robert Gair builds the first machine to make folding cardboard boxes.

Aug. 11, 1880 — "War is hell," declares William T. Sherman at a reunion celebrating the twenty-fifth anniversary of the end of the Civil War.

federal troops to restore order—and railroad service—by force, thus ending the first nationwide strike.

★ **Bland-Allison Act:** In February 1878, over Hayes's veto, Congress passed the Bland-Allison Act. This law made silver coins once again legal tender and required the government to purchase between two million and four million dollars' worth of silver each month for coinage purposes. The Bland-Allison Act temporarily compromised the dispute raging between western farmers on the one side and eastern bankers on the other over unlimited coinage of silver. The farmers wanted unlimited coinage because it would increase the money supply and make their debts easier to repay. The bankers (and Hayes) wanted to limit inflation by keeping the nation on the gold standard.

There can be no permanent disfranchised peasantry in the United States. Freedom can never yield its fullness of blessings so long as the law or its administration places the smallest obstacle in the pathway of any virtuous citizen.

James A. Garfield

20th President • 1881

JAMES GARFIELD CONSIDERED HIMSELF an intellectual, and his colleagues in Congress agreed. He was one of the few representatives who knew his way around the Library of Congress, and he often relaxed with a scholarly project, such as translating the work of the poet Goethe from the original German into English.

Garfield was drawn to intellectual pursuits because he felt a little nostalgic and a little guilty. Before the Civil War, he had taught Greek and Latin at a religious school run by the Disciples of Christ. After the war, he gave up both his scholarship and his religion for politics.

As a congressman, Garfield thrived within the "dirty cesspool," to quote Henry Adams, that was Washington politics during the Gilded Age. He was implicated in the biggest of the bribe scandals that rocked Congress during the Grant administration and, as leader of the House Republicans, sat on the electoral commission that stole the 1876 election from the Democrats. When he became president, however, the religious and scholarly side of Garfield's personality seemed to reassert itself.

Garfield hardly expected to be president. At the 1880 Republican convention, his job was to nominate Treasury Secretary John Sherman. Sherman didn't fare very well, but he did hold enough votes to keep the convention deadlocked between former president Grant, the candidate of the party's Stalwart faction, and Maine senator James G. Blaine. Finally, on the thirty-sixth ballot, the anti-Grant forces united behind Garfield, and he became the nominee.

Garfield knew, of course, that he would have to pay a price for party unity. After Grant's defeat, the convention nominated Stalwart lackey Chester A. Arthur for vice president, hoping to appease Sen. Roscoe Conkling of New York, Arthur's political boss and the leader of the Stalwarts. But Conkling had a more important demand in mind: He wanted Garfield to consult him before making federal civil service appointments in New York. As any experienced politician would have, Garfield agreed.

However, once he entered the White House, Garfield changed his mind. Ignoring Conkling's wishes, he made appointments in New York based on merit alone, causing a very public breach with the Stalwarts.

Garfield once explained the way he judged greatness in a man: "Did he drift unresisting on the currents of life, or did he lead the thoughts of men to higher and nobler purposes?" For nearly his entire political career, Garfield drifted. However, during his brief, stormy presidency, an earlier Garfield resurfaced. Perhaps the presidential Garfield would have become a man of higher and nobler purpose, but a madman's bullet ended all such speculation.

• True Belief

A precocious child, Jimmie Garfield was reading the Bible by the time he was three. Fatherless since infancy, he was raised on the Ohio frontier by his mother, a devoted member of the Disciples of Christ. Among the core beliefs of this group was that its members should remain detached from worldly matters, especially politics.

After his own conversion in March 1850, the eighteen-year-old Garfield became a true believer. In his diary, he wrote: "I am exceedingly disgusted with all the wire-pulling of politicians and the total disregard of truth in all their operations."

Soon after he entered Williams College in 1854, however, Garfield's religious fervor began to wane. The sophistication of his fellow students made him even more aware of how limited his experience of life had been: He was nineteen, for example, before he heard a piano played for the first time and twenty-three before he had eaten his first banana. He became worried that a career in the ministry would continue to limit him. Instead, he decided to become a teacher.

Garfield, shown here in his Civil War uniform, was the last president who could truthfully claim to have been born in a log cabin.

A reflective Garfield with his daughter Mollie.

• Public Speaking

When Garfield was in his early twenties, he paid for his education by giving weekly sermons at local churches. These sermons earned him a gold dollar apiece and boosted his self-confidence. It soon become clear to him that by speaking he could sway people.

When he entered politics after the Civil War, Garfield made good use of his oratorical talent and became one of the great stump speakers of his generation. His style comfortably blended his evangelical training with a more recently discovered sense of humor. During his seventeen years in Congress, Garfield became famous for his addresses on the floor of the House. It was often difficult for members to be heard above the chamber's unruly din—but, one journalist observed, "*Garfield's* voice is heard. Every ear attends.... His eloquent words move the heart, convince the reason, and tell the weak and wavering which way to go."

Garfield delivered his greatest speech at the 1880 Republican convention. Meant to nominate John Sherman of Ohio, it contained the rhetorical question, "What do we want?" During the brief pause that followed, a voice from the gallery yelled back, "We want Garfield!"

★ ★ ★ ★ ★ ★ ★ ★ ★ ★ ★

• Assassination

Charles J. Guiteau was a failed evangelist who thought that he might have a future in politics. During the 1880 presidential campaign, he attached himself to the Stalwart wing of the Republican party and wrote a speech supporting Grant for a third term. When Garfield became the Republican nominee, Guiteau made a few minor changes and renamed the speech "Garfield against Hancock."

Guiteau never actually gave this speech, though he did have several hundred copies printed up. No one paid any attention, but after the election, Guiteau sent Garfield a copy of the speech with a note that read, "It was *this*...that resulted in your election." He requested the ministry to Austria as a suitable reward.

During March and April, Guiteau appeared at the White House on a daily basis to press his case. In the meantime, he was running out of money. He began to turn up the collar of his coat to hide the fact that his only shirt was now ragged.

Finally, in mid-May, Guiteau had a vision: After reading several vicious attacks on Garfield in the Stalwart press, he decided that, for the country's sake, Garfield had to be "removed." Borrowing some money, he bought a ten-dollar ivory-handled pistol. (Guiteau passed up a cheaper wood-handled gun because he thought the fancier model would look better in the museum case for which it was destined.) He also began to stalk Garfield, which was easy. Presidents

Garfield's desk calendar, which hasn't been reset since the day he was shot.

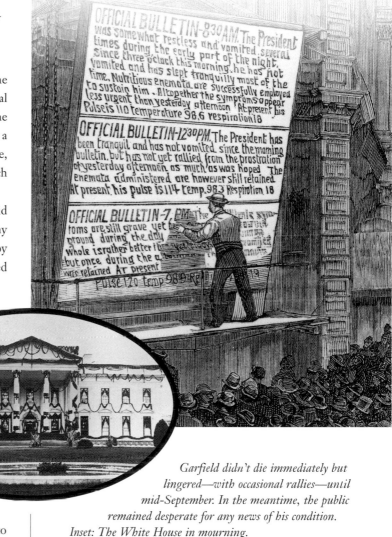

Garfield didn't die immediately but lingered—with occasional rallies—until mid-September. In the meantime, the public remained desperate for any news of his condition. Inset: The White House in mourning.

didn't begin to receive Secret Service protection until the 1890s, and Garfield didn't even have a bodyguard.

Guiteau had plenty of opportunities to kill Garfield, but he often passed them up, lacking the nerve. The day that he finally shot Garfield—July 2, 1881—was perhaps the last of his chances. The president was leaving Washington for a summerlong vacation, and Guiteau was in no financial or emotional position to wait until he returned. That morning, Guiteau staked out the Baltimore & Potomac railroad station, from which the president's train was scheduled to leave. As Garfield crossed the waiting room floor, Guiteau walked up behind him and shot him twice in the back. "I am a Stalwart," Guiteau told the policeman who grabbed him, "and now Arthur is president!"

★ ★ ★ ★ ★ ★ ★ ★ ★ ★ ★ ★ ★ ★ ★ ★ ★

• Lucretia Garfield

ON THE MORNING OF JUNE 18, 1881, President and Mrs. Garfield rode from the White House to the Baltimore & Potomac railroad station, where they planned to (and did) board a train for the New Jersey coast. Charles J. Guiteau, the man who would shoot Garfield two weeks later, was waiting at the station with a loaded pistol. When he saw the first lady, however, he decided not to shoot the president. "Mrs. Garfield looked so thin, and she clung so tenderly to the president's arm, that I did not have the heart to fire upon him," Guiteau recalled at his trial.

James Garfield first began to court Lucretia Rudolph sometime around 1854, when they were both students at the Eclectic Institute, a school run by the Disciples of Christ in Hiram, Ohio. Although Garfield had known Lucretia—he called her Crete—for nearly five years, it took him at least that long to appreciate her quiet modesty. Theirs was a relationship that began simply but grew much stronger as the years passed.

Guiteau thought that Mrs. Garfield looked thin in June 1881 because she was still recovering from a recent serious illness, perhaps malaria. On July 2, the day her husband was shot, Mrs. Garfield was recuperating at the seashore in Long Branch, New Jersey. Learning the news by telegram, she took a special train back to Washington, arriving at seven in the evening. She went immediately to the president's room, where the doctors told her (incorrectly) that he wouldn't live through the night. Only with the help of others could she stand. But she gathered herself and entered the bedroom. When Garfield began to tell her what she must do after his death, she stopped him. "You are not going to die," she told him with all the courage she could muster. "I am here to nurse you back to life."

MAJOR POLITICAL EVENTS

★ **Roscoe Conkling:** The day after his inauguration, President Garfield took on Roscoe Conkling directly when he named Conkling's Stalwart rival William H. Robertson to Chester Arthur's old job at the New York Customhouse. This appointment flagrantly broke the Treaty of Fifth Avenue, a deal made by Garfield and Conkling during the 1880 presidential campaign. (The Treaty of Fifth Avenue traded Conkling's active support in exchange for Garfield's promise that he would consult Conkling before making federal patronage appointments in New York State.) With his political career on the line, Conkling plotted with Vice President Chester Arthur to prevent the Senate from confirming Robertson's nomination. In a bold move, Conkling resigned his own Senate seat, hoping to win vindication from the New York state legislature. The gamble backfired, however, when the state legislature refused to reappoint him. Garfield's victory broke Conkling's hold over the Republican party in New York and greatly reduced the pressure to deliver patronage jobs felt by every Republican president since the Civil War.

★ **Star Route Scandal:** During his first week in office, Garfield ordered Postmaster General Thomas L. James to investigate charges that mail route contracts in the West had been awarded through a system of fraud, bribes, and kickbacks. The charges related specifically to "star routes" in the Far West, along which mail was carried by private stagecoaches and wagons under contract to the government. Although a New York Stalwart, James

About the 20th President

Born: November 19, 1831
Birthplace: Orange, OH
Died: September 19, 1881
Party: Republican
Children: Eliza, Harry, James, Mary, Irvin, Abram, Edward

★ ★ ★ ★ ★ ★ ★ ★ ★ ★ ★ ★ ★ ★ ★

During the Garfield Administration

May 21, 1881 — *Nurse Clara Barton, known during the Civil War as the Angel of the Battlefield, founds the American Red Cross.*

July 4, 1881 — *The Tuskegee Institute opens in Alabama under the leadership of Booker T. Washington. The all-black school—which has two small buildings, little equipment, and almost no money—focuses on teaching its thirty students basic job skills.*

July 14, 1881 — *During the night, Sheriff Pat Garrett shoots Billy the Kid in the bedroom of a house in Fort Sumner, New Mexico.*

July 19, 1881 — *After escaping to Canada following the 1876 battle of the Little Bighorn, Sitting Bull leads his starving band of 186 Sioux back across the border to surrender.*

Sep. 4, 1881 — *The world's first centralized electric power plant, designed by Thomas Edison, goes into operation on Pearl Street in New York City. Its generator supplies power to eighty-five paying customers.*

1881 — *Helen Hunt Jackson's* A Century of Dishonor *reveals the injustices to which Indians have been subjected by the U.S. government.*

1881 — *Showman P. T. Barnum offers a London zoo ten thousand dollars for the elephant Jumbo, the largest creature in captivity. The elephant's name, taken from an African word for elephant, comes to mean "extra large."*

1881 — *Charges of indecency force the publisher of Walt Whitman's* Leaves of Grass *to withdraw copies of the new edition.*

remained independent of Roscoe Conkling and pursued his inquiry diligently. A preliminary investigation turned up evidence that a number of Republicans (including several prominent Stalwarts) had indeed taken bribes. When James asked Garfield for permission to pursue a detailed examination of the records, the president gave his approval without hesitation. "Go ahead regardless of where or whom you hit," Garfield told James. "I direct you not only to probe this ulcer to the bottom, but to cut it out." An assistant postmaster general and a senator from Arkansas were among those indicted, although no one was ever convicted in the scandal that James estimated cost the taxpayers four million dollars.

Chester A. Arthur

21st President • 1881–1885

CHESTER ARTHUR DELIGHTED in the trappings of power: He dressed impeccably, indulged himself with fine food and drink, and relished being the head of New York City's most powerful political organization. He was a dishonest politician as well as a successful one, for whom living well was part of the job. This sort of corruption was common during the high-flying Gilded Age of the 1870s—so common that it probably never occurred to Arthur that he should give up any of it.

His base of operations was the Customhouse. In 1871, President Ulysses Grant, a fellow Republican, had appointed Arthur to the lucrative post of customs collector for the port of New York. Arthur then used the patronage (and bank accounts) of the Customhouse to enrich his party. This, too, was hardly unusual for the time, but when Rutherford Hayes replaced Grant, the presidential attitude toward patronage changed. In 1878, Hayes removed Arthur from office. (For the sake of Republican party unity, criminal charges were never pursued.)

Arthur was still smarting in 1880, when he became the Republican candidate for vice president. (James Garfield was the party's presidential nominee that year.) Arthur thought that a national campaign might improve his image, but people continued to see him for what he was: a corrupt machine politician. This impression was strengthened when, after shooting Garfield, patronage seeker Charles Guiteau declared that he had removed the president so that Arthur could take his place (and presumably find Guiteau a job).

Although no one would have predicted it, Garfield's assassination began a transformation within Arthur. During the ten weeks between the shooting and the president's death, Arthur displayed a great deal of decency and poise. Then, once he took office, he surprised everyone with the honesty and efficiency of his administration. As president, he was the great organizer he had been since childhood, and the public marveled at his remarkable about-face.

Arthur's popularity was helped by the same amiable personality that he had displayed as a charming accomplice of the New York political bosses. His easygoing style, gracious manners, and skill as a raconteur all contributed to his new public image as a man of dignity and wit. "Though few would have guessed it of this urbane politician," biographer Thomas C. Reeves has written, "Arthur was a deeply emotional, even romantic person, capable of great loyalties and easily brought to tears." At his death in 1886, a close friend called him "an extremely tender-hearted man."

• Organization

One of the earliest accounts of Arthur's 1830s childhood describes his natural talent for organizing. "You might see him in the village street after a shower, watching boys building a mud dam," a classmate recalled many years later. "Pretty soon he would be ordering this one to bring stones, another sticks, and others sod and mud to finish the dam."

In 1860, as one of the lesser lieutenants in the New York City Republican organization, Arthur helped reelect Gov. Edwin Morgan. Morgan rewarded Arthur with a political job in the New York state militia. According to one Arthur biographer, "Had his expectations been realized, he would have served through Governor Morgan's term with no more onerous demands upon his time than to wear gold braid on a few public occasions."

Instead, the Civil War began, and Arthur became responsible for feeding, clothing, housing, and equipping thousands of enlisted men. Because of his superb organizational skills, he was promoted often. By the summer of 1862, he had risen to the post of quartermaster general, which carried with it the rank of brigadier. That year, however, a Democrat became governor and Arthur was forced to resign.

Top: Arthur in his Civil War uniform, ca. 1862. Below: Arthur's birthplace in Fairfield, Vermont.

★ ★ ★ ★ ★ ★ ★ ★ ★ ★ ★ ★ ★ ★ ★ ★ ★ ★ ★

• Mr. Vice President

Arthur was the "gentleman boss" of New York City, but like every other Republican in the state he answered to Sen. Roscoe Conkling. At the 1880 Republican convention, Conkling supported former president Grant. And, of course, so did Arthur.

Although Grant lost the nomination, Conkling was too important a politician for the party to shut out. As a consolation, he was offered the power to choose James Garfield's running mate. Conkling wasn't impressed. He didn't care about the vice presidency. However, Arthur did.

Certain that Garfield would lose, Conkling told Arthur, "You should drop it as you would a red hot shoe from the forge."

"There is something else to be said," Arthur replied.

"What, sir, you think of accepting?" Conkling exploded.

"The office of the Vice-President is a greater honor than I ever dreamed of attaining," Arthur insisted. "In a calmer moment you will look at this differently."

Arthur was right. Conkling could easily have blocked his nomination, yet the senator reconsidered and eventually went along with Arthur's wishes.

Throughout his political career, Arthur feared and hated the press. As president, he had no regular dealings with reporters and granted very few interviews.

Tiffany's work on the Blue Room.

• He Had Taste

By the time he became president, Arthur's hearty appetite for luxury was well known. He looked down on shabbiness and always conducted himself with the greatest personal elegance. He considered the White House beneath the standards of a third-rate Manhattan hotel. During a tour of the poorly maintained mansion several weeks after Garfield's death, he announced, "I will not live in a house like this."

For the first three months of his presidency, he lived elsewhere while supervising, on a daily basis, thirty thousand dollars' worth of redecoration. Shortly before moving in, however, he announced that the work was only temporary.

Early in 1882, he asked Congress for enough money to demolish and rebuild the White House. Preservationists blocked the plan, but Arthur got another eighty thousand dollars for more extensive renovation work. To carry out his plan, he hired Louis Comfort Tiffany, the most fashionable designer in New York City. During the summer of 1882, Tiffany transformed the White House into the showplace that Arthur had wanted. "History remembers only a few things about [Arthur]," White House historian William Seale has noted, but "one is that he had taste."

• Bright's Disease

In October 1882, the Associated Press reported that the president was suffering from Bright's disease, a then-fatal kidney ailment. Arthur, desperate to protect his privacy, denied the report. Whenever the disease left him too fatigued to work, the White House said that he had a cold. Once his doctor told reporters that Arthur was suffering from overexposure to the sun. However, to himself Arthur couldn't deny the fact that he was slowly dying.

Knowing that his condition would get only worse, he decided that he couldn't, in good faith, run for another term. In February 1886, about a year after he left office, Arthur's family leaked to the press news of his rapidly declining condi-

Although Arthur is generally associated with the pleasures of city life, he was also an avid hunter and fisherman.

tion. A month later, the fifty-six-year-old Arthur made out his will.

The day before he died, Arthur asked that all his public and private papers be burned. His son Alan watched as large garbage cans were repeatedly filled and set aflame.

Some historians have speculated that Arthur's awareness of his fatal illness probably contributed to his moral transformation as president. However, the destruction of his private papers has made such claims nearly impossible to prove.

★ ★ ★ ★ ★ ★ ★ ★ ★ ★ ★ ★ ★ ★ ★ ★ ★ ★

• Ellen Arthur

ELLEN HERNDON MET Chester Arthur in 1856, when she came to New York City to visit some relatives. Nell, as she was called, had spent most of her life in Washington, D.C., but she had been born in Virginia, could trace her ancestry in that state back to the seventeenth century, and considered herself a southerner. Nell and Chester became emotionally attached early on in their courtship, but Nell's southern sympathies became something of a problem once the Civil War began.

After their marriage in 1859, the Arthurs moved into Nell's mother's house on West Twenty-first Street in New York City. They moved out again in April 1861, however, because of Mrs. Herndon's open support for the South. Nell shared her mother's viewpoint—which is understandable, given that most of her family was fighting for the Confederacy—yet she kept her sympathies to herself. Still, her feelings caused such obvious stiffness in her mar-riage that Arthur felt the need to laugh it off with jokes about his "little rebel wife."

In the years after the war, this source of conflict was replaced by another: Arthur's habit of feasting with his political cronies until very late at night. Nell enjoyed the money and the social status that Arthur's political activities pro-duced—in fact, her social ambitions demanded as much—but she felt abandoned. According to their son, the Arthurs were on the brink of separating when Nell died sud-denly in January 1880.

While Arthur was away on political business, Nell attended a concert. She came down with a cold while waiting outside for a carriage, and the cold quickly became pneumonia. A telegram recalled Arthur, but when he arrived home, he found that Nell's doctor had already given her morphine. Arthur remained at her bedside for the next twenty-four hours, even though his wife never regained consciousness.

MAJOR POLITICAL EVENTS

★ **Chinese Immigration:** After the Civil War, Chinese immi-grants arrived in large numbers to work in western mines and on railroad construction crews. When these industries tapered off, the Chinese began competing with less recent immigrants for jobs—often with violent consequences. Gangs of Irish-Americans began assaulting Chinese immigrants in San Francisco, causing Congress to pass an 1879 bill banning further Chinese immigration. Hayes vetoed this bill because it violated the Burlingame Treaty of 1868 and instead negotiated an 1880 treaty with China that gave the United States the right to "regu-late, limit, or suspend"—but not end—Chinese immigration. In 1882, Congress passed another Chinese Exclusion Act, suspend-ing immigration for twenty years. President Arthur vetoed the bill, but the time period was reduced to ten years and the revised bill became law.

★ **Pendleton Civil Service Act:** A decade of agitation and the recent murder of a president by a disappointed office seeker finally persuaded Congress to enact civil service reform. The Pendleton Act of 1883 sought to weaken the control that politi-cal parties had over federal jobs by requiring competitive exams for many jobs and establishing a merit system for promotion. It also created an independent Civil Service Commission to oversee the government workforce and banned the practice of soliciting campaign contributions from federal employees. An unintended consequence of the Pendleton Act was that it forced the political

About the 21st President

Born: October 5, 1829
Birthplace: Fairfield, VT
Died: November 18, 1886
Party: Republican
Children: William, Chester Alan Jr., Ellen

★ ★ ★ ★ ★ ★ ★ ★ ★ ★ ★ ★ ★ ★

During the Arthur Administration

Oct. 26, 1881	*The three Earp brothers and Doc Holliday battle the Clanton gang at the O.K. Corral in Tombstone, Arizona. The famous gunfight symbolizes the struggle between businessmen and cattle ranchers in the West.*
Jan. 2, 1882	*Thirty-nine oil companies turn over their stock to a board of trustees headed by John D. Rockefeller. The Standard Oil trust allows Rockefeller to run the U.S. oil industry as though it were his own company.*
May 1, 1882	*Clara Barton persuades the Senate to ratify the Geneva Convention of 1864, which outlaws attacks on hospitals and requires proper care for injured soldiers, no matter which side they fought on.*
May 17, 1883	*Buffalo Bill Cody's Wild West Show opens in Omaha, Nebraska. The revue glorifies a way of life that is already fading.*
May 24, 1883	*Using field glasses, chief engineer Washington Roebling watches the opening of the Brooklyn Bridge from the window of his bedroom. He has directed work on the bridge from that same bedroom since an 1872 work accident crippled him.*
Nov. 18, 1883	*Canadian and U.S. railroads adopt a system of standardized time zones to solve scheduling problems. Four zones are established, each separated by one hour.*
1885	*Work is completed on the world's first skyscraper, the Home Insurance Company building in Chicago. Architect William Le Baron Jenney uses an iron-and-steel frame to support the ten-story structure.*

parties to find new sources of funding. Without the kickbacks that patronage provided, the parties turned to big business for campaign contributions. Large corporations, eager to influence lawmakers, happily provided the money the politicians needed.

★ **Mongrel Tariff:** In 1882, Arthur appointed a commission to study tariff reform. Its report concluded that tariffs should be reduced sharply. However, the bill that Congress finally produced was such a hodgepodge of special-interest exemptions that congressmen called it the Mongrel Tariff. The bill, which Arthur signed, lowered rates by less than 2 percent and satisfied no one. It did, however, begin a decade-long fight over tariff rates, with the Republicans defending protectionism and the Democrats advocating free trade.

He who takes the oath today to preserve, protect, and defend the Constitution of the United States only assumes the solemn obligation which every patriotic citizen—on the farm, in the workshop, in the busy marts of trade, and everywhere—should share with him.

Grover Cleveland

Grover Cleveland

22nd & 24th President • 1885–1889/1893–1897

WINNING ELECTION AFTER ELECTION made Gilded Age Republicans arrogant. By 1884, they thought that they could nominate just about anybody and still beat the Democrats. That year, they picked former secretary of state James G. Blaine, a man tainted by railroad money. Blaine was so hated by Republican reformers that a group of them, nicknamed the mugwumps, abandoned the party and announced that they would support any Democrat who was honest.

The Democrats wondered what to do. Would electing an honest man be worth the trouble? Could they force him to grant the patronage that made political parties run? In the end, party leaders decided that the chance to elect the first Democratic president since the Civil War was too good to pass up. They looked around for an honest man and found Grover Cleveland.

At the time, Cleveland was governor of New York, where he had recently taken on New York City's corrupt Tammany Hall machine. A forty-seven-year-old bachelor, Cleveland was hardworking, conscientious, and methodical; on the other hand, he was also single minded and stubborn. Reporters didn't know what to make of him. "He just eats and works," one journalist remarked of the 260-pound New Yorker.

During his first term as president, Cleveland performed admirably, but his introverted manner hurt him politically. He often fought with members of his own party, refusing out of hand to do anything he considered dishonest or wasteful.

A remarkably consistent man, Cleveland firmly supported low tariffs throughout his career. This position got him into trouble during the 1888 election, which he lost to Benjamin Harrison. However, it later won him the 1892 election, after a tariff hike supported by Harrison stalled the economy.

Sadly, Cleveland's second term was an unqualified disaster. Just as he returned to office, the financial panic of 1893 triggered a severe economic depression, during which labor unrest rocked the country. Cleveland, giving in to his narrow-mindedness, insisted on order at all costs. When the Pullman strike of 1894 shut down mail trains running in and out of Chicago, he sent in federal troops. "If it takes the entire army and navy of the United States to deliver a postal card in Chicago," the president declared, "that card will be delivered."

The situation worsened, yet Cleveland's stubbornness and rigidity kept him from exercising creative leadership. Instead, he lost nearly all his public support and left office deeply hurt. In his last years, however, his reputation was restored as people began to recall with affection the high standard of personal integrity that he had brought to government service.

• The Only Way to Get It Done Right

Grover Cleveland believed in doing things himself. As sheriff of Erie County, New York, during the early 1870s, he became famous for ending routine payoffs. And he changed a regular practice at the Buffalo jails: Unlike previous sheriffs, Cleveland personally sprang the traps on convicts sentenced to death by hanging. He hated the task but thought it cowardly to delegate the responsibility to someone else.

A decade later at the White House, this personality trait contributed enormously to Cleveland's heavy workload. Presidents need a great deal of help to keep the government running, yet Cleveland had little trust in his subordinates and spent many hours micromanaging them. Incredibly, during his first term, Cleveland even answered the White House telephone himself.

The private Cleveland was much less of a drudge than the public one. On Sundays, for example, instead of attending church, he usually played poker.

To the Republican chant, "Ma, ma, where's my pa?" the Democrats replied, "Gone to the White House, ha, ha, ha!"

• The Illegitimate Child

With Cleveland as their standard-bearer in 1884, the Democrats sensibly ran an integrity-based campaign that called attention to Blaine's poor reputation. Meanwhile, the Republicans, put on the defensive, searched for something on Cleveland that they could use for a counterattack. What they discovered was that Cleveland had perhaps fathered an illegitimate child.

On July 21, a disreputable Buffalo newspaper broke the story that Cleveland had once kept company with a woman named Maria Halpin and that Halpin had an illegitimate son. According to Halpin, Cleveland was the father.

When party leaders asked Cleveland what to do, the candidate replied, "Tell the truth." Cleveland himself immediately admitted the relationship, which wasn't particularly immoral because both he and Halpin had been single at the time. As Cleveland later told a friend, he really didn't know whether he was the boy's father, but because all the other possible fathers were married, he had agreed to assume financial responsibility for the child's welfare.

According to the Reverend Kinsley Twining, a respected minister who investigated the scandalous charges, "After the preliminary offense, [Cleveland's] conduct was singularly honorable, showing no attempt to evade responsibility, and doing all that he could to meet the duties involved, of which marriage was certainly not one."

• White House Wedding

Throughout his public life, Cleveland carefully guarded his privacy. On June 2, 1886, however, the public caught a fleeting glimpse of his personal life when the forty-nine-year old president got married at the White House. To keep down the publicity, the engagement wasn't announced until five days before the ceremony. The president's bride was twenty-one-year-old Frances Folsom.

Cleveland scheduled the small Blue Room ceremony for seven o'clock in the evening so that he could work as usual on his wedding day. He had already revised and condensed the service, changing the bride's vow from "love, honor, and obey" to "love, honor, and keep." John Philip Sousa and his Marine Band provided the music. Reporters begged for wedding trivia to feed a hungry public, but they were given little information. So they made up some of their own. One baseless rumor suggested that Cleveland was a habitual drunkard and beat his new wife. Another claimed that she beat him.

Cleveland wasn't the first president married while in office (Tyler had done that), but he was the first married at the White House. Afterward, he sent out pieces of the wedding cake (left) as gifts.

★ ★ ★ ★ ★ ★ ★ ★ ★ ★ ★ ★ ★ ★

• Vetoes

Cleveland entered the White House opposed by a Republican Congress and a Washington bureaucracy grown accustomed to scandal. It's not surprising that he stuck to principles and procedures that had served him well in the past: He made appointments based on merit rather than party loyalty, closely inspected all appropriations bills, and without hesitation vetoed ones that he didn't like.

During his first term, Cleveland vetoed 304 bills, more than all of his predecessors combined. Most of these bills granted Civil War pensions to men who had supposedly been injured fighting for the Union. Pension bills were typically passed several hundred at a time, and previous presidents hadn't even bothered to look at them before adding their sig-

Cleveland's second inauguration in 1893. He's the only president ever to serve two nonconsecutive terms.

natures. But Cleveland read every one. What he learned was that some pensions were being handed out to men who had been injured years after the war and to others who had never even served in the army.

Cleveland's vetoes angered a great many congressmen, because on Capitol Hill it was generally believed that a man who couldn't get a friend a Civil War pension was hardly worth being called a man at all.

★ ★ ★ ★ ★ ★ ★ ★ ★ ★ ★ ★ ★ ★ ★ ★

• Frances Cleveland

DURING THE SUMMER OF 1864, when Grover Cleveland was a twenty-seven-year-old assistant district attorney, he went to visit his friend (and future law partner) Oscar Folsom, whose wife had just given birth to a girl. Eleven years later, Folsom died suddenly in a carriage accident. Because he left no will, the court appointed Cleveland to administer his estate. Thereafter, he felt a special duty to Mrs. Folsom and her daughter, Frances.

No one knows when Cleveland's feelings for Frances took on a romantic quality. However, a year before entering the White House, he asked Mrs. Folsom's permission to correspond with her daughter, and in August 1885, shortly after her graduation from Wells College, he proposed marriage by letter. Frances accepted immediately, but they kept their engagement secret to protect their privacy.

Twenty-one years old on the day she was married, Frances Folsom was a tall, pretty girl with dark hair, dark eyes, creamy skin, and a rosy coloring that suggested robust health. She spoke well and had an excellent sense of humor that she wasn't afraid to use in public. (As she left the White House in March 1889, she defiantly turned to a butler and predicted, correctly as it turned out, "We'll be back!")

During their years in Washington, the Clevelands kept as low a profile as they could, given that they were president and first lady. They accomplished this primarily by spending a great deal of time at Red Top, an estate on the outskirts of the city (near the present Washington Cathedral) that Cleveland had purchased a week before the wedding. Unlike most presidential "second homes," Red Top wasn't a summer cottage but a year-round retreat from the pressures of the White House. Desperate reporters still roamed the forests around the house, though Cleveland built a gatehouse and hired a gatekeeper to keep them at a distance.

MAJOR POLITICAL EVENTS

★ **Panic of 1893:** In February 1893, a month before Cleveland's second inauguration, the Philadelphia & Reading Railroad was turned over to a court-appointed receiver. Before the end of the year, twenty-three more railroads had failed, along with six hundred banks and thousands of other businesses. The depression caused by the panic of 1893 lasted throughout Cleveland's second term, but he had a more immediate problem: a run on federal gold reserves. Under the Sherman Silver Purchase Act of 1890, the government was required to redeem devalued silver certificates for gold. To stop the run, Cleveland called Congress into emergency session to repeal the Sherman Act. He got his way but, in the process, split the Democratic party between conservative "goldbugs," who favored the gold standard, and populist "silverites," who wanted free coinage of silver.

★ **Pullman Strike:** In May 1894, railroad workers called a strike against the Pullman Palace Car Company to protest a 30 percent wage cut. In support of the strike, Eugene V. Debs, president of the American Railway Union, organized a nationwide boycott of trains containing Pullman cars. By the end of June, railroad traffic in and out the midwestern hub of Chicago had dropped by 75 percent. On July 2, Cleveland instructed Attorney General Richard Olney to apply for a court order restoring railroad service on the grounds that the boycott interfered with mail deliveries. When Debs defied the court order, he was arrested and jailed. Meanwhile, on July 3, Olney sent federal troops to

About the 22nd & 24th President

Born: March 18, 1837
Birthplace: Caldwell, NJ
Died: June 24, 1908
Party: Democrat
Children: Ruth, Esther, Marion, Richard, Francis

Chicago to force an end to the Pullman strike. At the peak of the violence, fourteen thousand soldiers patrolled Chicago's streets and railroad yards.

★ **Plessy v. Ferguson:** In May 1896, the Supreme Court ruled in the case of *Plessy v. Ferguson*. Its decision upheld the southern Jim Crow laws that permitted "separate but equal" facilities for black and white citizens. The defendant in the case, Homer Plessy, was a black railroad passenger who had refused to leave a whites-only car despite a Louisiana law that required whites and blacks to travel separately. Plessy's attorneys argued that this law violated the Fourteenth Amendment, which forbade states to deprive citizens of any "privileges" because of their race. Instead the Court decided that laws "requiring their separation...do not necessarily imply the inferiority of either race."

★ ★ ★ ★ ★ ★ ★ ★ ★ ★ ★ ★ ★ ★ ★

During the Cleveland Administrations

May 4, 1886
Someone throws a bomb during a labor rally in Chicago's Haymarket Square. The blast kills several policemen and causes the rest to open fire on the crowd. One hundred people are injured, about half of them police. Although no evidence is ever presented to link them with the bomb thrower, eight anarchist labor leaders are later convicted of conspiracy to commit murder.

Oct. 28, 1886
French sculptor Frédéric-Auguste Bartholdi *dedicates* Liberty Enlightening the World in New York Harbor. The Statue of Liberty is a gift from France to the United States.

Mar. 12, 1888
The Great Blizzard of 1888 paralyzes the East Coast with a blanket of snow fifty inches deep in some areas.

Aug. 29, 1893
Whitcomb L. Judson patents his "slide fastener." In 1912, Gideon Sundback improves the design and sells it to the B. F. Goodrich Company, which calls it a zipper.

Sep. 21, 1893
Brothers Charles and Frank Duryea test their "gasoline buggy" in Springfield, Massachusetts. It is the first American-built gasoline-powered automobile.

1894
Percival Lowell builds the Lowell Observatory in Flagstaff, Arizona. An amateur astronomer, he predicts the existence of Pluto thirty years before its discovery in 1930.

1895
Bottle-cap salesman King C. Gillette invents the first safety razor with a disposable blade.

Apr. 23, 1896
The first public screening of a motion picture takes place at Koster and Bial's Music Hall in New York City.

I do not mistrust the future. Dangers have been in frequent ambush along our path, but we have uncovered and vanquished them all. Passion has swept some of our communities, but only to give us a new demonstration that the great body of our people are stable, patriotic, and law-abiding.

Benjamin Harrison

23rd President • 1889–1893

EXCEPT FOR HIS FAMOUS LAST NAME, there was nothing special about Benjamin Harrison. He looked like many other bearded statesmen of the late nineteenth century—Rutherford Hayes, in particular. And his mind was equally undistinguished: Face to face with people, Harrison was dull, stiff, and surprisingly naive.

Soon after the 1888 election, Harrison met with his campaign manager, Matt Quay, the notorious political boss of Pennsylvania. Grabbing Quay's hand, Harrison declared triumphantly, "Providence has given us the victory!"

"Think of the man!" a disgusted Quay said later. "He ought to know that Providence hadn't a damn thing to do with it." Still, Quay continued, the upright Harrison "would never know how close a number of men were compelled to approach the gates of the penitentiary to make him president."

Harrison became president, it seems, largely because his grandfather William Henry Harrison had been. And like his grandfather, Benjamin Harrison was a political puppet, elected by a party—in this case, the Republicans—that wanted a rubber stamp in the White House. According to one presidential historian, Benjamin Harrison was among "the best examples in American history of the bland nonentity who is the politician's ideal for president—both because he is easiest to elect and because he makes least trouble after being elected." Benjamin Harrison made no trouble at all.

As a politician, he had three chief assets: his family name, his popularity among Civil War veterans, and his talent as a public speaker. It may seem surprising, given his otherwise bland personality, but Harrison apparently had a genuine ability to move audiences emotionally.

However, the magnetism that he possessed in front of crowds deserted him during more personal encounters, when he seemed cold, distant, and sometimes rude. "He can make a speech to ten thousand men and every man will go away his friend," one colleague lamented, but "let him meet the same ten thousand men in private, and every one will go away his enemy." Less sympathetic people called Harrison a "human iceberg" and "as glacial as a Siberian stripped of his furs."

As president, Harrison was hampered by his dislike for the deal making and arm twisting that went on every day in Congress. (He never seemed to understand that this same arm twisting had made him president.) Even so, he might have served another term if he hadn't dutifully supported the 1890 McKinley Tariff, which raised rates to their highest peacetime level ever. Big Business was thrilled, but the American people were furious. In 1892, they threw Harrison out and returned Grover Cleveland to office for another four years.

• Grandfather's Hat Fits Ben

Given Benjamin Harrison's lifelong distaste for the rough-and-tumble of professional politics, it's odd that he had a political career at all. But he was born in the house of a president, and sometimes one's destiny can be difficult to escape.

Even though his grandfather had been president, Harrison's childhood in North Bend, Ohio, was typical for its time and place. His father, John Scott Harrison, wasn't a wealthy man. In fact, he was a downwardly mobile farmer, so all his children were expected to work.

Benjamin's chores included hauling wood and water, washing the dishes, and feeding the livestock.

After learning to apply himself at an early age, he was quickly recognized as the brightest of his father's children. He was taught by tutors at home and also attended a nearby one-room schoolhouse. Despite his family's difficult financial circumstances, Harrison was sent first to a college preparatory school in Cincinnati and later to Miami University in Oxford, Ohio.

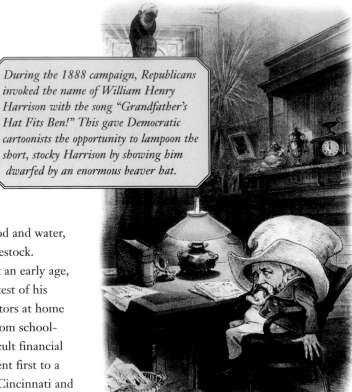

During the 1888 campaign, Republicans invoked the name of William Henry Harrison with the song "Grandfather's Hat Fits Ben!" This gave Democratic cartoonists the opportunity to lampoon the short, stocky Harrison by showing him dwarfed by an enormous beaver hat.

★ ★ ★ ★ ★ ★ ★ ★ ★ ★ ★ ★ ★ ★ ★ ★

• A "Plain Hoosier Colonel"

Harrison's early years as a lawyer in Indianapolis were difficult. Business was slow, and he often had to borrow money from friends and relatives to pay his bills. In 1857, however, his situation changed when he ran successfully for city attorney of Indianapolis. The twenty-four-year-old Harrison had no strong desire to serve the public, but he did crave the job's four-hundred-dollar annual salary. Thus began his political career.

Then, like everyone else, Harrison had his life interrupted by the Civil War. He served with some distinction, rising from second lieutenant to brigadier general in three years. He fought with Joseph Hooker in Georgia and won an important victory that allowed William T. Sherman to continue his backbreaking advance on Atlanta.

"I am not a Julius Caesar," Harrison wrote, "nor a Napoleon, but a plain Hoosier colonel, with no more relish for a fight than for a good breakfast and hardly so much." This modesty aside, Harrison was revered by his troops, and their devotion to him proved useful in his later political life.

Harrison poses for Mathew Brady, 1864.

• Gone Hunting

From the beginning of his presidency, Harrison made it a point to escape Washington on a regular basis. In late 1889, for example, he made two hunting trips: In mid-November he visited the Benjies Point Ducking Club outside Baltimore, and in late December he traveled to Cypress Swamp on the James River below Richmond, Virginia.

Hunting was Harrison's favorite sport. More often than not, he went after

ducks, but he occasionally hunted raccoons as well—"coons," he called them. Because Harrison was less experienced in coon hunting, he often used dogs to track the raccoons for him.

Few people noticed that Harrison had even left town during his November 1889 trip, though the December hunt made national news when the president mistakenly shot a pig owned by a farmer named Gilbert Wooten. The blunder made Wooten momentarily famous and Harrison seem foolish.

• Old Whiskers

Harrison's grandchildren with Old Whiskers.

During his one and only term, President Harrison spent little time in his office; instead, he usually worked until noon and then took the rest of the day off. His favorite pastime was an afternoon walk around Washington. He also spent a great deal of time playing with his grandchildren, many of whom had moved with their families to the White House.

Harrison allowed his grandchildren to keep as many pets as they wanted, including a goat named Old Whiskers. A special cart was built so that Old Whiskers could haul the smaller children around the White House grounds. Once, however, with three Harrison grandchildren in tow, the goat escaped through an open gate. Holding onto his top hat and waving his cane, the president ran off down Pennsylvania Avenue after them. The goat didn't stop until several bystanders, seeing the president panting and howling, caught Old Whiskers by his reins.

★ ★ ★ ★ ★ ★ ★ ★ ★ ★ ★ ★ ★ ★ ★ ★ ★ ★ ★

• Caroline Harrison

FRIENDS OF THE TEENAGE Benjamin Harrison remembered him as somber and lacking a sense of humor. He was also socially clumsy, but Caroline Scott offset this awkwardness with her own energy and irreverence. Harrison began courting her in 1850 while he was a student at Miami University.

A pious Presbyterian, Harrison refused to commit the sin of dancing, though Caroline dragged him to school dances anyway, and he sat on a bench while she flirted with the other boys. Harrison preferred to court Caroline in a different manner: He visited her nearly every evening and sat with her for hours on her father's front porch. Around campus, he was known as the "pious moonlight dude."

At the time of their marriage on October 20, 1853, Harrison was just twenty years old and his bride only twenty-one. He later admitted that they should have waited until he had finished his legal studies and established a practice. Yet he couldn't stand the thought of being away from her, and his desire overcame whatever misgivings he might have had.

Although her husband sleepwalked through most of his presidency, Caroline Harrison was an active first lady. Her greatest cause was the refurbishment of the White House, which had once again become dilapidated. She personally developed plans to construct two massive wings that would have tripled the building's size, but the Senate turned her down in March 1891.

In October 1892, just two weeks before the election, Caroline Harrison died of tuberculosis. Her husband spent the next four years trying unsuccessfully to adjust to life without her. Finally, he remarried. The sixty-two-year-old former president chose for his second wife Mary Dimmick, a niece of Caroline's who was nearly thirty years his junior. This second marriage caused a break with his older children, but Harrison didn't seem to care, and the following year, he became a father for the third time.

MAJOR POLITICAL EVENTS

★ **Sherman Anti-Trust Act:** During the 1880s, near monopolies were created in a number of key industries. The first and most important of these was the Standard Oil trust, formed by John D. Rockefeller in 1882. In his inaugural address, President Harrison warned that the government might be forced to discipline the trusts. A year later, Congress passed the Sherman Anti-Trust Act of 1890, which made it illegal to form trusts in order to eliminate competition or restrict trade. However, lawyers soon found ways around the Sherman Act. "What looks like a stone wall to a layman is a triumphal arch to a corporation lawyer," political humorist Finley Peter Dunne joked.

★ **Sherman Silver Purchase Act:** Silver strikes were common during the 1880s, when western boomtowns such as Tombstone, Arizona, thrived. At the same time, the increase in silver production drove down silver prices. The only way to keep the price up was to expand the market for silver, so miners began lobbying the government to buy more of the metal. In July 1890, Congress passed the Sherman Silver Purchase Act, which replaced the Bland-Allison Act of 1878. Under this new law, the government was required to buy 4.5 million ounces of silver each month, or nearly the entire output of the western mines. To pay for all this silver, the government issued paper money that was redeemable in gold. Eastern financial and manufacturing interests, which typically opposed silver coinage because of the inflation it produced, agreed to the bill in exchange for western support for higher tariffs.

About the 23rd President

Born: August 20, 1833
Birthplace: North Bend, OH
Died: March 13, 1901
Party: Republican
Children: Russell, Mary, Elizabeth

★ **McKinley Tariff:** Tariff rates had been abnormally high ever since the early 1860s, when Lincoln raised them to pay for the Civil War. After the war, rates remained high to protect U.S. industry from foreign competition. By the late 1880s, however, the U.S. economy was booming, and the Treasury had a large surplus. Even so, the McKinley Tariff of 1890, sponsored by future president William McKinley, raised tariff rates to their highest peacetime level ever. It was the Harrison administration's gift to the eastern businessmen who had funded the president's campaign. The stated purpose of the McKinley Tariff was to make foreign goods more expensive than similar products made in the United States. However, many greedy manufacturers simply raised their prices to match those of the imports. Two years later, irate consumers chased Harrison from office.

During the Harrison Administration

Apr. 22, 1889
At noon, a gunshot signals the opening of the Indian Territory to white settlers. Thus begins the Oklahoma land rush.

May 31, 1889
Following heavy rains, the dam above Johnstown, Pennsylvania, breaks. Within an hour, the Johnstown Flood kills twenty-three hundred people.

Nov. 14, 1889
Reporter Nellie Bly departs on a round-the-world trip. Her goal is to beat the time set by fictional adventurer Phileas Fogg in Jules Verne's 1873 novel Around the World in Eighty Days. *Bly completes the trip in just over seventy-two days.*

1889
William Gray installs the first coin-operated public telephone in Hartford, Connecticut.

Aug. 6, 1890
New York becomes the first state to execute criminals in an electric chair. Officials maintain that electrocution is more humane than hanging.

1890
Photographer Jacob Riis publishes How the Other Half Lives, *which uses both text and pictures to detail the poverty and overcrowding on New York City's Lower East Side.*

May 5, 1891
Carnegie Hall opens in New York City. Steel baron Andrew Carnegie paid for construction of the million-dollar concert hall.

Jan. 1, 1892
Ellis Island in New York Harbor becomes the official entry point for the flood of immigrants arriving in New York City.

1892
William Painter patents the throwaway bottle cap as well as a machine to clamp the caps onto bottles.

We want no wars of conquest; we must avoid the temptation of territorial aggression. War should never be entered upon until every agency of peace has failed; peace is preferable to war in almost every contingency.

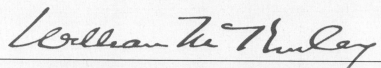

William McKinley

25th President • 1897–1901

WILLIAM MCKINLEY'S PERSONAL TRADEMARK was the pink carnation that he wore in his lapel, signifying both his warm personality and his easygoing manner. Frequently, he would pluck the carnation from his coat and give it to a guest. This sort of gesture made a lasting impression, especially when it came after a difficult meeting. "Mr. President," one senator said after just such a meeting, "I could not get mad at you if I tried."

Shrewd, attentive, and *pragmatic*—these are words that colleagues commonly used to describe McKinley the politician. One word they would never have used was *stubborn,* because McKinley made a career of modifying his policies to fit the desires of voters and the tenor of the times.

Although he was ambitious and made no secret of his desire to hold high public office, he was respected for his integrity and admired for his personal charm. A religious man, he was himself a model of moral rectitude: He once advised a nephew, in all sincerity, to "look after your diet and living, take no intoxicants, indulge in no immoral practices. Keep your life and your speech both clean, and be brave." McKinley spent four years in the Union army during the Civil War but never learned to swear, drink, or smoke. He was the complete Christian gentleman, with one interesting subtlety: He consciously understood how useful such an image could be.

McKinley's career in public office began in 1869, when he was elected district attorney of Stark County, Ohio. During the next three decades, he served a dozen years in the House of Representatives and four more as governor of Ohio. In 1896, he won the Republican presidential nomination on the first ballot and beat Democrat William Jennings Bryan in the general election.

While he was in Congress, his specialty had been the tariff, and he had worked hard to become an expert on the subject. Yet McKinley was no intellectual: He studied the tariff in order to learn facts that might be useful in a floor debate, not because he was fond of learning. On the rare occasions that he discussed economic theory, his ideas were usually foolish.

Ideas were never McKinley's strength. Even though his parents had raised him as a Methodist, he was a sentimentalist at heart. He believed in a divine loving-kindness, and this faith gave him an inner serenity that lasted his entire life. His vocabulary was small, but his heart was big—so big that the entire nation noticed. As president, McKinley was more than popular. He was beloved.

When the United States acquired the Philippine Islands from Spain, many newspapers accused McKinley of imperialism. "We are all jingoes now," the New York Sun crowed, "and the head jingo is the Hon. William McKinley."

• Remember the *Maine*!

The Cuban revolt against Spanish rule began in 1895. Grover Cleveland, who was president at the time, refused to interfere, and McKinley continued Cleveland's policy. As the revolt escalated, however, many Americans began to side with the rebels and call for a U.S. invasion. Remembering his own service in the Civil War, McKinley worked hard to persuade Spain to grant Cuban independence. He genuinely wanted peace: "I have been through one war," McKinley said. "I have seen the dead piled up, and I do not want to see another."

Historians have often criticized McKinley for pandering to the will of the people, but in this case (at least initially) he rejected the popular demand for war. Newspapers paraded their extreme, aggressive patriotism (also known as jingoism), yet McKinley told former inte-

rior secretary Carl Schurz, "You may be sure that there will be no jingo nonsense under my administration." Still, the pressure was immense. Within the navy itself, a hotheaded assistant secretary named Theodore Roosevelt screamed privately for war and even called his reluctant commander in chief a "white-livered cur."

McKinley believed that the greatest threat to peace was the possibility that Americans in Cuba might be attacked. As a deterrent, he sent the battleship *Maine* on a courtesy call to Havana in January 1898. The ship was expected to remain only about a week, but the Spanish were so hospitable that the *Maine* lingered.

On the night of February 15, the battleship exploded and sank, killing more than 250 sailors. The navy immediately formed a board of inquiry to investigate the cause of the explosion. Meanwhile, the president counseled calm and restraint. "I don't propose to be swept off my feet by the catastrophe," he told one senator. Sadly, he was.

The navy's report was thorough yet inconclusive: Although the investigators found no evidence of Spanish involvement, the navy still refused to admit the possibility of an accident. This left the press free to concoct wild stories of Spanish treachery.

Diplomacy might have preserved the peace, but McKinley no longer had the strength to stand up to the jingoes. Worried about splitting his party and losing the next election, the president finally agreed in April 1898 to ask Congress for a declaration of war.

Although the official navy report concluded that the Maine *had been sunk by an external explosion, probably caused by an underwater mine, one recent study conducted by naval experts concluded that the real cause was, as the Spanish had claimed, an accident inside the ship.*

• Presidential Mentor

McKinley first met Rutherford Hayes in June 1861 after enlisting in Hayes's Civil War regiment, the Twenty-third Ohio Volunteers. A short time later, when the regiment's guns arrived, Major Hayes had to put down a small rebellion. Because of rampant shortages at the start of the war, the Twenty-third Ohio had been sent muskets made originally for the War of 1812. The recruits were furious, but Hayes finally persuaded them to accept the muskets, if only for the purposes of drill.

"From that very moment," McKinley wrote, "he had our respect and admiration, which never weakened but ever increased during the four eventful years that followed." After the war, McKinley often wrote to his former commander for advice, and Hayes, as a presidential candidate in 1876, played an important role in launching McKinley's political career.

★ ★

• Assassination

McKinley took great pride in his appearance, and on the morning of September 6, 1901, he dressed in his usual finery: a boiled white shirt with starched collar and cuffs, a black satin cravat, pinstriped trousers, and a black frock coat. He was in Buffalo for the Pan-American Exposition, and that afternoon he attended a public reception at the exposition's Temple of Music. Because he was such a popular president, people had waited in line for hours for the privilege of shaking his hand.

A squad of Buffalo police assisted the three Secret Service agents on duty with the president, but it was common knowledge that public handshaking exposed the president to danger. Even the Secret Service admitted beforehand that it couldn't protect McKinley from a determined assassin who was prepared to give up his life.

At seven minutes past four, as McKinley reached for another hand, the Secret Service agents heard two sharp cracks: A deranged young anarchist named Leon Czolgosz had shot the president. Czolgosz, who had very large hands, had concealed a short-barreled revolver in his palm and covered it with a handkerchief. Because it was a sweltering day, the agents had relaxed the rule that the hands of everyone in line must be exposed and empty before reaching the president.

Czolgosz was immediately knocked to the ground and dragged to the center of the hall. As McKinley was helped to a chair, he kept staring at Czolgosz. "Don't let them hurt him," the president said.

McKinley arriving at the Temple of Music about fifteen minutes before he was shot. "I didn't believe one man should have so much service, and another man should have none," Czolgosz said later. "I killed the president because he was the enemy of the people—the good working people."

★ ★ ★ ★ ★ ★ ★   ★ ★ ★ ★ ★ ★ ★

• Ida McKinley

THE THOUGHTFULNESS AND consideration that McKinley showed in public was even more evident in his private life. When he married Ida Saxton in 1873, she was a vivacious twenty-three-year-old, beautiful and charming. Within a very short time, however, she lost both her health and her spirit. During the mid-1870s, Ida McKinley had two difficult pregnancies. The first child lived only three years; the second died in infancy. She never recovered from the strain.

It's difficult to know whether a specific illness caused her physical and emotional decline, but at some point she developed epilepsy. Being an epileptic was difficult during the nineteenth century, because no treatment existed and epileptic symptoms were considered shameful. Whatever its root cause, Ida's condition left her frail and demanding. From that point on, she insisted on (and got) McKinley's full attention.

Only people very close to him knew what a burden his marriage placed on him, especially because he typically put his wife's substantial needs before his own. For example, in 1896, while William Jennings Bryan energetically toured the country, McKinley waged his famous "front porch" campaign, never leaving his Ohio home because he refused to leave Ida's side.

During her tenure in the White House, Ida McKinley attempted to perform some of the social duties required of the first lady, but concessions had to be made. For instance, although protocol dictated otherwise, she was always seated next to the president at formal dinners in case she had a seizure. When she did, McKinley calmly placed a napkin over her head until the seizure passed. This way, he shielded his guests from the sight of his wife's transfixed eyes and foaming mouth.

Even after he was shot, McKinley continued to display an enduring concern for his wife. Raising his hand from his belly and seeing the blood on it, McKinley whispered to his private secretary, "My wife—be careful, Cortelyou, how you tell her—oh, be careful!"

MAJOR POLITICAL EVENTS

★ **Hawaii:** In January 1893, Sanford B. Dole and several other American sugar planters overthrew the independent Hawaiian government of Queen Liliuokalani. Their goal was to annex Hawaii to the United States and therefore avoid high U.S. import tariffs on sugar. Although an annexation treaty was drawn up and submitted to the Senate, Cleveland withdrew the treaty in March 1893, five days after his second inauguration, because of U.S. complicity in the coup d'état. Once McKinley replaced Cleveland, however, he ordered Secretary of State John Sherman to negotiate a new treaty of annexation, which was signed in June 1897.

★ **Treaty of Paris:** Although the fighting stopped in July 1898, the formal end to the Spanish-American War didn't come until December, when the United States and Spain signed the Treaty of Paris. The terms of this treaty, dictated by the American negotiators, included independence for Cuba and the sale of the Philippine Islands to the United States for twenty million dollars. In addition, Puerto Rico and Guam became U.S. possessions. Fearing that the Germans might soon invade the Philippines, McKinley ordered U.S. troops to occupy the island chain. This, in turn, provoked a rebellion by Filipino nationalists—which the United States brutally suppressed using many of the same methods that it had recently criticized the Spanish for using in Cuba. Meanwhile, anti-imperialists, who opposed the creation of a U.S. empire in the Pacific, nearly defeated the Treaty of Paris in the Senate.

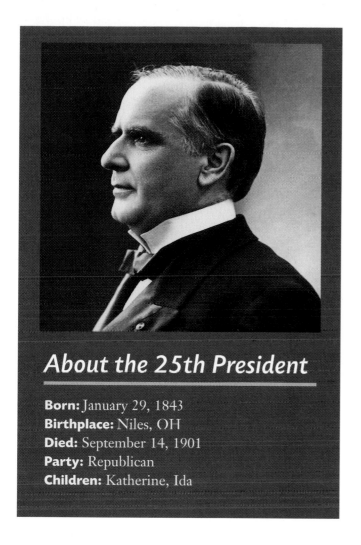

About the 25th President

Born: January 29, 1843
Birthplace: Niles, OH
Died: September 14, 1901
Party: Republican
Children: Katherine, Ida

★ **Open Door Policy:** In September 1899, Secretary of State John Hay sent diplomatic notes to six world powers proposing an "open door" policy toward China. Hay suggested that rather than carve up China into competitive "spheres of influence," the international community agree to keep the markets of China open to all nations. Although China was the most populous country in Asia, it was militarily and politically weak. Hay worried that the Western imperial powers, along with Japan, would divide up China, leaving nothing for the United States. In March 1900, he happily announced an international agreement that permitted every country to trade with China on an equal basis. Thus, when in June 1900 Chinese nationalists staged the Boxer Rebellion to drive foreigners from their country, an international army of U.S., British, French, Russian, and Japanese troops responded to the crisis.

★ ★ ★ ★ ★ ★ ★ ★ ★ ★ ★ ★

During the McKinley Administration

Sep. 1, 1897 — *The first U.S. subway opens in Boston. Nearly two miles long, it uses streetcars running along underground track.*

Sep. 21, 1897 — New York Sun *editor Francis P. Church replies to a letter from eight-year-old Virginia O'Hanlon asking whether or not Santa Claus exists. "Yes, Virginia, there is a Santa Claus," Church assures the girl.*

1897 — *Twin brothers Francis and Freelan Stanley introduce the Stanley Steamer, a new automobile that features a steam engine.*

1897 — *Simon Lake builds the* Argonaut, *the first submarine to operate in the open sea. It travels on wheels along the ocean bottom.*

1899 — *Frank Norris publishes* McTeague, *the story of a man who becomes a drunkard and a murderer. Norris's novel influences American fiction away from historical romances toward more naturalistic themes.*

1899 — *Black pianist Scott Joplin, called the King of Ragtime, composes the "Maple Leaf Rag."*

Apr. 30, 1900 — *Rather than leaping to safety, engineer John Luther "Casey" Jones stays aboard his locomotive so that he can slow it down before it reaches a stalled freight train. Although Jones dies in the crash, his bravery saves the lives of many passengers.*

1900 — *Chicago newspaperman L. Frank Baum publishes* The Wonderful Wizard of Oz.

1900 — *Eastman Kodak introduces the affordable, easy-to-operate Brownie Box Camera, which makes photography accessible to amateurs.*

Justice and generosity in a nation, as in an individual, count most when shown not by the weak but by the strong. While ever careful to refrain from wrongdoing others, we must be no less insistent that we are not wronged ourselves. We wish peace, but we wish the peace of justice, the peace of righteousness.

Theodore Roosevelt

26th President • 1901–1909

WHEN A THEODORE-ROOSEVELT-FOR-VICE-PRESIDENT movement swept the 1900 Republican national convention, President William McKinley's chief political adviser, Mark Hanna, exploded: "Don't any of you realize there's only one life between this madman and the White House?" Of course, Hanna's words were prophetic. "Now look," he seethed after McKinley's September 1901 assassination, "that damned cowboy is president of the United States!"

The man who succeeded McKinley couldn't have had a more different temperament. Whereas the cautious McKinley respected the political status quo, Roosevelt demanded change. He was a brash reformer and an activist in the most literal sense: He rarely sat still.

The first president to be known commonly by his initials, TR was a great believer in centralized authority—especially when *he* was the authority. Three traits in particular marked his presidency: his charismatic energy, abundance of will, and boyish conviction that he always knew what was best for the country.

The story of the Panama Canal is an instructive one: In 1903, Roosevelt began negotiating for the purchase of a canal zone across the Colombian province of Panama. In August, he offered the Colombians ten million dollars, but they wanted more. "Those contemptible little creatures in Bogotá ought to understand how much they are jeopardizing things and imperiling their own future," Roosevelt wrote to his secretary of state.

On November 3, with U.S. encouragement, the Panamanians revolted. The State Department immediately recognized the new government, and Roosevelt sent warships to protect it. Two weeks later, Panama signed the same treaty recently rejected by Colombia.

Around this time, Roosevelt read to his cabinet a detailed legal analysis that he had prepared defending America's right to the canal zone. When he was finished, he asked whether he had clarified his actions relating to Panama. "You certainly have, Mr. President," Secretary of War Elihu Root assured him. "You have shown that you were accused of seduction, and you have conclusively proved that you were guilty of rape."

As a general rule, when TR's worldview differed from reality, Roosevelt worked to change reality. Several years after leaving office, he told a crowd, "I took Panama and left Congress to debate, and while the debate goes on the canal does also."

Of course, Roosevelt had to work his way up to such cockiness. Immediately after McKinley's assassination, the forty-two-year-old vice president humbly pledged to respect his predecessor's conservative, probusiness policies. However, Roosevelt came to power at the height of the Progressive movement, and his desire for reform simply couldn't be contained.

• The Rough Riders

The unlikely chain of events that brought Theodore Roosevelt to the presidency began in 1897, with the start of the first McKinley administration. As a favor to Sen. Henry Cabot Lodge, McKinley made Roosevelt assistant secretary of the navy.

Although war with Spain over Cuba seemed likely, the president favored peace and resisted the war drums being beaten in the press. Not TR. Roosevelt was eager to fight, and as soon as Congress declared war in April 1898, he quit the navy to organize a regiment of volunteers. These were the Rough Riders, a colorful cross section of gung-ho types, including college athletes, Dakota cowboys, Long Island polo players, and New York City policemen.

The public's voracious appetite for stories about the Rough Riders overshadowed the fact that the regiment saw little action—only one day's hard fighting. Nevertheless, the Spanish were firing very real bullets that day as Roosevelt charged up Kettle Hill, and he later remembered it as the greatest of his life. "I killed a Spaniard with my own hand, like a jackrabbit," he wrote home. "Oh, but we had a bully fight!"

Top: Colonel Roosevelt and the Rough Riders in Cuba. Inset: TR's spurs.

With his first wife, Roosevelt had a daughter, Alice, named for her mother. With Edith, he had (in order of age): Theodore Jr., Kermit, Ethel, Archie, and Quentin.

• The Fun-Loving Roosevelts

Americans thoroughly enjoyed having Theodore Roosevelt as president. They loved his sparring sessions with boxing champion John L. Sullivan in the White House gym and his "obstacle walks," which typically left namby-pamby congressmen and overweight ambassadors panting in TR's wake. The Roosevelt family was also a source of great joy and humor. Newspapers filled their pages with stories of TR's pillow fights with his children and the time that Quentin rode his pony upstairs to cheer up his brother Archie, who was sick.

Alice, the president's eldest daughter, caused quite a stir when it was learned that she smoked in public *and* bet on horses. "I can do one of two things," Roosevelt said. "I can be president of the United States, or I can control Alice. I cannot do both."

For his own part, Roosevelt believed that he had more fun being president than any man before him. He craved the attention more than anything, and he regularly cultivated the press to get it. According to one relative, "When Theodore attends a wedding, he wants to be the bride, and when he attends a funeral, he wants to be the corpse."

• The Great Conservationist

Roosevelt's interest in nature began during his childhood, when he spent many hours collecting all sorts of small animals, especially insects. He preserved their carcasses, examined them, and cataloged his collection. He called it the Roosevelt Museum of Natural History.

After the death of his first wife, TR moved temporarily to the Dakota Territory, where he spent a good deal of time hunting buffalo, bear, and elk. His experiences out west later motivated him as president to preserve 125 million acres of public land in national forests.

Roosevelt's most memorable hunting trip was his postpresidential safari to Africa. Accompanied by a team of Smithsonian naturalists and taxidermists, he spent eleven months in the East African interior. Overall, the expedition bagged 512 animals, including 20 rhinos, 17 lions, 11 elephants, 9 giraffes, and 8 hippopotamuses. Roosevelt later emphasized that he had killed only specimens requested by the scientists or animals that were needed for food.

★ ★ ★ ★ ★ ★ ★ ★ ★ ★ ★ ★ ★ ★

• Decline and Fall

Beginning in 1910, it has been said, Roosevelt became "an unkind caricature of his better self." He returned from Africa no longer jovial but harshly vindictive. Part of the reason was that he was only fifty years old when he left office, and TR couldn't find a satisfying substitute for his energetic public career. In 1912, he returned to politics and challenged his protégé, William Howard Taft, for the presidency. Failing at that, he later attacked President Woodrow Wilson for opposing U.S. entry into World War I. He even called Wilson a coward on occasion.

When war finally came, the fifty-eight-year-old TR asked permission to lead a division to France. Two hundred thousand men quickly volunteered to go with him, but Wilson rejected the plan. Instead, a frustrated Roosevelt spearheaded Liberty Bond drives and took some comfort in the knowledge that all four of his sons were fighting. In July 1918, however, he learned that his son Quentin, a pilot in the Army Air Corps, had been shot down behind German lines.

With Quentin's death, the boyishness that had long sustained Theodore Roosevelt left him. He became ill on Armistice Day—November 11, 1918— and died in his sleep two months later. "Death had to take him sleeping," Vice President Thomas R. Marshall told the press, "for if Roosevelt had been awake, there would have been a fight."

Roosevelt, two months before his death, wears a black arm-band to mourn the death of his son Quentin.

★ ★ ★ ★ ★ ★ ★ ★ ★   ★ ★ ★ ★ ★ ★ ★ ★ ★

• Edith Roosevelt

EDITH CAROW GREW UP NEXT DOOR to Theodore Roosevelt on East Twentieth Street in New York City. She was one of the best friends of his younger sister, Corinne, and his first real playmate outside the family. As adolescents, he and Edith developed a romantic attraction, but they drifted apart after he went off to Harvard and met his first wife, Alice Lee.

Roosevelt married Alice in October 1880, a few months after his Harvard graduation. The couple settled in New York, where Roosevelt attended law school at Columbia. He didn't much like the law, however, and a year later joined the local Republican club, soon winning election to the state assembly.

Roosevelt's legislative career was cut short on February 14, 1884: That day, his mother succumbed to typhoid fever, and a few hours later his wife died of complications related to the birth of their first child. Leaving his infant daughter in the care of his sisters, a distraught TR fled to the Dakota Territory, where he had recently purchased an interest in two cattle ranches.

A year after Alice's death, Teddy returned to New York and ran into Edith. At first, he avoided her out of respect for the memory of his late wife. But he fell in love despite himself and proposed to Edith on November 17, 1885. They were married a year later in a small ceremony in London. TR later recalled that the fog was so thick that day it filled the church.

While the tall, elegant Alice had been "enchanting," "flowerlike," and "radiant," the freckled, red-haired Edith was more serious, more literary, and more temperamental. During one of TR's regular outdoor "scrambles," he allowed his children to go swimming with their clothes on. When they arrived home, a furious Edith immediately sent them to bed with a dose of ginger syrup. "There's nothing I can do," the president told his protesting children. "I'm lucky that she didn't give me a dose of ginger, too."

MAJOR POLITICAL EVENTS

★ **Northern Securities Case:** President Roosevelt wanted to protect workers from capitalism's most flagrant abuses. He also wanted to protect big business from itself. Roosevelt believed that unless the industrialists were contained, their excesses might lead to socialism in the United States. In his first speech to Congress, he indicated that the most ruthless trusts needed to be reformed. In March 1902, his administration filed suit against the Northern Securities Company, a railroad trust run by J. P. Morgan. Roosevelt's "trust-busting" campaign won a significant victory two years later when the Supreme Court ordered the breakup of the Northern Securities trust.

★ **Roosevelt Corollary:** Roosevelt's foreign policy was called Big Stick Diplomacy because of the president's often-quoted maxim that one should "speak softly and carry a big stick." In December 1904, he announced the Roosevelt Corollary to the Monroe Doctrine. Nearly a century earlier, Monroe had warned Europeans against further colonization of the Western Hemisphere. Now Roosevelt extended this doctrine to justify U.S. intervention in the affairs of Latin American countries. According to Roosevelt, the Monroe Doctrine obligated the United States to promote stability in the region. "Chronic wrongdoing, or an impotence which results in a general loosening of the ties of civilized society, may...ultimately require intervention," Roosevelt declared. "The Monroe Doctrine may force the United States, however reluctantly,...to the exercise of an international police power."

About the 26th President

Born: October 27, 1858
Birthplace: New York, NY
Died: January 6, 1919
Party: Republican
Children: Alice, Theodore Jr., Kermit,
    Ethel, Archibald, Quentin

★ **Meat Inspection and Pure Food and Drug Acts:** Upton Sinclair's 1906 novel, *The Jungle*, told the story of a Lithuanian immigrant working in a meatpacking plant in Chicago. Although the character was fictional, the dangerous slaughterhouse practices described by Sinclair, including the canning of dead rats, were very much real. Meanwhile, other muckraking journalists exposed similar threats to public health. Responding to the widespread disgust, Roosevelt called for the federal regulation of food and drugs. In June 1906, Congress passed two new laws: The Meat Inspection Act provided for the federal inspection of fresh meat and required canned meat to be accurately dated and labeled. The Pure Food and Drug Act established national standards to prevent manufacturers from adding harmful preservatives and other unhealthful ingredients to food and drug products.

★ ★ ★ ★ ★ ★ ★ ★ ★ ★ ★ ★ ★ ★

During the Roosevelt Administration

Oct. 16, 1901
President Roosevelt invites black educator Booker T. Washington to dinner at the White House. Southern racists react to the gesture with violent attacks against blacks.

Dec. 12, 1901
Italian inventor Guglielmo Marconi receives the first transatlantic radio message at his antenna station in Newfoundland, Canada.

1902
Binney & Smith introduces multicolored wax markers under the brand name Crayola crayons.

Dec. 17, 1903
Bicycle mechanics Orville and Wilbur Wright make the world's first flight in a heavier-than-air machine.

1904
Health officials in New York City trace a typhoid epidemic to cook Mary Mallon. Nicknamed Typhoid Mary, she is herself immune to the disease.

1905
Albert Einstein presents his special theory of relativity. From this he has derived the equation $e = mc^2$.

Apr. 18, 1906
An earthquake rocks San Francisco. Fires burn for three days, destroying two-thirds of the city and leaving half a million people homeless.

July 8, 1907
The Ziegfeld Follies opens in New York City. Florenz Ziegfeld's vaudeville spectacular combines dancing girls with such popular performers as W. C. Fields, Will Rogers, and Fanny Brice.

Oct. 1, 1908
The Ford Motor Company introduces the Model T, an $850 car that Henry Ford calls "a motorcar for the multitudes."

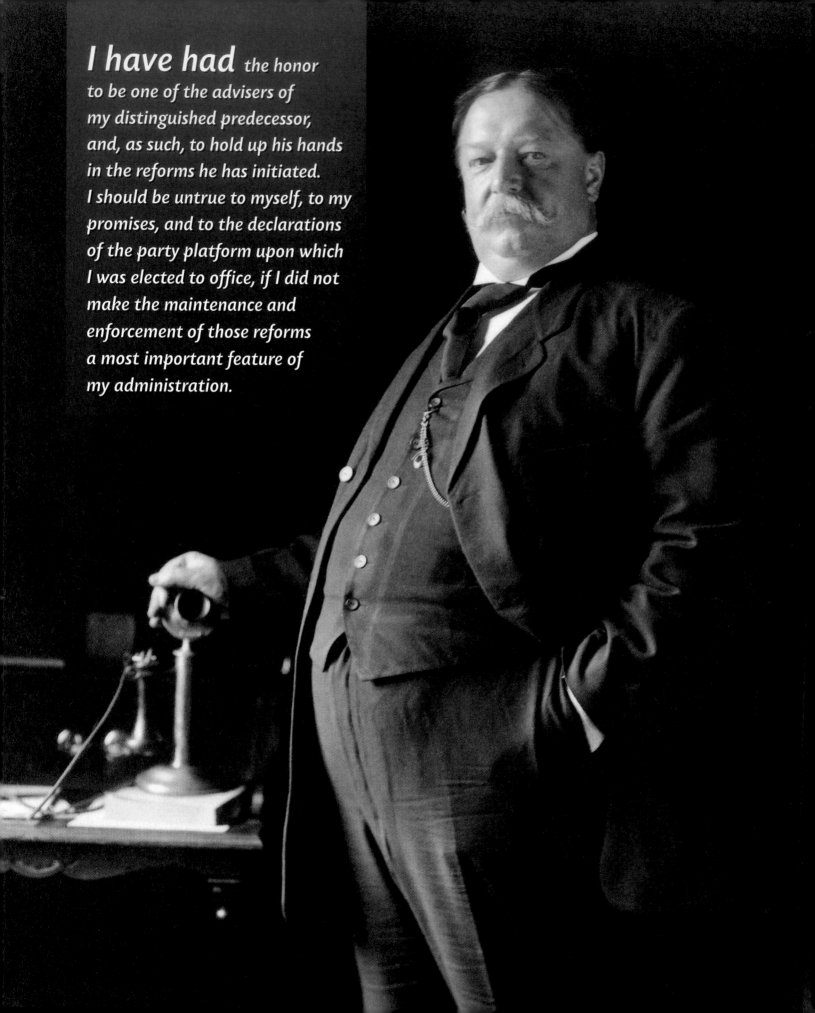

I have had the honor to be one of the advisers of my distinguished predecessor, and, as such, to hold up his hands in the reforms he has initiated. I should be untrue to myself, to my promises, and to the declarations of the party platform upon which I was elected to office, if I did not make the maintenance and enforcement of those reforms a most important feature of my administration.

William Howard Taft

27th President • 1909–1913

WARM-HEARTED WILLIAM HOWARD TAFT was unquestionably likable. A friend once compared his expansive smile to "a huge pan of sweet milk poured over one." Other people who knew Taft well cited his patience, tolerance, and enormous capacity for affection. It isn't difficult to understand why most Americans, when they thought of Taft, pictured a jolly fat man.

The origin of this always smiling, always friendly (perhaps a little lazy) "good old Bill" image can be traced to the years between 1904 and 1908, when Taft served as Theodore Roosevelt's secretary of war. Many people contributed to the Taft legend, but none more so than Roosevelt himself. When TR went off on a hunting trip a month after his 1905 inauguration, he told the press corps that all would be well in Washington because he had "left Taft sitting on the lid."

Taft was guilty himself of perpetuating this jolly-fat-man stereotype because he loved telling humorous stories at his own expense. One of his favorites involved a telegram that he sent in 1901 to Secretary of War Elihu Root. "Took long horseback ride today; feeling fine," Taft cabled from Manila, where he was serving as governor-general of the Philippines. Root immediately cabled back: "How is the horse?"

What many people didn't know about Taft, the devoted public servant, was that he hated politics. During his life, he ran for only one elective office: the presidency. Given a choice, he much preferred the judiciary. All he really wanted to be was a Supreme Court justice.

He hoped that Roosevelt might appoint him, but TR had other plans: Specifically, Taft would succeed TR as president and thereby preserve the magnificent Roosevelt legacy. When Mrs. Taft and Taft's brothers agreed, it was decided that Taft would run. It didn't seem to matter that Taft himself had once declared that "a national campaign for the presidency is to me a nightmare."

Temperamentally, Taft wasn't suited for the White House. Running the War Department according to Roosevelt's wishes had been one thing; having to cope with Congress by himself was quite another. Taft especially missed Roosevelt's goading and prodding.

Sadly, after 1910, Taft's relationship with Roosevelt soured, and his remaining years in office became difficult and nervous. "The amiable, sunny Taft vanished," one historian has noted, "and in his place appeared an irritable man." After leaving office in 1913, Taft became a professor of law at Yale, his alma mater, where he waited patiently for a Republican to regain the White House. Eight years later, the call he had been waiting for all his life finally came: President Harding had appointed him chief justice of the United States.

• In TR's Shadow

Taft and Roosevelt first became friendly around 1896, when Taft was a federal judge and TR police commissioner of New York City. After McKinley's election, Taft met with the new president to plead Roosevelt's case for an executive appointment.

When Roosevelt became president, he made Taft his secretary of war. According to Taft biographer Henry F. Pringle, the relationship that developed between the two men was "based on mutual respect, admiration, even love." However, the passive, somewhat lazy Taft was clearly dependent on the energetic Roosevelt for advice and encouragement. As a member of Roosevelt's cabinet, Taft did everything he was told and agreed with everything TR said.

Although Roosevelt could have easily won reelection in 1908, he chose instead to help Taft win the White House. Then he left on a yearlong African safari. Roosevelt's plan was to give Taft some breathing room, but when he returned

Taft as St. Patrick driving the evildoers from U.S. commerce.

home in 1910, TR began criticizing Taft for abandoning their progressive policies. Roosevelt may have sincerely believed his harsh, unfair charges, but at their root must have been Roosevelt's deep conviction that no one could run the country as well as he could. The break that he caused in their friendship was never healed.

• Taft's Golf Game

Taft was the first president to take up golf. He found the sport relaxing and, conscious of his weight, thought the walking was good for his health. During the 1908 campaign, however, his golf game caused a minor political flap. Apparently, many western voters—the same ones who equated Taft's Unitarianism with atheism—thought that his golf playing was immoral or at least indecent.

"I don't suppose you will have the chance to play until after [the] election and whether you have the chance or not, I hope you won't," Roosevelt advised him. "It is just like my tennis. I never let any friends advertise my tennis, and never let a photo of me in tennis costume appear."

Later, as president, Taft made no effort to hide his love for the links. In fact, on June 25, 1909, the *New York Times* reported that Taft's devotion to the sport had caused a golf boom that doubled the number of players at some public courses.

The Tafts in 1909 with their children Charlie and Helen.

• Big Bill

What most people remembered about Taft was his weight. As president, he weighed between 300 and 350 pounds, and his size made him the target of many "fat man" jokes. For example: Taft was the most polite man in Washington. One day he gave up his seat on a streetcar to three women. Or: Taft was bathing one day off the coast of Massachusetts when one of his neighbors suggested a swim. "Perhaps we'd better wait," said another. "The president is using the ocean."

In truth, Taft was so large that he literally got stuck if he tried to use a standard-size bathtub. (He once had to be pried out of one.) To accommodate the president, a special bathtub was installed in the White House. It was seven feet long and nearly four feet wide and weighed one ton.

Taft's own attitude toward his weight was one of amusement mixed with annoyance. The Japanese apparently shared this opinion. On a voyage to the Philippines, where he had been sent to establish a new government after the Spanish-

American War, Taft stopped over in Japan and took a rickshaw to visit the Nikko temples high in the mountains.

"The road was steep and got steeper," Taft recalled. "I had one 'pusher' in addition to the jinrikisha man when I began, another joined when we were halfway up, and it seemed to me that [when] we struck the last hill the whole village was engaged in the push. The Japanese seemed to look upon me with great amusement…. They gathered in crowds about me, smiling and enjoying the prospect of so much flesh and size."

The Taft bathtub was so large that it could easily hold three ordinary men.

★ ★ ★ ★ ★ ★ ★ ★ ★   ★ ★ ★ ★ ★ ★ ★ ★ ★

• Nellie Taft

DURING HIS LATER YEARS, a contented William Howard Taft looked back on his life. From his elevated vantage point as chief justice of the Supreme Court, he decided that his wife had not only brought him boundless happiness but also given him the will to succeed.

Both Taft and Nellie Herron (her given name was Helen) grew up in Cincinnati, where Nellie's father was a U.S. attorney. They met during a bobsledding party in 1879. Although Taft didn't date her for another three years, it was immediately obvious that Nellie was a highly intelligent girl.

Since his youth, Taft had always liked intelligent, outspoken women. While in high school, he had written a remarkably progressive essay on women's suffrage, in which he declared, "However different man and woman may be intellectually, coeducation…shows clearly that there is no mental inferiority on the part of the girls."

During their courtship, Taft wrote Nellie, "So far from holding your opinions lightly, I know no one who attaches more weight to them or who more admires your powers of reasoning than the now humbled subscriber." This is exactly what Nellie wanted to hear, and when Taft finally proposed to her in April 1885, she accepted.

Despite Taft's often-stated preference for the judiciary, Nellie urged him to pursue his many opportunities in politics. "Quick-witted and energetic," White House historian William Seale wrote, "she was less a charmer than her husband, and more of a pusher when it came to having her way." A stroke that she suffered two months after Taft took office temporarily sidetracked her, but by 1911, she was largely herself again. "She is quite disposed to sit as a pope and direct me as of yore," a relieved Taft wrote of Nellie during her convalescence, "which is an indication of the restoration of normal conditions."

MAJOR POLITICAL EVENTS

★ **Dollar Diplomacy:** President Taft generally accepted Roosevelt's "big stick" approach to foreign affairs, but he recast Roosevelt's method to suit his own purposes. Taft's Dollar Diplomacy, carried out by Secretary of State Philander C. Knox, used the military might of the United States to promote U.S. business interests overseas. Rather than take over Latin American countries, as Roosevelt had advocated, Taft encouraged Americans to invest in them. He invited U.S. banks to rescue debt-ridden Honduras and encouraged U.S. corporations to make investments in Haiti. However, when rebels threatened to overthrow the Nicaraguan government in August 1912, Taft without hesitation sent in marines to stabilize Nicaragua's conservative, pro-U.S. regime.

★ **Busting the Standard Oil Trust:** The most famous antitrust case of the Taft years involved John D. Rockefeller's Standard Oil Company. In May 1911, the Supreme Court found that Rockefeller's oil trust violated the 1890 Sherman Anti-Trust Act because its monopoly of oil refineries allowed Rockefeller to control oil prices. Although Roosevelt later accused Taft of having abandoned Roosevelt-style "trust-busting," Taft was actually more successful at breaking up trusts than Roosevelt had been. In addition to persuading the Supreme Court to dismantle Standard Oil, Taft succeeded in forcing the breakup of the American Tobacco Company, James B. Duke's powerful tobacco trust.

About the 27th President

Born: September 15, 1857
Birthplace: Cincinnati, OH
Died: March 8, 1930
Party: Republican
Children: Robert, Helen, Charles

★ ★ ★ ★ ★ ★ ★ ★ ★ ★ ★ ★ ★

During the Taft Administration

Apr. 6, 1909
Naval engineer Robert E. Peary reaches the North Pole and becomes the first person to stand on "the roof of the world."

Aug. 7, 1909
The U.S. Mint replaces the old Indian head penny with a new Lincoln penny.

Sep. 10, 1909
Dr. Sigmund Freud begins a lecture tour of the United States, during which he discusses his controversial theories about human psychology.

Apr. 1910
President Taft starts an executive tradition when he throws out the first ball of the new baseball season.

July 4, 1910
Flamboyant black heavyweight champion Jack Johnson successfully defends his title against Jim Jeffries, a former champion who has been billed as the Great White Hope. Johnson's victory causes race riots in which ten people die.

Mar. 25, 1911
A fire at the Triangle Shirtwaist Company in New York City kills 146 workers. An investigation reveals that factory owners had locked the building's doors to keep the workers at their machines. The deaths spur labor unions to demand greater worker safety.

Oct. 29, 1911
In his will, newspaper publisher Joseph Pulitzer leaves money for the creation of prizes in the fields of fiction, poetry, history, and journalism.

1912
Mack Sennett founds the Keystone Company and begins producing silent comedy films. The most popular of these films feature Sennett's slapstick Keystone Kops.

★ **Constitutional Amendments:** The Sixteenth Amendment, which gave the federal government the power to levy income taxes, was passed by Congress and sent to the states for ratification in July 1909. It was declared effective as of February 25, 1913, and Congress approved the first graduated income tax as part of the Underwood Tariff eight months later. (The new income tax applied only to individuals earning more than three thousand dollars a year.) The Seventeenth Amendment, which provided for direct election of U.S. senators, passed Congress in May 1912. It was declared effective in May 1913, two months after Taft left office. Previously, senators had been elected by the legislatures of their states. Direct election of senators was one of many voting reforms urged by progressives, who also championed recall petitions, the secret ballot, and women's suffrage.

Here muster, not the forces of party, but the forces of humanity. Men's hearts wait upon us; men's lives hang in the balance; men's hopes call upon us to say what we will do. Who shall live up to the great trust? Who dares fail to try?

Woodrow Wilson

28th President • 1913–1921

WOODROW WILSON WAS OFTEN LIKENED to the stern Presbyterian minister that his father had been. In public, both were cold, self-righteous, and aloof. Journalist William Allen White once said that shaking Wilson's hand was like grasping "a ten-cent pickled mackerel in brown paper." After Wilson became president, his reserve increased. When interacting with the public, he always wore his most serious face.

Wilson's personal philosophy was also very much influenced by his father's beliefs. Like Lincoln, Wilson believed strongly in predestination, but he was much more certain than Lincoln of God's will. After his election in 1912, Wilson met with William F. McCombs, chairman of the Democratic National Committee, who reminded the president-elect of his services during the campaign. "God ordained that I should be the next President of the United States," Wilson nearly shouted. "Neither you nor any other mortal could have prevented that!"

According to commentator Walter Lippmann, Wilson believed deeply that he was being "guided by an intelligent power outside himself." This lack of doubt made Wilson less flexible than Lincoln had been and also less tolerant of other people's opinions. His ambassador to England, Walter Hines Page, recalled once briefing Wilson in Washington during World War I. When Page persisted in making a point that contradicted Wilson's views, the president "sprang up, stuck his fingers in his ears, and, still holding them there, ran out of the room." Wilson himself said that there were two sides to every issue: "the right and the wrong."

In private, however, Wilson was a completely different man. At home, he liked to dance, sing, and play parlor games; he went out often to the theater and especially liked the new "moving pictures."

His family was the center of his personal life, and it brought out his exuberance and silliness. Wilson's daughter Nell remembered him waking up on the morning of his first inauguration and staging an impromptu vaudeville dance around her mother, singing, "We're going to the White House—*today*!"

A year after his first wife's death, while he was courting his second, Wilson often walked back to the White House late at night. According to the Secret Service agent who was assigned to him: "We walked briskly, and the President danced off the curbs and up them when we crossed streets." Pausing at corners, Wilson "whistled softly, through his teeth, tapping out the rhythm with restless feet. 'Oh, you beautiful doll! You great big beautiful doll!'"

Although Wilson attempted to rid Princeton of class bias, he refused to support a black applicant's right to be admitted to the university.

• Wilson's First Presidency

In September 1875, an eighteen-year-old southerner named Thomas W. Wilson (Tommy to his friends) arrived at the College of New Jersey. Around 1881, at his mother's request, Tommy began calling himself by his middle name, Woodrow. In 1896, the College of New Jersey, its reputation and ambitions growing, changed its name to Princeton University. And in 1902, Woodrow Wilson became president of Princeton University.

Before taking over the presidency, Wilson had taught political science at Princeton, so he knew the university well. Immediately, he set about reorganizing it. His reforms included a new curriculum and a new method of teaching that replaced large impersonal lectures with much smaller reading groups, or preceptorials. Wilson was less successful in doing away with Princeton's "eating clubs," fraternitylike societies that segregated students by class. Opposition to Wilson's efforts was so strong that, when the New Jersey Democratic party offered to back him for governor in September 1910, Wilson resigned his post at the university.

★ ★ ★ ★ ★ ★ ★ ★ ★ ★ ★

• Southern Sympathies

The first feature film ever shown at the White House was D. W. Griffith's *The Birth of a Nation*. When this Reconstruction saga premiered in 1915, Wilson asked for a private screening. Using actors in blackface, Griffith's film told a story that dramatically portrayed the threat he believed Negroes posed to white womanhood.

According to historian Leon F. Litwack, the film was "an appropriate one for a president who embraced the ideology of racial segregation and maintained a discreet silence on the triumph of white terrorism in his native South." After viewing *The Birth of a Nation*, Wilson said, "It is like writing history in lightning. My only regret is that it is all so terribly true."

Throughout his political career, Wilson had tried to evade the issue of race relations. His sympathies were undeniably those of the South, but the Democratic coalition that elected him also included northern progressives who wanted equal rights for blacks. "I hope with all my heart," Wilson wrote a southern senator after nominating a black for a federal judgeship, "that my course will be understood and supported…. I know the dangers involved and deplore them just as much as you do."

The Wilson family at their Princeton home in 1912.

Crowds in the rue Madeleine greeting Wilson on December 14, 1918. Inset: As a memento, Clemenceau presented Wilson with a piece of the tablecloth used as a white flag by the Germans when they surrendered.

• The Quest for Peace

In December 1918, at the end of World War I, President Wilson left Washington for the Paris Peace Conference. Although no sitting president had ever traveled to Europe before, Wilson decided to attend the conference personally because world peace had become his obsession.

Almost a year earlier, Wilson had set forth fourteen points on which he believed peace had to be based. "I really think," British prime minister David Lloyd George recalled, "that at first the idealistic President regarded himself as a missionary whose function was to rescue the poor European heathen from their age-long worship of false and fiery gods."

"God gave us his Ten Commandments, and we broke them," French premier Georges Clemenceau said. "Wilson gave us his Fourteen Points—we shall see."

When Wilson returned in July 1919 and submitted the Treaty of Versailles to the Senate, he declared, "The stage is set, the destiny disclosed. It has come about by no plan of our conceiving, but by the hand of God, which led us into this war." However, some senators saw more of Wilson's handiwork than God's in the treaty, and they wanted changes. In September, Wilson began a strenuous cross-country speaking tour to promote his version of the treaty.

However, the sixty-two-year-old president, not a well man to begin with, didn't have the strength for such an undertaking. He collapsed a little over three weeks into the tour.

The top hat and white gloves that Wilson took with him to Versailles.

Once back at the White House, Wilson seemed to improve, but on October 2 he suffered a stroke that paralyzed his left side.

To protect her husband's health, the first lady placed herself firmly between Wilson and the outside world. Beginning what she called her "stewardship," she ordered that all presidential business cross her desk first: "I studied every paper…and tried to digest and present in tabloid form the things that, despite my vigilance, had to go to the President."

In December, the Senate Foreign Relations Committee insisted on sending a delegation to visit the president and determine his condition. Senators Gilbert Hitchcock (a Wilson friend) and Albert Fall (an enemy) appeared at the White House on December 5 and were escorted to the presidential bedroom. At their end of the brief interview, Fall said, "Well, Mr. President, we have all been praying for you." "Which way, Senator?" was Wilson's famous reply.

The president used this portable typewriter on ships and trains during his western trip campaigning for ratification of the Treaty of Versailles.

Ellen Wilson

Edith Wilson

★　★　★　★　★　★　★　★　★　★

• The Two Mrs. Wilsons

BECAUSE WOODROW WILSON socialized rarely and had few male friends, he became emotionally dependent on his first wife, the Savannah-born Ellen Axson. They met in April 1883 at the home of Wilson's cousin in Rome, Georgia, and became engaged five months later.

Unlike most first ladies, Ellen Wilson cared little for the glamour of her public position. She was content to remain in the background, but those who knew the president best thought that Ellen Wilson was her husband's closest adviser. Because she preferred painting, reading, and gardening to socializing (the Rose Garden was her idea), the housekeeper

of the White House described her as a "day-dreamer." Yet she was the first person the president consulted when he had to sift through the advice and opinions of others, and when she died of Bright's disease in August 1914, Wilson was devastated. During the long train ride home to Georgia, Wilson rode in the same compartment with her coffin.

Wilson remained distraught until about seven months later, when he happened to meet a Washington widow named Edith Bolling Galt. He was so captivated by Mrs. Galt that he abandoned his mourning in order to court and wed her. Less than two months after their first meeting, Wilson proposed. "Oh, you can't love me, for you don't really know me," Edith said. The loss of his wife had made him miserable, Wilson replied, but now he was ready to live again. In October 1915, their engagement was announced to the press, and marriage followed two months later.

Edith Wilson lacked the shrewdness and intellectual depth of the president's first wife. However, as Wilson still had the same need to bring his work home with him, Edith was prepared early for the role of presidential adviser. While they were still courting, Wilson gave her important documents to read, and when he suffered a stroke in 1919, the second Mrs. Wilson took on even more decision-making responsibility.

MAJOR POLITICAL EVENTS

★ **Mexican Revolution:** In 1913, two years after the start of the Mexican Revolution, military dictator Victoriano Huerta came to power. Refusing to recognize Huerta's regime, President Wilson continued his policy of "watchful waiting." In April 1914, Mexican troops arrested U.S. sailors in Veracruz. Although the sailors were released with an apology, Wilson ordered the occupation of Veracruz. Huerta resigned two months later. In March 1916, however, Mexican revolutionary Pancho Villa raided Columbus, New Mexico. Gen. John J. Pershing hunted Villa for nearly a year before Wilson recalled Pershing to lead the American Expeditionary Force to France.

★ **World War I:** During the first three years of World War I, the United States stayed out of the fighting. However, Wilson's policy of cautious neutrality became more and more difficult to maintain once the German navy began torpedoing U.S. ships bound for England. In May 1915, public opinion turned strongly against the Germans when a U-boat sank the British passenger liner *Lusitania*. Nearly 1,200 people drowned, including 128 Americans. At first, the Germans backed down and suspended U-boat operations. In January 1917, however, they announced a resumption of unrestricted submarine warfare in British waters. On February 3, Wilson broke off relations with Germany. A month later, U.S. newspapers published the text of an intercepted telegram from German foreign minister Arthur Zimmermann to the German ambassador in Mexico. In the telegram, Zimmermann proposed an alliance between Germany and

About the 28th President

Born: December 28, 1856
Birthplace: Staunton, VA
Died: February 3, 1924
Party: Democrat
Children: Margaret, Jessie, Eleanor

Mexico should the United States enter the war. On April 2, Wilson asked Congress to declare war on Germany.

★ **Prohibition:** By the time the Eighteenth Amendment was ratified in January 1919, most southern and western states already had prohibition laws. In October 1919, Congress passed a national law (over Wilson's veto) to enforce the Eighteenth Amendment. The Prohibition Enforcement, or Volstead, Act established specific penalties for the manufacture, transportation, and sale of alcohol, beginning January 16, 1920.

★ **Women's Suffrage:** Ratified in August 1920, the Nineteenth Amendment gave American women the right to vote just in time for the 1920 presidential election. Millions of new women voters helped elect Warren Harding.

During the Wilson Administration

Sep. 1, 1914	*The last of the passenger pigeons dies at the Cincinnati Zoo. These birds, flocks of which once darkened the North American skies, have been hunted into extinction.*
1914	*For his second film, Charlie Chaplin develops his Little Tramp character. Chaplin uses a bowler hat, a cane, and baggy clothing to evoke the sadness and helplessness that underlie the Little Tramp's appeal.*
1914	*Edgar Rice Burroughs publishes* Tarzan of the Apes, *which becomes so popular that it spins off twenty-two sequels.*
May 20, 1916	*The first cover illustration by Norman Rockwell appears on the front of the* Saturday Evening Post. *The magazine soon features ten Rockwell covers a year.*
Apr. 6, 1917	*Showman George M. Cohan writes the song "Over There" after reading a newspaper account of the U.S. entry into World War I.*
May 15, 1918	*Lt. George Boyle of the Army Signal Corps makes the first airmail flight. He takes off from Washington, D.C., for Philadelphia, but a course error forces him to land in a Maryland cow pasture.*
Oct. 1919	*Eight Chicago White Sox players receive payments from gamblers to throw the World Series. Those banished from baseball for life as a result of the Black Sox scandal include "Shoeless" Joe Jackson.*
Nov. 2, 1920	*Pittsburgh station KDKA begins the first regular radio broadcasts with its coverage of the 1920 presidential election results.*

Our supreme task is the resumption of our onward, normal way. Reconstruction, readjustment, restoration—all these must follow. I would like to hasten them.

Warren G. Harding

29th President • 1921–1923

WARREN HARDING WAS THE SORT OF POLITICIAN who made people feel good about themselves. Although his mind may have been weak and undisciplined, his "people" skills were extraordinary. Personal contact and gentle persuasion were his favorites, and he made use of them often. His private secretary, George Christian Jr., once estimated that Harding had shaken the hands of 250,000 people in his political career.

When Christian suggested cutting back on the president's public appearances, Harding refused: "I *love* to meet people. It is the most pleasant thing I do; it is really the only fun I have. It does not tax me, and it seems to be a very great pleasure to them."

The distinguished-looking Harding was somewhat vain about his appearance. He kept his heavy, dark eyebrows trimmed, was partial to jewelry, and had so many clothes that new closets had to be built in the White House. Yet all the public saw was the result, apparent ease and charm.

Harding had a personal magnetism that attracted both men and women—not the charisma of a great leader but the engaging personality of a cherished next-door neighbor. According to Harding biographer Robert K. Murray, he was "typical of that America whose tastes were the movies and popular magazines, who knew only what appeared in the paper, and who after work desired to go home and be entertained by the inanities of the radio."

A former newspaper editor, Harding cultivated the best relationship any president has had with the press. He knew many of the White House correspondents personally and called them all by their first names. As a result, throughout his presidency, he always received extremely favorable coverage, making him very popular with the voters.

After his death, however, Harding's public image changed dramatically. The exposure of the Teapot Dome oil-leasing scandal (and others), along with revelations about his extramarital affairs, created a "bad" Harding who quickly supplanted the "good" Harding of the early 1920s. It's the fallen Harding that the history books remember today.

Harding never took any bribes himself, though, like Grant, he placed too much trust in cronies who betrayed him for their own gain. Harding considered loyalty to be the foremost virtue of any politician, but his own virtue misled him. As Harding himself admitted to the National Press Club in 1922, his father had told him that he was lucky he hadn't been born a girl. When he asked why, his father said, "Because you'd be in the family way all the time. You can't say, 'No.'"

Harding's diamond-studded cigarette case.

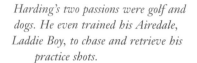

Harding's two passions were golf and dogs. He even trained his Airedale, Laddie Boy, to chase and retrieve his practice shots.

• The "Bad" Harding

After his death, stories began to appear in the press about Harding's "questionable" lifestyle while in the White House. For instance, although he was careful never to be photographed with a cigarette or a Scotch in his hand, it was well known that Harding both smoked and drank. Sunday school teachers regularly wrote to him, urging him to give up tobacco because their backsliding students used the president's habit as an excuse.

The drinking, however, was even worse, because Prohibition was the law and Harding himself had voted for it. The truth was, of course, that Harding had supported Prohibition only for political reasons and, like most Americans, didn't think the law applied to him.

Another cause of belated concern were the poker parties that Harding held twice weekly at the White House. Regular players included Attorney General Harry M. Daugherty and Interior Secretary Albert G. Fall, both of whom were later implicated in major scandals. Commerce Secretary Herbert Hoover played once but not thereafter. "It irked me," Hoover said, "to see [poker playing] in the White House."

Even so, by far the worst of the posthumous revelations were the affairs, particularly the one Harding allegedly had with a longtime friend's daughter, Nan Britton, who was more than thirty years Harding's junior. In 1927, Britton wrote a book that included many erotic details of their relationship, as well as her claim that Harding had fathered her daughter. Particularly shocking were her descriptions of their trysts in the White House, which took place in a private "telephone booth" adjacent to the Oval Office.

The president's silk pajamas.

• A Compulsive Joiner

Warren Harding very much wanted to be liked. Some biographers have described his need for friends as "compulsive," caused by his insecurity and lack of faith in his own abilities. Whatever the reason, Harding was certainly a compulsive joiner.

Beginning early in his political career, he joined nearly every organization that would have him—from the Sons of Union Veterans to the Concatenated Order of the Hoo Hoo (a fraternal organization for lumbermen). The only group that wouldn't have him was the Masons—which distressed Harding greatly, because he wanted to be a Mason most of all. Not until August 1920, when Harding was about to become president, did his hometown lodge raise him to the Sublime Degree of Master Mason. "You know that I have longed to be a Mason for twenty years," Harding said. "I am glad that my ambition has been fulfilled."

The red fez on Harding's head symbolizes member-ship in the Aladdin Temple, Ancient Arabic Order of Nobles of the Mystic Shrine. The Shriners weren't specifically a Masonic order, but they admitted only the most elite Masons.

Harding's Masonic ring.

★ ★

Stopping off in Sitka, Alaska, in late July 1923, Harding helped paint a local house despite obvious signs of physical decline.

• Death in Office

Harding's health began to decline during the spring of 1923, when he lost his usual ruddiness and appeared tired and worried. With hindsight, historians have concluded that Harding's nervousness was caused by his fear that several administration scandals would soon be exposed.

The president's schedule that summer included a trip to Alaska, which his doctor thought was a good idea, provided that Harding got some rest along the way. The Republican party, however, saw the trip as an opportunity for the president to stump the nation in advance of the 1924 campaign. Despite his doctor's warning, Harding agreed to a tiring schedule of cross-country speeches. By the time he boarded a train from Seattle to San Francisco on July 27, he was near collapse.

That night, when he complained of nausea and pains in his chest, his doctors diagnosed heart trouble and wired ahead for a specialist. When Harding arrived in San Francisco on Sunday morning, July 29, he felt well enough to dress himself, though that night his condition worsened.

He died four days later. The doctors agreed that the cause of death was probably a cerebral hemorrhage, but they wanted to perform an autopsy. Mrs. Harding steadfastly refused. Later, her refusal sparked rumors that she had poisoned the president to spare him the indignity of facing up to the scandals.

★ ★ ★ ★ ★ ★ ★ ★ ★ ★ ★ ★ ★ ★ ★ ★ ★

• Florence Harding

WARREN HARDING CALLED HIS WIFE THE DUCHESS. He meant the nickname affectionately, but it also captured her haughty manner and the emotional distance that separated them. A log-cabin sort of president, Harding admired his wife's fine pedigree—she was the daughter of the richest man in town—and her gracious manner as a hostess. Yet Florence Harding was also a tough, ambitious lady and a hard worker.

Five years Harding's senior, she was a twenty-nine-year-old divorcée with a young son when they first met. Within about a year, she had chased him down and married him. Afterward, she helped him build his newspaper, the *Marion* (Ohio) *Star*, into a financial success and encouraged his political career. However, on a personal level, their marriage was much less successful. It lacked intimacy, and Harding regularly abandoned his wife for other, younger women.

As first lady, Mrs. Harding, like her husband, was very popular. She gave lawn parties for wounded World War I veterans and restored to White House social life some of the old gaiety that had been missing during the tenure of the publicly grim Wilsons. The grandes dames of Washington society, however, considered her a provincial and gossiped maliciously about her overuse of makeup, her excitability, and her visits to a local astrologer named Madam Marcia.

One Harding biographer has described Florence as "sexless, with the brittle quality of an autumn leaf after the chlorophyll has receded." Another has pointed out that "Mrs. Harding's hold on her husband…always rested more on her tenacity and sense of purpose than on coyness or charm." In her defense, Florence Harding's nagging and prodding often provided the resolve that Harding so often failed to muster himself.

MAJOR POLITICAL EVENTS

★ **Immigration:** Responding to public fears that the country was being overrun by poor immigrants, President Harding signed into law the Immigration Restriction Act of 1921. This act imposed the first general limits on immigration to the United States. Specific quotas were set for each country at 3 percent of the number of people from that country already in the United States as of the 1910 census. The total number of immigrants allowed in during any given year was capped at 357,000. In comparison, between 1905 and 1910, nearly 1,000,000 immigrants per year entered the country. In May 1924, the Johnson-Reed Act further limited immigration to 164,000 people per year.

★ **Washington Conference:** Harding's most important accomplishment came in the field of foreign affairs. With the victorious World War I powers already maneuvering for advantage in the postwar world, Harding convened the Washington Conference for the Limitation of Armament, held in the U.S. capital beginning in November 1921. Participants included the United States, Great Britain, France, Italy, and Japan. After three months of talks, these nations agreed to limit the size of their navies according to specific ratios. Under this agreement, the United States and Britain were granted the largest navies, while the size of the Japanese fleet was capped at slightly more than half the size of the U.S. and British fleets. The conference also produced the Four Power Pact among the United States, Great Britain, Japan, and France. According to this treaty, all four nations agreed to respect one another's territories in Asia.

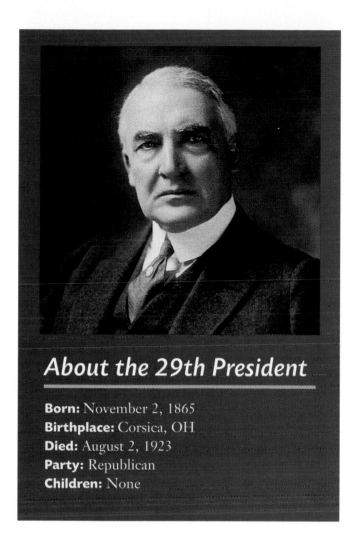

About the 29th President

Born: November 2, 1865
Birthplace: Corsica, OH
Died: August 2, 1923
Party: Republican
Children: None

★ **Teapot Dome Scandal:** In April 1922, Harding's interior secretary, Albert G. Fall, granted the Mammoth Oil Company exclusive rights to the government's Teapot Dome oil fields in Wyoming. In exchange, Fall received more than three hundred thousand dollars in cash and government bonds. Having heard rumors about the deal, a number of senators began looking into it, but the complete story didn't emerge until after Harding's death in August 1923. In October 1923, the Senate Public Lands Committee launched an in-depth investigation that revealed a number of payoffs. Although Fall and Mammoth owner Harry Sinclair were both acquitted on conspiracy charges, Sinclair was jailed for jury tampering and contempt of Congress, while Fall paid a large fine and served a year in prison for bribery.

★ ★ ★ ★ ★ ★ ★ ★ ★ ★ ★ ★ ★ ★ ★

During the Harding Administration

Sep. 7-8, 1921   Local businessmen sponsor the first Miss America Pageant in Atlantic City, New Jersey. They hope it will extend the tourist season beyond Labor Day.

Aug. 28, 1922   New York City radio station WEAF broadcasts the first paid radio commercial.

Oct. 24, 1922   Mayor James Curley bans Isadora Duncan from performing in Boston after the twenty-four-year-old dancer declares her sympathy for Communism while exposing herself on stage.

Nov. 7, 1922   In Egypt, British archaeologist Howard Carter discovers the tomb of the boy pharaoh Tutankhamen. Treasures from the tomb tour the world. Meanwhile, in the United States, people are captivated by Tutmania.

1922   Italian immigrant Angelo Siciliano changes his name to Charles Atlas. Then, after winning the World's Most Perfectly Developed Man contest, he begins marketing a physical fitness program. In his advertising, he claims (dishonestly) that he was once a "ninety-seven-pound weakling."

1922   Emily Post publishes a best-selling guide to etiquette that she hopes will raise the social standards of ordinary Americans.

Mar. 3, 1923   Henry R. Luce and Briton Hadden, both recent Yale graduates, begin publishing the weekly newsmagazine Time.

Apr. 18, 1923   Babe Ruth hits a home run on opening day at the new Yankee Stadium. The ballpark is nicknamed the House That Ruth Built because Ruth's popularity has paid for it.

Here stands our country, an example of tranquillity at home, a patron of tranquillity abroad. Here stands its government, aware of its might but obedient to its conscience. Here it will continue to stand.

Calvin Coolidge

30th President • 1923–1929

BOVE ALL THINGS, CALVIN COOLIDGE cherished stability. If his Puritan New England upbringing had taught him anything, it was the importance of thrift and caution. One historian has called him "a man bred and trained to avoid daring." After the tumultuous years of the Harding administration, however, a dose of reliability was exactly what the populace craved.

Personally, Coolidge was about as far from Harding's good fellowship as one could get. After meeting Coolidge one evening, a White House guest remarked that his smile "was like ice breaking up in a New England river." Alice Roosevelt Longworth liked to say that he had been "weaned on a dill pickle," with a personality to match his sour appearance.

From his father, a prosperous Vermont farmer and storekeeper, Coolidge had inherited tightness with a dollar and with his lips. He was famous for smoking expensive cigars given to him as gifts while offering his guests three-cent stogies that he'd bought himself. His Silent Cal reputation was equally well deserved. Yet these negative characteristics were often redeemed by Coolidge's remarkable wit, which he often used to squelch conversations that displeased him.

In politics as well as his private life, Coolidge was modest and self-confident. He had great faith in the ability of average people to conduct their own affairs and tried to do as little as possible to upset the natural course of things.

According to H. L. Mencken, Coolidge's "ideal day is one on which nothing whatever happens." Or as a more recent historian pointed out, "The country wanted nothing done, and he did nothing." Coolidge's laissez-faire philosophy of government can account for much of this lack of initiative. He believed in fattening the golden goose of Big Business so that it could provide for all Americans. One of his most famous sayings was "The business of America is business."

Coolidge was efficient, logical, and organized, but he never looked ahead for troubles down the road. Instead, "while he yawned and stretched," Mencken wrote, "the United States went slam-bang down the hill—and he lived just long enough to see it fetch up with a horrible bump at the bottom."

During the Great Depression, New Dealers denounced Coolidge's laissez-faire policies and the fact that he'd spent more time vacationing than any other president. The respect he had returned to the presidency after the Harding scandals was forgotten, and he was simply dismissed as a churchwarden from a rural parish who had "accidentally strayed into great affairs." When he died of a sudden heart attack in 1933, Dorothy Parker quipped, "How can they tell?"

• The Oath of Office

News of President Harding's death in San Francisco reached Vice President Coolidge in a roundabout way. First the message traveled to Washington, D.C., where it was rerouted to Bridgewater, Vermont. This was the telegraph station closest to the Plymouth Notch home of Coolidge's father, where the vice president was spending his summer vacation. From Bridgewater, it traveled by car, because John Coolidge refused to have a telephone in his house.

"I was awakened by my father coming up the stairs calling my name," Coolidge remembered. "He [was] the first to address me as President of the United States."

Coolidge immediately dressed and went downstairs. By that time, a herd of reporters had arrived. Coolidge dictated a public statement, and they all rushed off to file their stories. Meanwhile, Coolidge went across the road to a store and spoke by telephone with Secretary of State Charles Evans Hughes, who urged him to take the oath of office immediately.

Reading from a well-thumbed copy of the Constitution, Coolidge's father, who was a notary public, administered the oath of office to his son at 2:47 A.M. Coolidge signed the oath in triplicate and then went back to sleep. The simplicity of this ceremony, a senator later remarked, "fired the public imagination."

Top: During visits to his father's farm, Coolidge would often reenact boyhood chores for the benefit of news photographers. Right: The family Bible on which Coolidge took the oath of office.

★ ★

• Fast Asleep

Noted curmudgeon H. L. Mencken once wrote of the thirtieth president that "Nero fiddled while Rome burned, but Coolidge only snores…. His chief feat during five years and seven months in office was to sleep more than any other president."

Coolidge typically slept at least ten hours a day: from ten o'clock at night until six the next morning and then another two or three hours after lunch. (As president, he used to joke that his lengthy afternoon naps were good for the country because he couldn't initiate anything while asleep.)

On one of his infrequent evenings out, Coolidge went to a Washington theater to see the Marx Brothers in the stage version of *Animal Crackers*. Noticing the president in the audience, Groucho Marx called out to him, "Isn't it past your bedtime, Calvin?"

Coolidge loved publicity because it was good politics and because it was fun. Although he usually emphasized his personal dignity, he would nevertheless occasionally dress up in strange costumes to please voters and get his picture in the paper.

• Giddyap!

Coolidge's exacting, demanding nature made him efficient but also irritable. In public, he suppressed his anger. Later, in private, he (and his wife) paid the emotional price.

Biographers have speculated that Coolidge's chronic lack of exercise contributed to this buildup of tension. Although his high metabolism kept his weight down (and necessitated all that sleep), it didn't provide the physical or emotional release that he needed.

What little exercise the president did get came from a stationary mechanical horse that he rode in the White House three times a day. Early in his presidency, Coolidge had ridden a flesh-and-blood horse, but

he had switched to an electric model to save time and because he was allergic to horse dander.

In the summer of 1927, while vacationing in the Black Hills of South Dakota, Coolidge temporarily returned to nonmechanical mounts. Because he was always given a responsive horse to ride, the president soon began to think that his hobbyhorse riding had made him an excellent equestrian. His confidence became so strong that he decided to ride a wild horse. Fortunately, his wife stopped him before he could hurt himself.

This electrically operated horse became embarrassing to Coolidge when it was revealed that he liked to whoop and holler like a cowboy as he rode it.

• Silent Cal

During his presidency, anecdotes clung to Calvin Coolidge like iron filings to a magnet. People made fun of his aloofness, his thriftiness, and especially his famous silence. Yet it was always the witty Coolidge who supplied the punch lines.

One day, Massachusetts governor Channing Cox visited then–Vice President Coolidge to compare notes. Cox pointed out that as governor of Massachusetts, Coolidge had been able to see an extraordinary number of visitors and still leave work by five o'clock. Cox was frustrated because, even though he saw fewer people, he often found himself at work until nine. "You talk back," Coolidge explained.

The Silent Cal story that the first lady most enjoyed telling concerned a woman who approached her husband at a dinner party. "You must talk to me, Mr. Coolidge," she said. "I made a bet today that I could get more than two words out of you." "You lose," Coolidge replied.

★ ★ ★ ★ ★ ★ ★ ★ ★ ★   ★ ★ ★ ★ ★ ★ ★ ★ ★ ★

• Grace Coolidge

THE FIRST TIME Grace Goodhue saw Calvin Coolidge was through an open window in Northampton, Massachusetts. (They lived on the same street.) He was standing in his underwear, wearing a hat and shaving. She laughed. Coolidge heard her and later asked to be introduced. On their first date, he explained that he had an undisciplined lock of hair that often got in his way when he shaved. He used the hat to anchor the lock.

Although both were Vermonters away from home, they made a strange couple. Grace was extremely outgoing, with a genuine interest in people, while Coolidge was Coolidge. As one biographer later observed, "She did almost everything, and he did almost nothing."

Socially, Grace Coolidge provided an important buffer between her husband and the outside world—in other words, she did nearly all the talking, though never about government matters. Coolidge appreciated his wife's social abilities, but he was also very strict with her. As first lady, she wasn't allowed to dance in public, bob her hair, or wear slacks.

She bore the brunt of his tantrums, which were the price that they both paid for Coolidge's constant public composure. During their Black Hills vacation in 1927, she went hiking with her Secret Service bodyguard. Misjudging the time and distance, they returned two hours late. Coolidge was so furious that he transferred the Secret Service agent and refused to speak to his wife for several days.

Sometimes Grace rebelled. It particularly irked her that Coolidge made plans for her without letting her know in advance. One morning at breakfast she said, "Calvin, look at me. I find myself facing everyday a large number of engagements about which I know nothing. I wish you'd have your Secret Service prepare for me each day a list of the engagements for the coming week, so that I can follow it." Coolidge peeked out from behind his newspaper and replied, "Grace, we don't give out that information promiscuously."

MAJOR POLITICAL EVENTS

★ **Commercial Aviation:** Among President Coolidge's successful probusiness policies was his encouragement of commercial aviation. Although the aviation industry had grown by great leaps since the first Wright brothers flight in 1903, passenger flights didn't become available until the 1920s. In 1926, Congress passed the Air Commerce Act, which made commercial aviation subject to government regulation. It also approved the first two commercial airline routes. The Transcontinental Airway linked New York with Los Angeles and San Francisco by way of Cleveland, Chicago, Iowa City, Des Moines, North Platte, Cheyenne, and Salt Lake City. The Southwestern Airway between Chicago and Dallas included stops at Fort Wayne, Moline, St. Joseph, Kansas City, Wichita, Tulsa, and Oklahoma City.

★ **Farm Relief:** Coolidge was notably successful at defeating bills he didn't like. In 1927 and again in 1928, Congress passed the McNary-Haugen farm bill. Both times Coolidge vetoed the bill because of its allegedly socialist aspects. The McNary-Haugen farm bill would have created an independent federal corporation to purchase surplus crops from farmers at a price equal to the world price plus the tariff amount. These surpluses would then be stored and sold—domestically, if the price rose, or abroad at any price. The purpose of the bill was to protect farmers from price fluctuations and guarantee them a profit. Coolidge responded that the government had no business fixing crop

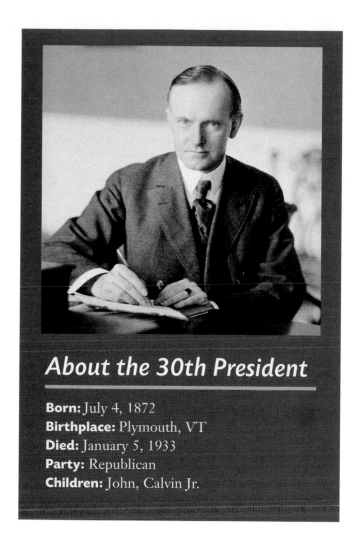

About the 30th President

Born: July 4, 1872
Birthplace: Plymouth, VT
Died: January 5, 1933
Party: Republican
Children: John, Calvin Jr.

★ ★ ★ ★ ★ ★ ★ ★ ★ ★ ★ ★ ★ ★

During the Coolidge Administration

Feb. 12, 1924 *George Gershwin debuts his* Rhapsody in Blue, *the first jazz composition written for the concert hall.*

July 1925 *The state of Tennessee tries biology teacher John T. Scopes for teaching his students about Darwin's theory of evolution and thus violating a state law banning any theory that denies creationism. Scopes is convicted and fined one hundred dollars.*

1925 *Clarence Birdseye uses techniques that he has learned from the Eskimos to develop and market frozen food.*

Mar. 1926 *Harry Scherman starts the Book-of-the-Month Club for rural readers who live far away from bookstores and well-stocked libraries. He prints less expensive editions of current books selected by a panel of judges.*

Aug. 6, 1926 *Gertrude Ederle of New York City, a 1924 Olympic gold medalist, becomes the first woman to swim the English Channel. Her time of fourteen hours, thirty-one minutes beats the old record by more than two hours.*

May 21, 1927 *Charles Lindbergh completes the first solo transatlantic flight in his single-engine monoplane, the* Spirit of St. Louis.

1927 *The Continental Baking Company begins to sell Wonder Bread, which becomes the nation's first sliced bread in 1930.*

Feb. 14, 1929 *Al Capone sends killers dressed as police to wipe out a rival gang led by Bugs Moran. The St. Valentine's Day Massacre helps Capone win control of the illegal liquor trade in Chicago.*

prices, which should move up and down freely according to the laws of supply and demand. The president's refusal to stabilize farm prices later contributed to the devastation of U.S. agriculture during the Great Depression.

★ **Kellogg-Briand Pact:** Coolidge's foreign policy was one of isolationism, with one exception: the international peace treaty negotiated by Secretary of State Frank Kellogg and French foreign minister Aristide Briand. In August 1928, fifteen nations signed the ambitious Kellogg-Briand Pact, which outlawed war as a tool of national policy. Eventually, all but five of the world's nations signed the treaty, which was celebrated as the beginning of a new era of international peace. However, the Kellogg-Briand Pact contained neither an enforcement mechanism nor sanctions for those nations that dared to break it.

In no nation *are the institutions of progress more advanced. In no nation are the fruits of accomplishment more secure. In no nation is the government more worthy of respect. No country is more loved by its people. I have an abiding faith in their capacity, integrity, and high purpose. I have no fears for the future.*

Herbert Hoover

31st President • 1929–1933

ALTHOUGH HERBERT HOOVER EVENTUALLY embraced public service with a moralistic fervor, he wasn't a career politician or even a lawyer. Instead, he was a mining engineer—one of the world's best. After his graduation from Stanford University in 1895, Hoover supervised mining operations in Australia, China, and Burma, where a silver mine made him rich enough to start his own international engineering firm. Warren Harding once called Hoover "the smartest geek I know."

Hoover entered public service during World War I, when he and several other wealthy young men organized the Committee for the Relief of Belgium. Operating without any government support, Hoover's group raised a billion dollars to feed and clothe starving Belgians.

Hoover's straightforward humanitarianism and stunning results made him internationally famous *and* an attractive political candidate. Although the shy, selfless Hoover tried to discourage publicity, journalists couldn't help writing about him. Walter Lippmann declared that Hoover "incarnates all that is at once effective and idealistic in the picture of America," and Hoover's political career took off from there. In 1921, Harding made him secretary of commerce. Seven years later, he became the Republican presidential nominee.

Hoover was elected because he was a technocrat. Voters believed that he represented a new, modern leader: a self-made millionaire who could use his business skills to organize the government more efficiently. Hoover himself believed that technology could solve the world's problems. Even in 1938, as the world prepared for another war, he told a group of engineering students in Vienna that by improving industrial production they could provide, more than any statesmen, "the things that make peace."

So why was this brilliant, generous man such a failure as president? The Great Depression was, of course, not his fault—the crash had been building for years—but Hoover didn't know how to respond to it. As one biographer has written, Hoover was "born to the backstage." Terrified of public speaking, he had a "low voltage" personality, as journalist William Allen White wrote. But the depression was a high-voltage problem, and Hoover proved incapable of coping with it.

The man whose name had once inspired families to "hooverize," or ration, their food consumption now presided over a nation of Hoovervilles, shantytowns thrown up by the homeless unemployed. The stigma of the depression never quite left him, but his reputation was somewhat restored after World War II, when his efforts to combat postwar famine reminded many of his humanitarian successes during the First World War. It also helped that Hoover remained active well into his eighties. Or, as he put it, "I outlived the bastards."

• Hooverizing

Hoover earned his reputation as one of the world's great humanitarians during and immediately after World War I. From 1914 until 1919, he headed the private, charitable Commission for the Relief of Belgium and for two years after that directed the American Relief Administration. His efforts resulted in the distribution of thirty-four million tons of American food, clothing, and supplies to needy Europeans.

Once the United States entered the war in 1917, Hoover entered public service as head of the U.S. Food Administration. From the start, the new food administrator urged his countrymen to conserve. Hoover's slogan was "Food Will Win the War."

Because of Hoover's relentless promotion of meatless Mondays and wheatless Tuesdays, a new word entered the language. To *hooverize* meant to ration one's consumption voluntarily. "I can hooverize on dinner and on lights and fuel too, but I'll never learn to hooverize when it comes to loving you," read the message on one 1918 Valentine's Day card.

Belgian schoolchildren receiving one of Hoover's food shipments, ca. 1915. Many of those who received U.S. food shipments during World War I embroidered flour sacks and returned them to Hoover as tributes to his great humanitarianism.

★ ★ ★ ★ ★ ★ ★ ★ ★ ★ ★ ★ ★

• Gone Fishing

From the president's tackle box.

Hoover often said that he was most happy when he was fishing. His biographer Richard Norton Smith concluded that fishing was, for Hoover, "a pursuit of almost spiritual intensity and one that restored a sense of proportion in a period of excess."

Always the engineer, Hoover had a strategy for catching fish that was methodical and exhaustive. He would fish one spot from six in the morning until noon, eat a picnic lunch, and then drive as many as a hundred miles away before finding a suitable spot for his afternoon's angling.

"Fishing is the chance to wash one's soul with pure air, with the rush of the brook, or with the shimmer of the sun on the blue water," Hoover wrote. "It brings meekness and inspiration from the decency of nature, charity toward tackle makers, patience toward fish,…a quieting of hate, a rejoicing that you do not have to decide a damned thing until next week. And it is discipline in the equality of men, for all men are equal before fish."

• Hooverball

Hoover's routine as president included tossing a medicine ball around for thirty minutes every morning before breakfast. This White House regimen eventually became a daybreak ritual known as Hooverball. The rules were vaguely similar to those of volleyball—there were two sides and a net, for instance—but the heavy, bounceless medicine ball made for an entirely different sort of game.

When a group of government officials became Hooverball regulars, the press dubbed them the Medicine Ball Cabinet. These men included actual cabinet members, congressional leaders, friends, a journalist or two, and even a Supreme Court justice. The game on the South Lawn took place year round, no matter what the weather. Hoover particularly liked the game because it offered maximum exertion for the least investment of time.

Top: Hooverball on the White House lawn. The players, from left to right, are Agriculture Secretary Arthur Hyde, Interior Secretary Ray Lyman Wilbur, presidential aide Lawrence Richey, and Supreme Court Justice Harlan Fiske Stone. Left: An authentic "Hooverball" autographed by some of the regular players.

• The Elder Statesman

After leaving the presidency, Hoover appreciated and enjoyed his role as elder statesman. In 1938, the Belgian government invited him to visit the site of his earlier humanitarian triumphs, and Hoover accepted, extending the trip into a fifteen-nation European tour.

The journey was an eventful one: Hoover visited Vienna on March 3; nine days later, Nazi Germany annexed Austria. Then, while in Berlin on March 7, Hoover received an unexpected invitation from Adolf Hitler. At first, Hoover didn't want to go, but the American ambassador persuaded him that accepting the invitation would be a service to U.S. diplomacy.

During their seventy-five-minute meeting, Hoover and Hitler argued the merits of democracy versus dictatorship. Occasionally, such as when Hoover mentioned the word *Jew*, the German führer jumped up and ranted for several minutes,

mixing gutter language with his purple-faced shouting. At one point, Hoover simply told Hitler to sit down. "That's enough," Hoover said. "I'm not interested in your views." Hoover later told a friend that Hitler was "partly insane" but intelligent and well informed.

Although FDR cut Hoover out of World War II ("I'm not Jesus Christ," Roosevelt said. "I'm not raising the dead."), Harry Truman asked him to head famine relief efforts after the war. In March 1947, the seventy-two-year-old Hoover embarked on an eighty-two-day, thirty-eight-nation, round-the-world inspection tour, which included the stop in Warsaw pictured here.

"If your neighbors and their children were hungry, you would instantly invite them to a seat at the table," Hoover said in a speech to promote conservation at home. "These starving women and children are in foreign countries, yet they are hungry human beings—and they are also your neighbors.... Will you not take to your table an invisible guest?"

★ ★ ★ ★ ★ ★ ★ ★ ★ ★ ★ ★ ★ ★ ★ ★

• Lou Hoover

HERBERT HOOVER HAD ONE GREAT LOVE in his life: Lou Henry. A tall, tomboyish girl, she was the only female geology major at Stanford, and her ideas about a woman's role in life were as unconventional as her major. "It isn't as important what others think of you as what you feel inside yourself," she told another freshman. Lou and "Bert" met in 1894, during Hoover's senior year.

By the time Lou graduated in 1898, Hoover was already off in Australia, but he cabled her his marriage proposal and she accepted by return wire. They married in 1899 and then sailed for China, where Hoover had landed a new job. During the Boxer Rebellion of June 1900, Hoover helped defend the Western community at Tientsin against gangs of Chinese who hated foreigners. Lou even strapped on a Mauser pistol herself. (Later, at the White House, the Hoovers would often speak Mandarin when they didn't want others to understand them.)

As first lady, Lou Hoover became interested in the history of the White House. Using her own money, she hired a photographer to make a visual record of every piece of furniture in the mansion. She also took an interest in the White House staff. When she learned that a butler couldn't afford the milk and cream he needed for his ulcer, she arranged for their regular delivery. She also offered to pay the college bills for a young White House maid.

In June 1929, Lou became the center of a national controversy when she invited the wife of a black congressman to tea at the White House. Editors of some southern newspapers denounced her for "defiling" the presidential residence, and the Texas legislature formally censured her.

Hoover consoled his wife by telling her that the advantage of orthodox religion was "that it included a hot hell" and that cruel journalists and politicians would surely find "special facilities in the world to come."

MAJOR POLITICAL EVENTS

★ **Stock Market Crash:** On October 29, 1929, Wall Street collapsed. In just one day, companies listed on the New York Stock Exchange lost about nine billion dollars in value. The primary cause of the crash was stock speculation financed by borrowing. As long as prices kept rising, everyone made money. However, when prices began to fall, brokers called in their customers' debts. To pay the brokers, investors sold stock, which made prices fall even faster. A stampede quickly developed. Stock that had been trading at thirty or forty dollars a share one week earlier suddenly fell to pennies a share. The immediate effect of the crash was widespread bankruptcy on Wall Street, yet its lasting effects touched all Americans when five thousand banks failed, wiping out the savings accounts of nine million people.

★ **Smoot-Hawley Tariff:** Congress's first response to the Great Depression was the Smoot-Hawley Tariff of 1930. Despite the advice of a thousand economists that he veto the bill, President Hoover signed it because he thought that he had no other choice. The purpose of this bill, which raised U.S. tariff rates to record levels, was to protect domestic industry and American jobs. Sadly, as the economists had predicted, the Smoot-Hawley Tariff kicked off an international trade war that sharply reduced U.S. exports and caused even more people to lose their jobs. During the next two years, an average of one hundred thousand jobs were lost each week. Most Americans thought that the government should be providing direct aid to the unemployed, but

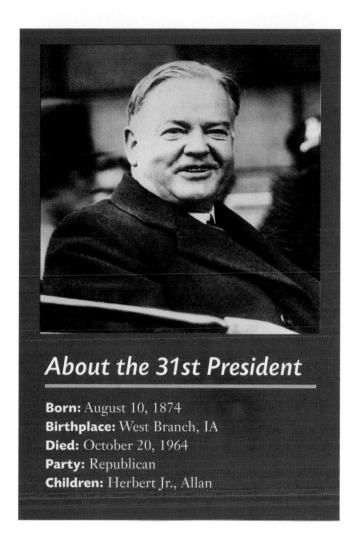

About the 31st President

Born: August 10, 1874
Birthplace: West Branch, IA
Died: October 20, 1964
Party: Republican
Children: Herbert Jr., Allan

During the Hoover Administration

1929	*Donald F. Duncan markets the first yo-yo, which he bases on a sixteenth-century weapon used by hunters in the Philippines.*
Feb. 18, 1930	*Astronomer Clyde Tombaugh discovers Pluto while comparing photographs taken at the Lowell Observatory in Arizona.*
May 15, 1930	*United Airlines introduces the stewardess when it assigns nurse Ellen Church to care for passengers during a flight from San Francisco to Cheyenne, Wyoming. Like her seven colleagues, Church is an attractive twenty-five-year-old who helps passengers overcome their fear of flying.*
Aug. 1930	*King Kullen, the first supermarket, opens in New York City. Before supermarkets, people shopped for groceries in small stores, where clerks brought them what they wanted.*
May 1, 1931	*The 102-story Empire State Building, the world's tallest structure, opens in New York City. Its construction has been made possible by the advent of inexpensive steel and fast electric elevators.*
Oct. 25, 1931	*The Port Authority of New York completes work on the George Washington Bridge across the Hudson River. Its length more than doubles that of the bridge that had previously been the world's longest.*
Mar. 1, 1932	*The infant son of Charles and Anne Lindbergh is kidnapped from their New Jersey home. The Lindberghs pay a fifty-thousand-dollar ransom, but the boy isn't returned. On May 12, a truck driver finds his body in a shallow grave. In 1936, Bruno Hauptmann is executed for the crime.*

Hoover feared that direct aid would make people overly dependent on the government.

★ **Bonus March:** In May 1932, nine thousand World War I veterans marched on Washington, D.C., to press their demand for Congress to accelerate payment of war bonuses promised them in 1924. These bonuses had been awarded in the form of insurance redeemable in 1945. However, as members of the Bonus Army pointed out, many of them might not be alive in 1945 unless the bonuses were paid immediately. When Congress turned the Bonus Marchers down, many went home, but some remained camped near the Capitol. In late July, a frustrated President Hoover ordered federal troops to drive out the Bonus Army. Soldiers used tear gas and fixed bayonets against the veterans, many of whom were injured and some even killed.

This great nation will endure as it has endured, will revive and will prosper. So, first of all, let me assert my firm belief that the only thing we have to fear is fear itself—nameless, unreasoning, unjustified terror which paralyzes needed efforts to convert retreat into advance.

Franklin D. Roosevelt

32nd President • 1933–1945

THE MAN YOUNG FRANKLIN DELANO ROOSEVELT most admired was his fifth cousin Theodore Roosevelt. Like Teddy, FDR was confident and self-assured. He also possessed the magnetic Roosevelt charm: His big, easy smile, according to one biographer, supplemented his "obvious and unfeigned love of company, conversation, and a good time."

However, whereas TR was utterly straightforward, FDR was complex. Alternately cheerful and sullen, exuberant and sober, FDR had so many moods that it was difficult to know which one would surface next. His friend playwright Robert E. Sherwood thought that no one had ever penetrated (or would ever penetrate) FDR's "thickly forested interior."

Roosevelt's great charm concealed a profound arrogance. He believed, as Teddy had, that he was the man best suited to run the country. As a result, he rarely questioned his own judgment and didn't like it when others did. Roosevelt's boldness infuriated well-to-do Americans, who objected to his "socialist" New Deal policies—such as Social Security, regulation of the stock market, and the minimum wage. However, when Roosevelt was elected president in 1932, the well-to-do weren't a very large voting bloc.

The haunted, frightened country that Roosevelt took over was in the fourth year of an economic crisis so deep that one in four workers had lost his or her job. Roosevelt responded with a bold activist mixture of idealism and practicality. "It is common sense," he said, "to take a method and try it. If it fails, admit it frankly and try another. But above all, try something."

According to Eleanor, her husband's greatest accomplishment was communicating to others his own sense of assurance. She believed that FDR's radio speeches, especially his "fireside chats," restored "people's sense of security and confidence in themselves," which made recovery possible. Roosevelt's use of the radio, still a new technology, made him a familiar presence in American homes, and his manner was comforting. In the words of Roosevelt biographer James MacGregor Burns, he was "unruffled in temper, buoyant of spirit, and, as always, ready with a wisecrack or a laugh."

Some have speculated that Roosevelt's struggle with polio may have helped him by making him appear more human to the public and increasing his sympathy for the troubled people of the world. Certainly he felt a close kinship with people. One of his first presidential orders concerned calls to the White House from people in need. He insisted that staff members taking these calls find some way of providing assistance. After FDR's death, Eleanor received a flood of letters from people who had called her husband during the worst days of the depression and gotten immediate help.

• Fear of Fire

Franklin Roosevelt was renowned for his courage and composure. "The only thing we have to fear is fear itself," he declared during his first inaugural address. Yet the president did have one irrational fear: He was deeply afraid of fire.

This phobia was most likely the result of a childhood trauma: When Roosevelt was two years old, his beautiful nineteen-year-old aunt Laura Delano accidentally set herself on fire and died. Roosevelt might not have actually seen his aunt ablaze, but he certainly heard her horrible screams.

After FDR contracted polio, his immobility apparently made his fear even more intense. He would sometimes lower himself down from his bed or wheelchair to practice crawling along the floor. As late as 1944, he became so worried about being trapped in his second-floor White House bedroom that Eleanor had plans drawn up for a chute that he could slide down unaided.

FDR in his thirties, when he served as assistant secretary of the navy (the same post TR once held).

★ ★ ★ ★ ★ ★ ★ ★ ★ ★ ★

• Paralysis

Most Americans knew that President Roosevelt suffered from polio, which he had contracted in 1921, but only those closest to him knew the full extent of his disability: He was completely paralyzed from the hips down. In private, he always used a wheelchair or was carried about by sturdy aides. When he had to make public appearances, the events were carefully choreographed to hide his paraplegia.

If FDR was required to stand—to give a speech, for example—he wore heavy steel leg braces that locked at the knees. He walked with a cane on one side and the support of an aide on the other. Even so, he couldn't manage more than a short distance.

By following an unwritten White House rule that the president never be photographed in his wheelchair, the press helped FDR maintain this deception. "You have to remember that he arrived during Depression days and remained into the war," one photographer explained. "These were hard times, and he was our hope. To have done anything to tear him down in the eyes of the public would have been unthinkable."

A rare family photograph of FDR in his wheelchair taken at the Roosevelt estate in Hyde Park, New York, in February 1941. Because the public never saw photographs of FDR in a wheelchair, most people assumed that he had limited use of his legs.

• Practical Jokes

According to his son James, FDR "loved life, and for all the burdens he bore, he got a lot of fun out of life." Much of this fun Roosevelt made for himself. He had a broad sense of humor and was an incorrigible (if not particularly clever) practical joker.

One of his favorite tricks was to send his longtime bodyguard, Gus Gennerich, up onto a roof for one invented reason or another. Meanwhile, he had a hired hand remove the ladder, stranding poor Gus!

Another of his cherished devices was the fake news bulletin. FDR, who loved the sea, often hosted voyages on the presidential yacht. During these trips, bulletins were delivered daily so that passengers might keep up with the news. One fictional bulletin concocted by FDR stated that the New York Supreme Court had just reversed every decision made by a "discredited" judge who was one of Roosevelt's guests. Another reported that all "quickie" divorces obtained in western states had been invalidated by the Supreme Court. If true, this story would have seriously (and perhaps criminally) inconvenienced a number of passengers.

While fishing in May 1937, Roosevelt jokes about "the one that got away."

• Wining and Dining

FDR hated the food at the White House. At first, he sent memos to Henrietta Nesbitt, the woman Eleanor had hired to run the kitchen. "Do not pluck fowl until just before cooking," read one.

When Mrs. Nesbitt ignored his wishes, FDR wrote to Eleanor directly: "Do you remember that about a month ago I got sick of chicken because I got it at least six times a week? The chicken situation has definitely improved, but 'they' have substituted sweetbreads and for the past month I have been getting sweetbreads about six times a week. I am getting to the point where my stomach positively rebels and this does not help my relations with foreign powers. I bit two of them today."

Although dinner caused FDR some consternation, the cocktail hour that preceded it was his favorite part of the day. Usually he mixed the drinks himself. The cocktail of the day was always chosen in advance—

Roosevelt's favorites were gin martinis and bourbon orange blossoms. One regular guest, playwright Robert E. Sherwood, observed that FDR "mixed the ingredients with the deliberation of an alchemist but with what appeared to be a certain lack of precision since he carried on a steady conversation while doing it."

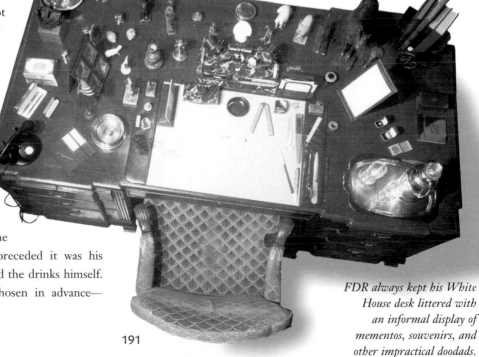

FDR always kept his White House desk littered with an informal display of mementos, souvenirs, and other impractical doodads.

★ ★

•Eleanor Roosevelt

IN 1903, WHEN FRANKLIN ROOSEVELT proposed to Eleanor Roosevelt, his fifth cousin once removed, many people congratulated him for making such an excellent match. Few people congratulated Eleanor, however. At the time, this was understandable: Franklin was a wealthy but insignificant member of an obscure branch of the Roosevelt family; Eleanor was the favorite niece of the president of the United States.

Many people have since wondered what the engaging, handsome FDR saw in the tall, sober Eleanor. The consensus among biographers is that, although she wasn't a beauty, Eleanor fascinated Franklin with her mind. Even so, FDR was undeniably attracted to her, especially admiring her long, gleaming blond hair.

Sadly, the marriage was a troubled one, and it nearly ended when Franklin had an affair with Eleanor's social secretary, Lucy Mercer. (The affair began during the mid-1910s when he was assistant secretary of the navy and was rekindled shortly before his death.) Although Eleanor offered to divorce Franklin, it was eventually decided that they would remain together for the sake of the children and his political career. Emotionally, however, the marriage was over. Franklin and Eleanor became business partners, their son James recalled, rather than husband and wife: "Mother swallowed her pride and permitted the marriage to endure, but it left a residue of bitterness that remained with her all her life."

The frustrations of her personal life led Eleanor to seek satisfaction in public service. In the White House, she became the principal spokesperson for civil rights, organized labor, tenant farmers, the poor, and women in general. "I had this horrible sense of obligation which was bred in me," she once explained. "I couldn't help it." Her energy was so great that in 1940 she delivered more than one hundred lectures nationwide and, though in her late fifties, occasionally worked through the night and then continued working all the next day.

MAJOR POLITICAL EVENTS

★ **Banking Crisis:** On March 4, 1933, the day of Roosevelt's first inauguration, a banking crisis swept the nation. At 4:30 A.M., New York governor Herbert Lehman joined nearly two dozen other governors in declaring a statewide banking holiday. These governors all feared that nervous investors would clean out their bank accounts and cause a systemwide collapse. On March 6, Roosevelt ordered a national banking holiday and called Congress into special session. Three days later, the House and Senate passed the Emergency Banking Act, which kept the banks closed until federal auditors could examine their books and declare them sound.

★ **Packing the Court:** By 1937, government spending had produced a limited recovery. However, Roosevelt remained frustrated because many of his bold emergency programs were being blocked by elderly justices on the Supreme Court. Among the laws struck down were the National Industrial Recovery Act, which permitted management and labor to set prices and production quotas, and the Agricultural Adjustment Act, which controlled crop surpluses by limiting the amounts that farmers could grow. In February 1937, Roosevelt proposed a reorganization of the Court that would add one justice for each of the six justices over seventy years old. The president said that he merely intended to reduce each justice's workload, but the Senate saw through his dodge and rejected the plan. Even so, the justices got the message. While the court-packing plan was still alive, a previously conservative justice began vot-

About the 32nd President

Born: January 30, 1882
Birthplace: Hyde Park, NY
Died: April 12, 1945
Party: Democrat
Children: Anna, James, Franklin, Elliot,
Frankin Delano Jr., John

★ ★ ★ ★ ★ ★ ★ ★ ★ ★ ★ ★ ★ ★ ★

During the Roosevelt Administration

Nov. 1933	*When a dust storm carries topsoil from South Dakota as far east as New York, erosion problems become a focus of concern. In May 1936, a similar storm in the dust bowl of Texas and Oklahoma eclipses the sun as far east as the Appalachians.*
Aug. 1936	*Black sprinter Jesse Owens wins four gold medals at the Berlin Olympics, disproving Hitler's theories that the white Aryans represent a master race.*
May 6, 1937	*The airship* Hindenburg *bursts into flame and explodes while landing at Lakehurst, New Jersey. The hydrogen-filled zeppelin began making regular transatlantic crossings in May 1936.*
July 2, 1937	*Pilot Amelia Earhart disappears over the South Pacific during her attempt to fly around the world. A naval search party finds no trace of her.*
Dec. 1937	*Walt Disney releases* Snow White and the Seven Dwarfs, *the first full-length animated feature.*
1939	*Pocket Books begins publishing paperback books in the United States.*
1941	*Lyle Goodhue and W. N. Sullivan develop the first disposable aerosol can.*
Nov. 1, 1941	*Workers complete the last of the drilling on Mount Rushmore in the Black Hills of South Dakota.*
1944	*Harvard mathematician Howard Aiken designs the first digital computer, which he builds with a large grant from IBM.*

ing with the Court's liberal bloc. His swing vote made the difference in 5–4 rulings upholding minimum wage laws and Social Security.

★ **World War II:** As during the First World War, isolationist pressures kept the United States out of the early fighting. However, unlike Wilson, Roosevelt actively looked for ways to help the Allied cause. In September 1940, a year after the invasion of Poland and three months after the fall of France, Roosevelt issued an executive order sending fifty destroyers to Great Britain in exchange for naval bases in British-controlled Newfoundland and Bermuda. In March 1941, he signed the Lend-Lease Act, which provided even more arms for Britain and deferred payment until after the war. The United States itself entered the war in December 1941 after the Japanese attack on Pearl Harbor.

Communism is based on the belief that man is so weak and inadequate that he is unable to govern himself, and therefore requires the rule of strong masters. Democracy is based on the conviction that man has the moral and intellectual capacity, as well as the inalienable right, to govern himself with reason and justice.

Harry S. Truman

33rd President • 1945–1953

WHEN FRANKLIN ROOSEVELT DIED in April 1945, a shock wave swept over the country. "To many it was not just that the greatest of men had fallen," historian David McCullough has written, "but that the least of men—or at any rate the least likely of men—had assumed his place." Most people thought Vice President Harry Truman was little more than a political hack. "If Harry Truman can be president," went the typical man-in-the-street reaction, "so could my next-door neighbor."

All his life, Truman had been, in his own words, the quintessential "simple man." (His modesty prevented him from saying much more.) He had grown up in rural Missouri, where his parents and teachers had instilled in him a straight-arrow Victorian morality. He valued fidelity in marriage, courage in battle, and honesty in business. He also developed a sense of personal honor that later made him uncomfortable when he had to deal with corrupt politicians and make questionable compromises.

As a young man, Truman worked at a variety of clerical jobs. After World War I, he opened a men's clothing store in Kansas City, but it closed during the recession of 1922. After this failure as an entrepreneur, Truman entered the rather low-status world of politics as a henchman for Democratic boss Thomas J. Pendergast. (When Truman was elected to the Senate from Missouri in 1935, he was jokingly referred to as the "senator from Pendergast.")

During most of his political career, Truman had to juggle the debt he owed Pendergast with his sincere devotion to honesty and efficiency. The psychological stress this caused him made him irritable, and his knowledge that he had failed as a businessman made his pride easily wounded. As a result, he often felt persecuted or at least insufficiently appreciated.

During Truman's presidency, people inevitably compared him to FDR, whose composure he lacked. Sometimes Truman's shrillness served him well, as during the 1948 campaign, when he came from behind to beat Thomas Dewey. At other times, he merely seemed erratic, petty, and not up to his responsibilities. According to one biographer, Truman displayed "an opinionated snappishness that would seem amusing to a later generation" but wasn't then considered the stuff of leadership.

Yet Truman was a great leader, a politician who stood for "common sense and common decency," according to McCullough. "He was not and had never been a simple, ordinary man. The homely attributes, the Missouri wit, the warmth of his friendship, the genuineness of Harry Truman, however appealing, were outweighed by the larger qualities that made him a figure of world stature, both a great and good man, and a great American president."

• Under Fire

After passing the army eye exam by memorizing the chart, Truman served with the 129th Field Artillery Regiment during World War I, rising in rank from lieutenant to major. He spent about a year in France, during which time he related to the French as a typical American tourist.

"I can tell 'em I don't understand and ask for des oeufs sur la plat, and that's about all," he wrote his fiancée, Bess Wallace. "I pronounce fromage frummage and say Angers like she's spelled, but the French insist on saying fromaag and Onjay. I'll never comprehend it."

As commander of Battery D of the 129th, Truman took part in the Argonne-Meuse offensive

Truman in France, 1918. He particularly disliked the extended multicourse meals that French officers insisted on eating before getting down to business. "It takes them so long to serve a meal that I'm always hungrier when I get done than I ever was before," he wrote Bess.

of September–November 1918 that forced Germany to surrender. "There was more noise than human ears could stand," he said of the shelling on the front lines. "Men serving the guns became deaf for weeks afterward. The sky was red from one end to the other."

Although Truman himself played but a small part in the war, his ability to remain composed under fire greatly increased his self-confidence. He later told his family that the war had changed him enormously.

★ ★

"Churchill talks all the time and Stalin just grunts but you know what he means," Truman wrote his mother and sister from Potsdam.

• Ending the War

Less than three months after becoming president, Truman traveled to Germany, where a meeting of the Big Three (the United States, Great Britain, and the Soviet Union) was scheduled to take place. On July 16, while Truman waited in the Berlin suburb of Potsdam for Soviet leader Joseph Stalin to arrive, the army conducted its first atomic bomb test. A coded telegram confirming the test's success arrived at Truman's headquarters on July 18. Over lunch that day, he informed British prime minister Winston Churchill, and together they decided to tell Stalin.

"The final decision of where and when to use the atomic bomb was up to me," Truman wrote later. "Let there be no mistake about it. I regarded the bomb as a military weapon and never had any doubt that it should be used."

Months later, after bombs were dropped on Hiroshima (August 6) and Nagasaki (August 9), the country's chief atomic scientist, J. Robert Oppenheimer, asked to see Truman privately. "Mr. President," Oppenheimer whimpered, "I have blood on my hands."

"The blood is on my hands," the president replied sharply. "Let me worry about that." After Oppenheimer left, a disgusted Truman told an aide, "Don't you bring that fellow around again."

• Musicality

The Trumans were an exceptionally musical family. As a teenager, President Truman had studied to be a concert pianist. He awoke every morning at five o'clock to practice for two hours before school and traveled into Kansas City twice a week for lessons.

In 1900, Ignace Paderewski gave a concert in Kansas City, and Truman was taken backstage to meet the great man. Paderewski even showed Truman how to play a special "turn" in his Minuet in G, which Truman later played for Churchill and Stalin at a dinner party in Potsdam.

Although he gave up the piano after high school when he ran out of money for lessons, Truman retained a lifelong interest in classical music and encouraged his daughter, Margaret, to pursue a musical career. She debuted as a singer before a national radio audience in March 1947. Three years later, she ended one of her concert tours with an appearance at Constitution Hall, where *Washington Post* music critic Paul Hume reviewed her performance.

"She is flat a good deal of the time," Hume wrote. "She communicates almost nothing of the music she presents….

Truman with Lauren Bacall at a stage show for servicemen in early 1945. "My choice early in life was either to be a piano player in a whorehouse or a politician," he once joked, "and to tell the truth there's hardly a difference."

The performance…was no more than a caricature of what it would be if sung by any one of a dozen artists today."

Reading Hume's review over breakfast the next morning, Truman reached for a sheet of stationery and fired off an immediate response. "I've just read your lousy review of Margaret's concert," he wrote. "It seems to me that you are a frustrated old man who wishes he could have been successful. When you write such poppycock as was in the *back* section of the paper you work for it shows conclusively that you're off the beam and at least four of your ulcers are at work.

"Some day I hope to meet you," Truman continued. "When that happens you'll need a new nose, a lot of beef steak for black eyes, and perhaps a supporter below!"

When Hume published the letter, Truman's staff became worried that the public would think the president had lost his mind. Truman himself believed that American parents would understand his motivation and predicted that the mail would run four to one in his favor—and he was right. "The trouble with you guys is that you just don't understand human nature," Truman told them.

Secretary of State Dean Acheson said that Truman's most inspiring quality was his "priceless gift of vitality, the life force itself."

Truman kept this sign, a gift from a friend, on his desk only a short time, but its message stayed with him permanently.

★ ★ ★ ★ ★ ★ ★ ★ ★ ★ ★ ★ ★ ★ ★ ★ ★ ★ ★ ★

• Bess Truman

BESS WALLACE'S FAMILY lived about two blocks away from the Trumans' house in Independence, Missouri. As children, Harry and Bess went to the same church and the same elementary school. Because their teachers liked to sit students alphabetically, year after year Bess sat directly behind Harry. "I only had one sweetheart from the time I was six," Truman later said. However, being extremely shy, he made his feelings known only very slowly.

As a young girl, Bess played baseball as well as any boy and tennis better than most. Because of his bad eyesight and fragile, expensive eyeglasses, Truman played neither. "If I succeeded in carrying her books to school and back home for her I had a big day," he later recalled.

Their extraordinarily long and methodical courtship lasted until 1917, when thirty-three-year-old Truman volunteered to serve in World War I. The knowledge that he might not survive finally gave him the courage to propose. Bess accepted and suggested that they marry immediately, but Truman insisted on waiting in case he came back maimed or crippled or not at all. "Sometimes I think that if World War I hadn't come along," their daughter, Margaret, wrote, "he might not have married her until he was forty or fifty, and I might never have gotten here."

Unlike Eleanor Roosevelt, First Lady Bess Truman preferred to remain in the background. Although reporters pleaded with her to hold press conferences and grant interviews, she rarely complied. The public didn't seem to mind. As one Washington cabbie said, "She seems to think Harry ought to run the country, not her."

During her years in the White House, Bess dressed as simply and conservatively as she had throughout her life. In fact, an article in *Time* once suggested that she would have blended in well with the crowd at the A&P.

MAJOR POLITICAL EVENTS

★ **Marshall Plan:** In March 1947, President Truman announced his intention to aid all countries threatened by Communist revolution. With this policy (soon labeled the Truman Doctrine) in mind, Secretary of State George Marshall tackled the problem of how to rebuild Europe. Marshall concluded that the only way to save the war-ravaged nations of Western Europe from Communism was to restore their economies with U.S. dollars. In June 1947, the former army chief of staff proposed that nearly fourteen billion dollars in foreign aid be sent to Europe during the next four years. The most controversial part of the Marshall Plan was that it included money to rebuild Germany.

★ **Berlin Airlift:** At Potsdam, postwar Germany was divided into four zones controlled by the Big Three and France. Although Berlin fell entirely within the Soviet zone, it was also divided into four sectors, one for each Allied power. In April 1948, the Soviets began a blockade of West Berlin, hoping to drive out the Western powers. Truman responded by ordering an airlift of supplies into the besieged city. A continuous shuttle of cargo planes provided West Berlin with food, coal, and other necessities until the Soviets lifted the blockade a year later. During its fifteen months of operation, the Berlin airlift delivered more than two million tons of supplies. The airlift also led to the chartering in April 1949 of the North Atlantic Treaty Organization so that the West could present a united front to the Soviets. In May 1949, the western zones of Germany were merged to form the new nation of West Germany.

About the 33rd President

Born: May 8, 1884
Birthplace: Lamar, MO
Died: December 26, 1972
Party: Democrat
Children: Margaret

★ **Korean War:** After World War II, Korea was divided along the thirty-eighth parallel into two countries: a Communist north and a capitalist south. On June 25, 1950, North Korea invaded South Korea. Given the Truman Doctrine, the president had little choice but to send U.S. troops. Even so, the war went badly for South Korea until Gen. Douglas MacArthur's September landing behind enemy lines at Inchon. By October, United Nations forces under his command had pushed the North Koreans back across the thirty-eighth parallel and nearly to the Yalu River border between North Korea and China. In late November, after MacArthur casually dismissed a number of warnings, the Chinese entered the war, chasing the UN forces back (again) across the thirty-eighth parallel. MacArthur regrouped, but the best he could now achieve was a stalemate. In April 1951, Truman fired the general for insubordination.

★ ★ ★ ★ ★ ★ ★ ★ ★ ★ ★ ★ ★ ★ ★

During the Truman Administration

1945 The town of Grand Rapids, Michigan, begins fluoridating its water supply after dental researchers report that small amounts of fluoride can reduce tooth decay in children.

Oct. 14, 1947 Test pilot Chuck Yeager becomes the first human to break the sound barrier when he flies a top-secret X-1 rocket plane past the speed of sound.

1948 Guitar maker Leo Fender begins selling the Broadcaster, the first mass-produced solid-body electric guitar.

Feb. 1950 Diners Club introduces the first credit card. It allows club members to charge meals at twenty-eight participating restaurants in New York City.

Oct. 15, 1951 I Love Lucy, starring Lucille Ball and Desi Arnaz, premieres on the CBS television network. During its six years on the air, the situation comedy never falls below third place in the popularity ratings.

Dec. 20, 1951 A reactor in Idaho Falls, Idaho, run by the Atomic Energy Commission produces the first electricity generated by nuclear fission.

1951 J. D. Salinger publishes The Catcher in the Rye. The novel's sixteen-year-old protagonist, Holden Caulfield, rejects the adult world because it's full of "phonies."

1952 Kemmons Wilson founds the Holiday Inn hotel chain after taking a summer vacation with his family and finding too few decent places to stay.

No people can live to itself alone. The unity of all who dwell in freedom is their only sure defense.... No nation can longer be a fortress, lone and strong and safe. And any people, seeking such shelter for themselves, can now build only their own prison.

Dwight D. Eisenhower

34th President • 1953–1961

EVEN THOUGH HIS RECORD during World War II had made him a certified national hero, Dwight David Eisenhower was easy to underrate. His wide grin, passion for dime novels, and often confusing way of speaking persuaded many Washington insiders that he was a political amateur, a military man who had risen above his proper place in the world. Throughout his presidency, as throughout his life, Ike was consistently underestimated by those around him.

In addition to being a natural leader, Eisenhower was acutely intelligent. His experiences as supreme commander of the Allied forces in Europe and later as head of NATO had provided him with a nearly complete mastery of the world situation. The 1950s, while a bland period in domestic politics, were filled with international crises, including the seizure of the Suez Canal and the Soviet invasion of Hungary, not to mention the fighting in Korea and the ongoing Cold War. Quietly and patiently, but with great skill and determination, Eisenhower found the safest path through these diplomatic minefields.

Unlike a number of military leaders, notably Douglas MacArthur, Eisenhower didn't covet the presidency. In fact, the job was all but forced on him by an adoring public. Nevertheless, he didn't shrink from the responsibility.

As president, he exhibited the strengths of the career soldier. Sturdy and authoritative, he was also a consensus builder, reaching out to every congressional faction as the need arose. With the public, he wasn't just popular but trusted. Americans embraced Ike's middle-class tastes and especially his hobbies—painting, fishing, and golf.

Some columnists made fun of the president's passion for golf, joking that he was more interested in his handicap than in foreign affairs. They never understood: Of course, Ike liked to play golf, but his apparent obsession with the sport was also a sleight of hand, a dodge. His drives and putts held the attention of the media while Eisenhower worked quietly—secretly, if possible—behind the scenes to exercise his will.

Ike preferred to work this way because he knew how to make use of the advantages that came from being underestimated. Even his reputation for ill use of the English language was a shrewd pose. (Although few remembered, Eisenhower had been a speechwriter for General MacArthur, whose silver-tongued orations were famous.)

It suited Ike to come across as folksy, goofy, and sometimes tongue tied. Once he was warned to reply "No comment" if a particularly sensitive issue came up at a press conference. "Don't worry," Eisenhower said, "If that question comes up, I'll just confuse them."

★ ★ ★ ★ ★ ★ ★ ★ ★ ★ ★ ★ ★ ★ ★

With the Tank Corps at Camp Meade, 1919. Eisenhower called these early tanks "coffins on wheels."

• Military Career

Eisenhower's parents were pacifists, yet they didn't object to his enrollment at West Point in 1911. Part of the reason may have been that their son was involved more in football than in soldiering. Eisenhower starred as a running back for Army until a knee injury ended his playing career.

He overcame this disappointment by immersing himself in the strategies of football, mastering them so thoroughly that he was asked to coach the junior varsity team. He "was born to command," one senior officer reported. This judgment was reinforced when Eisenhower finished first in his class of 275 at the elite Command and General Staff School at Fort Leavenworth, Kansas.

Like all dedicated soldiers, Eisenhower ached to prove himself on the battlefield. In 1917, when the United States entered World War I, he pleaded to be sent overseas. However, he was so talented at training and drilling troops that the War Department kept him stateside. He was crushed but performed his job flawlessly, always looking for ways to improve methods and morale. When one junior officer insisted that there wasn't a fault to be found in Eisenhower's unit, the major replied, "For God's sake, get out and find something wrong with the camp! It can't be as good as you say."

Eisenhower's long apprenticeship paid off once the Japanese attacked Pearl Harbor in 1941. Within days, he was summoned to Washington, where he joined the War Department's planning division under Army chief of staff George C. Marshall. Eisenhower's organizational abilities impressed Marshall as well as President Roosevelt and British prime minister Winston Churchill. Ike had a unique ability to

bridge the gap, normally so awkward, between military and civilian leaders. "Whenever I asked Ike for an opinion I got an answer," one statesman recalled. "It may not have been what I wanted to hear,…but it was always straightforward and honest." In 1942, Eisenhower led the Allied invasion of North Africa and within a few months was named supreme commander of all Allied forces in Europe.

He leapt from obscurity to world fame. Unlike so many generals, he had the common touch. When he met an enlisted man, Ike's first question was never about his specialty, training, or unit, but always "Where are you from?" This simple humanity, when added to his accomplishments as a commander, made Eisenhower an authentic American hero, the "soldier of democracy."

General Eisenhower gives last-minute encouragement to members of the 101st Airborne Division on June 5, 1944. Just after midnight on June 6, these paratroopers landed in France to begin the D-Day invasion.

• Painting

More than one biographer has noted the tension that Eisenhower felt between his natural gregariousness and his yearning for solitude. One way he resolved this tension was by painting. "It gives me an excuse to be completely alone and interferes not at all with what I am pleased to call my 'contemplative powers,'" he once said. Unlike Winston Churchill, Ike had no pretensions to being an artist. He called himself a "deliberate dauber" and often ran down his own work as banal and "woefully bad." (He did, however, search the walls of friends' houses to see whether his paintings were being properly displayed.)

As president, he painted with the help of army privates stationed in the bowels of the White House. Usually these men had been professional illustrators before being drafted. Whenever Eisenhower wanted to paint a particular subject, one of these men would sketch a rough outline onto the president's canvas—carefully, because Ike was fussy. For example, he liked the noses of his portraits placed exactly at the center of the frame.

Painting, like Ike's other hobbies, eventually became fodder for his public relations machine. In 1954, for example, presidential Christmas cards began to feature reproductions of his oil paintings.

• Heart Attack

Shortly after midnight on September 24, 1955, while vacationing in Denver, Eisenhower began feeling sharp chest pains. The next morning, after he was taken to the hospital, his doctor told the press that Ike had "suffered a digestive upset."

The following day, the truth was revealed: The president had suffered a heart attack—"neither mild nor serious [but] moderate," the country's top heart specialist said. On Monday, September 26, the Dow Jones stock index fell more than thirty points, its worst day since the crash of 1929.

Press Secretary Jim Hagerty asked his boss what he wanted done. Eisenhower told Hagerty to "tell the truth, the whole truth; don't try to conceal anything." And Hagerty did just that, inundating reporters with thrice-daily reports on the president's condition. Hagerty's medical bulletins were so thorough that they included specifics on

Eisenhower kept these miniature portraits of his wife and mother on his desk during his term in office.

the nature and frequency of the president's bowel movements. Not used to printing such information, newspapers struggled for euphemisms. Meanwhile, the public's attention remained fixed on the president's health.

Eisenhower steadily improved. He walked out of the hospital on November 11 and, two months after that, resumed his normal schedule. In the meantime, a joke went around Washington that when Vice President Richard Nixon greeted Ike on his return, Nixon said, "Welcome back, Mr. President. I'll race you to the top of the steps!"

During the first two weeks after Ike's heart attack, a distraught Mamie lost ten pounds. To keep herself busy, she decided to answer individually each of the thousands of cards and letters being sent to the hospital from all over the country.

★ ★ ★ ★ ★ ★ ★ ★ ★ ★ ★ ★ ★ ★ ★ ★

• Mamie Eisenhower

WHEN MAMIE DOUD FIRST MET DWIGHT EISENHOWER, she felt immediately attracted to him because he looked like "a bruiser." Ike, in turn, was aroused by Mamie's dainty appearance and saucy manner.

The year was 1915 and the place San Antonio, Texas, where Mamie's wealthy parents had a winter home. The eighteen-year-old Miss Doud had just completed her education at a finishing school in Denver, where she had learned how to flirt. Eisenhower was on his first tour of duty at Fort Sam Houston. He proposed on Valentine's Day 1916, and they were married four months later.

Having grown up with a full staff of servants, including a personal maid, Mamie had no domestic skills and no idea of what life would be on an army post with a first lieutenant's pay. She couldn't sew, cook, or make a bed properly. Either her husband cooked or they ate in the officers' mess. When Mamie became pregnant, it was Ike who let out the seams of her dresses.

Mamie also didn't take well to the constant moves, which averaged one a year until they settled into the White House. Rumors circulated on and off that she drank, but there's little evidence to support this. More than likely, the source of the rumors was her Ménière's disease, an inner-ear disorder that affected her balance and made her stumble as though she were drunk.

As first lady, Mamie got some rest. She seldom woke before ten and rarely got out of bed before noon. Even so, she closely supervised the White House, scanning newspapers every day for sales on supplies and telephoning in her orders. "I have only one career, and his name is Ike," she frequently declared. However, with Ike's busy schedule, she rarely saw him in daylight. She didn't play golf and wouldn't play bridge with him because he yelled at her whenever she misplayed.

MAJOR POLITICAL EVENTS

★ **McCarthyism:** In February 1950, Joseph McCarthy declared that Communists had infiltrated the federal government. The Wisconsin senator underscored his point by repeatedly waving a piece of paper that he claimed was a list of 205 "card-carrying Communists" currently at work in the State Department. McCarthy never revealed any of these names, but the charges brought him power. In April 1954, at the height of his arrogance, he began a series of televised hearings into whether Communists had subverted the army. On June 9, army lawyer Joseph Welch challenged McCarthy personally after the senator tried to smear one of Welch's young assistants. "You have done enough," Welch told McCarthy. "Have you no sense of decency, sir, at long last?" Welch's dignified rebuke seemed to break McCarthy's spell, and in December McCarthy was reprimanded by the Senate for "conduct unbecoming a member."

★ ***Brown v. Board of Education:*** The Supreme Court's decision in the *Brown* case, handed down in May 1954, outlawed racial segregation in public schools. In doing so, the Court unanimously reversed *Plessy v. Ferguson* (1896), which had upheld the constitutionality of "separate but equal" facilities. Important evidence was presented by psychologist Kenneth Clark, who showed that segregation itself made black children feel inferior. In one experiment, Clark gave black students two dolls: one black and one white. When he asked them to choose the "nasty" doll, nearly all picked the black one.

About the 34th President

Born: October 14, 1890
Birthplace: Denison, TX
Died: March 28, 1969
Party: Republican
Children: Dwight, John

★ **U-2 Incident:** In September 1959, Soviet premier Nikita Khrushchev made a goodwill tour of the United States. Although he was disappointed that security considerations prevented him from seeing Disneyland, he had a pleasant visit with Eisenhower at Camp David, during which the two leaders made plans for a summit in Paris the following May. Less than two weeks before the Paris summit was scheduled to begin, the Soviet Union shot down a U.S. spy plane over Soviet airspace. At first the State Department issued vague denials, but when the Soviets produced the plane's pilot, Eisenhower was forced to admit that U-2 planes had been making regular high-altitude flights over Soviet territory. Even worse, the early State Department denials planted in many Americans their first suspicion that their government might not be altogether truthful.

★ ★ ★ ★ ★ ★ ★ ★ ★ ★ ★ ★ ★ ★

During the Eisenhower Administration

1953   *The firm of C. A. Swanson & Sons introduces the first TV dinner, a frozen meal designed to be eaten in front of the set.*

Oct. 1954   *In response to hysterical fears that horror comics are damaging the minds of children, comic book publishers institute the Comics Code, which regulates the amount of violence in comic books.*

1954   *Marlon Brando stars in* The Wild One *as the leader of a motorcycle gang that terrorizes a California town. His performance appeals strongly to teenagers, who empathize with Brando's moody apathy.*

Sep. 30, 1955   *James Dean dies in an automobile crash at age twenty-four. He will be best remembered for playing the title role in* Rebel without a Cause, *scheduled for release next month.*

Sep. 9, 1956   *Elvis Presley's appearance on the Ed Sullivan television show sets a record for most viewers. Fifty-four million people watch Presley sing, but they don't see him shake his hips, because Sullivan has ordered his cameramen to show Presley only from the waist up.*

Oct. 4, 1957   *The Soviet Union launches Sputnik, the first man-made satellite. Its success undermines the widely held belief that the United States is technologically superior.*

1957   *Jack Kerouac publishes* On the Road, *which becomes the definitive novel of the Beat Generation.*

Mar. 1, 1959   *Mattel introduces the Barbie doll, the most popular toy in history.*

Let every nation know, whether it wishes us well or ill, that we shall pay any price, bear any burden, meet any hardship, support any friend, oppose any foe, in order to assure the survival and the success of liberty. This much we pledge—and more.

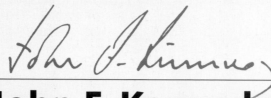

John F. Kennedy

35th President • 1961–1963

H E WAS AS MUCH A PHENOMENON AS A PRESIDENT. His administration, which glittered with academic and business celebrities, was dubbed Camelot by an adoring press corps. Youth flocked to his call for engagement with the world. He said that we would land a man on the moon by the end of the decade— and we did. Ask just about anyone: John Fitzgerald Kennedy was one of the great ones.

Historians are hesitant to agree. Some rate Kennedy highly; others, not so well. However, all tend to acknowledge that his assassination, the most pivotal moment in post-war American history, has so transformed our perception of him that the original man—the living president, not the martyred one—may be lost forever.

Some facts remain—the influence of his father, for instance. Joseph P. Kennedy promised himself that he'd become a millionaire by age thirty-five—and he did, many times over. He made his money in stocks during the 1920s, in liquor during Prohibition, and in Hollywood, where he carried on a long-term, poorly concealed affair with film star Gloria Swanson. No one doubted Pa Kennedy's wealth, smarts, or ruthlessness, and he endeavored to pass on all these traits to his children.

His son Jack was blessed with striking good looks, an easy manner, and a quick wit that made him instantly, irresistibly likable. "An idealist without illusions," JFK called himself. He thought his best quality was his curiosity and his worst, his irritability.

But there was also a darker side: He didn't treat his wife very well, and he could be two faced. Like Franklin Roosevelt, he kept his warts well hidden from the public—the health problems, the extramarital affairs. Yet even when these blemishes were revealed after his death, they never eclipsed the popular memory of his energy, his high spirits, and his force of will.

By dying, it has been suggested, Kennedy escaped blame for failing to meet the expectations he had raised. Perhaps this is so. Yet people still mourn his passing as though their own innocence died that day.

"I don't think there's any point in being Irish if you don't know that the world is going to break your heart," Assistant Secretary of Labor Daniel Patrick Moynihan said shortly after Kennedy's death. "[Columnist] Mary McGrory said to me that we'll never laugh again. And I said, 'Heavens, Mary. We'll laugh again. It's just that we'll never be young again.'"

In August 1943, a Japanese destroyer sliced Lieutenant Kennedy's PT boat in half. With his teeth grasping an injured crewman's life jacket, Kennedy—bad back and all—towed the man to the nearest island, four hours away. His superiors wanted to know why Kennedy had allowed his boat to be rammed and why he hadn't fired a single shot at the destroyer. Meanwhile, the press picked up on the story. "They had to give me a medal or throw me out," Kennedy joked. In fact, they gave him two medals.

• Health Problems

Believing that America's entrance into World War II was inevitable and that he needed to take part in what would become his generation's great shared experience, Kennedy joined the navy in September 1941. Later, friends of his father helped along his request for a transfer to active duty in the Pacific. However, as JFK biographer Richard Reeves has pointed out, "Kennedy had no business being in the military, much less on a PT boat. Prior to joining the navy, he was plagued by fevers, abdominal pain, venereal disease, back problems, and Addison's disease. He couldn't even obtain life insurance."

During the rest of his life, Kennedy continued to deceive people about his health. As a presidential candidate in 1960,

During his sickly childhood, Kennedy had bouts of bronchitis, tonsillitis, appendicitis, scarlet fever, whooping cough, and measles. His brothers joked that healthy mosquitoes took a big risk biting Jack.

he lied to reporters that his health was excellent, never admitting that as an adult he'd already received the last rites of the Catholic church at least four times. According to Reeves, "He was something of a medical marvel, kept alive by complicated daily combinations of pills and injections." In the White House, Kennedy often spent half the day resting in bed, and he was once so tortured by back pain that a crane was needed to lift him into Air Force One.

★ ★ ★ ★ ★ ★ ★ ★ ★ ★ ★ ★ ★

• Change of Clothes

When John F. Kennedy succeeded Dwight D. Eisenhower in January 1961, the youngest president ever elected took the place of the oldest man ever to serve. At the same time, the most stylish president replaced the stodgiest.

Kennedy's youthful, vigorous image had been very carefully built, and his clothes were an important part of the look. He dressed fashionably in European-cut two-button suits, which seemed more elegant and dapper than American suits with their three-button jackets.

As president, JFK owned eighteen suits in all, changing them several times a day. In fact, he liked to change clothes from the skin out as often as four times a day, sometimes going through as many as six shirts. His friend journalist Ben Bradlee said that Kennedy was shocked to learn from Bradlee that some men actually wore the same shirt two days in a row.

Kennedy in Berlin, June 1963. His interest in clothes never extended to hats, which he disliked wearing.

• Fatherhood

Although the Kennedys wanted their children's upbringing to be as normal as possible, the president and first lady knew that they couldn't keep Caroline and John Jr. hidden from public view. Photographs of John Jr. playing inside his father's desk were enormously popular with magazine editors, and so were pictures of Caroline riding her pony—named, of course, Macaroni.

JFK didn't have (or make) a great deal of time to spend with his children. Aside from family vacations in Palm Beach or Hyannis Port, he got by with mostly quick visits here and there. Sometimes Caroline and John Jr. (his parents never called him John-John) visited him during the day in the Oval Office. He might stop working and sweep them up into his arms. However, after a few moments of play, he'd press a special button on his desk to call their nanny, who would take them away.

• The Kennedy Wit

What made JFK such a master of the press conference were his relaxed self-confidence and peppery wit. The fact that he often mocked himself made it that much easier for him to brush aside an awkward question with a joke.

For instance, during the early days of the 1960 campaign, Minnesota senator Hubert Humphrey complained that competing against the wealthy Kennedys was "like an independent retailer running against a chain." JFK succeeded in muting this attack by composing an imaginary telegram from his father: "Dear Jack: Don't buy one vote more than necessary. I'll be damned if I'll pay for a landslide."

Later, he was scolded for appointing his younger brother Bobby to head the Justice Department. The critics had a point: Thirty-five-year-old Robert Kennedy's résumé was rather light for the post of attorney general. Yet the president was able to mute the opposition to Bobby's appointment with a single coy remark: "I can't see that it's wrong to give him a little legal experience before he goes out to practice law."

"Mr. President, how did you become a war hero?" a child once asked Kennedy (shown here with Vice President Lyndon Johnson). The president replied, "It was absolutely involuntary. They sank my boat."

• Jackie Kennedy

SHORTLY AFTER WINNING ELECTION to the Senate from Massachusetts in 1952, thirty-five-year-old Jack Kennedy, the capital's most eligible bachelor, became engaged. The girl he chose to marry had attended Miss Porter's School, Vassar College, and the Sorbonne. When she made her society debut in 1947, one columnist named her Queen Deb of the Year. Since her graduation from college in 1951, she had kept herself busy working as the *Washington Herald*'s Inquiring Camera Girl. Her name was Jacqueline Bouvier. A child of wealth and privilege like Kennedy, she didn't need the job's $42.50 weekly salary to make ends meet.

Before their September 1953 marriage, Kennedy had been considered a smartly dressed man-about-town. However, this impression belied the fact that about the house he was notoriously messy. (Columnist Joseph Alsop once found a half-eaten hamburger behind some books on Kennedy's mantel.)

Jackie smartened him up. "I brought a certain amount of order to his life," she recalled. "He no longer went out in the morning with one brown shoe and one black shoe on. His clothes got pressed, and he got to the airport without a mad rush."

As first lady, she used her beauty and grace to enhance Kennedy's public image. The chic Jackie Look—simple skirted suit, restrained bouffant hairstyle, pillbox hat—came to dominate American fashion, and Jackie herself became an important arbiter of taste. After forty-seven million people watched her host a televised tour of the White House in 1962, one critic called her "our uncrowned queen."

On the surface, Jack and Jackie seemed the perfect couple. Yet the small public satisfactions that he allowed her never made up for the fact that he largely shut her out of his political life. Even worse, "we had no home life whatsoever," she once admitted.

MAJOR POLITICAL EVENTS

★ **Peace Corps:** Created in March 1961 as an agency of the State Department, the Peace Corps came to symbolize the enthusiastic acceptance of social responsibility that President Kennedy had called for in his inaugural address. The purpose of the program was to send recent American college graduates to developing nations around the world. Youthful volunteers lived with local people and shared their expertise in fields such as education, agriculture, engineering, and public health.

★ **Bay of Pigs:** During the final year of the Eisenhower administration, the Central Intelligence Agency began planning an invasion of Cuba. Communist revolutionary Fidel Castro had overthrown the Cuban government of corrupt president Fulgencio Batista in February 1959, and since then Castro's increasingly close relationship with the Soviet Union had made the U.S. national security establishment nervous. After Kennedy became president, he went along with the plan, which called for fifteen hundred CIA-trained Cuban exiles to land at the Bay of Pigs. It was believed that the creation of a beachhead there would trigger a popular uprising against Castro. The exiles were also led to believe that U.S. troops would support them, if necessary. However, on the day of the invasion, Kennedy refused even to provide air cover. After three days of fighting, eleven hundred survivors surrendered to Castro. The United States arranged their release in 1962 in exchange for fifty-three million dollars in food and medical supplies.

About the 35th President

Born: May 29, 1917
Birthplace: Brookline, MA
Died: November 22, 1963
Party: Democrat
Children: Caroline, John Jr., Patrick

★ **Cuban Missile Crisis:** On October 22, 1962, Kennedy went on national television to announce that U.S. spy planes had taken photographs of Soviet nuclear missile sites under construction on the island of Cuba. Kennedy demanded that the Soviets remove the missiles immediately. Meanwhile, he ordered a naval blockade of Cuba to prevent any more offensive weapons from reaching the island. Days passed as Soviet ships steamed closer to the blockade line and the world waited for a possible nuclear exchange. Finally, on October 28, Kennedy accepted an offer from Soviet premier Nikita Khrushchev that ended the Cuban Missile Crisis. The Soviet Union agreed to remove the missiles if the United States removed similar missiles from Turkey and pledged not to invade Cuba.

During the Kennedy Administration

Apr. 12, 1961
Soviet cosmonaut Yuri Gagarin becomes the first human in space when his Vostok capsule completes a single orbit of the earth. Three weeks later, Alan Shepard becomes the first American in space, flying aboard the Mercury capsule Freedom 7.

1961
After buying the McDonald's restaurant chain from its founders, Ray Kroc greatly expands the fast-food business and starts McDonald's Hamburger University to train new employees.

Apr. 5, 1962
Marilyn Monroe is found dead in her Los Angeles home. Police rule her death a suicide, caused by an overdose of sleeping pills.

Sep. 1962
In Silent Spring, biologist Rachel Carson warns of the dangers posed by environmental pollution. She singles out the damage being caused by chemical pesticides such as DDT, which is soon banned.

June 11, 1963
Alabama governor George Wallace stands "in the schoolhouse door" at the University of Alabama. His gesture fulfills a campaign promise to keep black students from enrolling there.

Aug. 28, 1963
Martin Luther King Jr. delivers his "I Have a Dream" speech before 250,000 people at the March on Washington, the largest civil rights demonstration yet.

1963
Psychologist Betty Friedan publishes The Feminine Mystique, which explores the dissatisfaction being experienced by many suburban housewives. Friedan's book attacks the cultural values that encourage women to seek fulfillment in the family alone.

I do not believe that the Great Society is the ordered, changeless, and sterile battalion of the ants. It is the excitement of becoming—always becoming, trying, probing, falling, resting, and trying again—but always trying and always gaining.

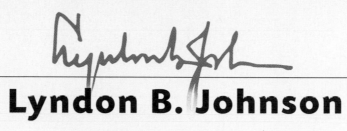

Lyndon B. Johnson

36th President • 1963–1969

LYNDON BAINES JOHNSON'S CHARACTER WAS SHAKESPEAREAN in its scope and complexity: He was both the imperial Henry V and the boorish Falstaff squeezed into a single body. According to Press Secretary Bill Moyers, "He was proud, sensitive, impulsive, flamboyant, sentimental, earthy, mean at times, bold, euphoric, insecure, magnanimous, the best dancer in the White House since Washington, but temperamental, melancholy, and strangely ill at ease as well." In other words, he had a Texas-size personality and an ego to match.

Johnson had one goal in life—to be the greatest president doing the greatest good in history. His energy was boundless, his personal presence overwhelming. He had both an instinct for power and a gift for wielding it, sometimes in unusual ways. For example, he was a master of vulgarity, which he used both to intimidate and to entertain.

"When he had to go to the bathroom in the middle of a conversation, it was not unusual for him to move the discussion there," historian (and former White House Fellow) Doris Kearns Goodwin recalled. "Johnson seemed delighted as he told me of 'one of the delicate Kennedyites who came into the bathroom with me and then found it utterly impossible to look at me while I sat there on the toilet. You'd think he had never seen those parts of the body before.'"

Although Johnson appreciated authority for its own sake, he had, in the words of biographer Robert Caro, "a rare gift for mobilizing the powers of government to raise up the downtrodden." Even as a young schoolteacher in Texas, LBJ had persuaded the all-white school board to buy playground equipment for his all-Mexican school. That way, the students, many of whom didn't have lunches to eat, could at least play sports during lunch hour.

As president, he strong-armed Congress into accepting civil rights, voting rights, and War on Poverty legislation that John Kennedy could never have passed. Most historians believe that LBJ would have become one of the greatest presidents in history had it not been for the Vietnam War.

The escalation of the war in Southeast Asia made Johnson's tragic flaw clear. The self-confidence that had carried him to the White House now gave way to its darker side, arrogance.

Johnson gradually came to believe that he was powerful enough and clever enough to fund both "guns and butter"—that is, to fight a war overseas at the same time he pressed ahead with his Great Society program at home. Of course, no one could do both, and in the end, like Othello and Hamlet, he came to ruin and sorrow by his own hand.

• Texas Politics

In 1941, Rep. Lyndon Johnson took on Texas governor Pappy O'Daniel in a special election for the U.S. Senate. It was a typical Texas campaign: Wheeling and dealing mattered more than issues, and money mattered most.

Johnson bribed voters to attend rallies, handing out free tickets for a defense-bond raffle at the end of each speech. Behind the scenes, he bought votes directly in San Antonio and the rest of South Texas for two to five dollars apiece.

At first, Johnson appeared to win the election by five thousand votes. His staff sent out telegrams that read "ELECTION BUREAU CONCEDES ELECTION UNLESS MIRACLE HAPPENS…. LOOKS LIKE WE'RE IN." However, a few

A signed photograph of the senatorial candidate.

days after the voting, as late results came in, it became clear that O'Daniel's supporters had done a more effective job of cheating.

LBJ's first impulse was to steal the election back, so he called George Paar, the political boss of Duval County in South Texas, and asked for some "corrected" returns of his own. Paar refused. "Lyndon," he said, "I've been to the federal penitentiary, and I'm not going back for you." Seven years later, though, Duval County came through with enough votes to win "Landslide Lyndon" his Senate seat. This time, Johnson defeated a different governor by eighty-seven ballots out of nearly one million cast.

• Him and Her

Before he became president, Johnson owned a dog that he called Little Beagle Johnson—because, he said, "It's cheaper if we all have the same monogram." Later, when he moved into the White House, he brought with him two new beagles named Him and Her. These dogs soon became as popular as their master, but in April 1964 an incident involving the hounds hurt Johnson's soaring popularity.

After a meeting with some bankers, LBJ casually picked up both beagles by their ears. When photographs of Johnson picking up one of the dogs appeared on the front pages of most newspapers the next day, dog lovers were furious. Organizations such as the ASPCA demanded an explanation for the president's behavior. "To make them bark," LBJ said disgustedly. "It's good for them." Then former president Harry Truman rose to Johnson's defense: "What the hell are the critics hollering about? That's the way to handle hounds."

• Vietnam

In December 1967, LBJ's daughter Lynda married Marine Capt. Charles S. Robb in a White House ceremony. Four months later, Robb shipped out to Vietnam.

"When I left for Vietnam, the President gave me a small battery-operated tape recorder and several blank tapes so that I could send Lynda occasional recordings and could play back tapes she sent me," Robb recalled. "Most of the tapes Lynda and I exchanged had a lot of the talk you might expect from a recently married couple. I can only trust that the tapes her father found of particular interest were ones in which I described the operations we had participated in. If so, I think they gave him some of the texture of the war at company levels."

Alone in the Cabinet Room, Johnson listens to a tape made by his son-in-law in Vietnam.

★ ★ ★ ★ ★ ★ ★ ★ ★ ★ ★ ★ ★ ★

• The Johnson Treatment

"As a human being he was a miserable person…a bully, sadist, lout, and egotist," White House staff member George Reedy observed of his former boss. The president's "lapses from civilized conduct were deliberate and usually intended to subordinate someone else to his will. He did disgusting things because he realized that other people had to pretend that they did not mind. It was his method of bending them to his designs."

Reedy wasn't the first to notice that LBJ would do just about anything to get what he wanted from people. His methods, both verbal and physical, were collectively known as the "Johnson treatment." A tall, imposing man at six feet three inches and 210 pounds, he liked to stand close to people so that he could intimidate them with his powerful physical presence. Sometimes he'd poke at them, paw them, bark in their faces, snarl, curse, and spit. At other times, he'd laugh, wheedle, and cajole his targets. In any cause, whether people got the "good" Johnson treatment or the "bad," it made them reluctant to say no.

Even his vice president, Hubert Humphrey, wasn't immune. Humphrey once rolled up his trouser leg to show some friends the result of an encounter with LBJ: cuts and bruises on his shins where the president had kicked him several times before yelling, "Get going now!"

★ ★ ★ ★ ★ ★ ★ ★ ★ ★ ★ ★ ★ ★ ★ ★ ★ ★ ★

• Lady Bird Johnson

LYNDON JOHNSON, WHO GREW up dirt poor, was determined to marry into money. As a student at Southwest Texas State Teachers College, he dated two girls seriously. Each of their fathers was the richest man in his town. In September 1934, he met Claudia Taylor, known as Lady Bird, from Karnack, Texas. According to biographer Robert Caro, "Whether or not…her father's position was the explanation, or any part of the explanation, for Lyndon Johnson's interest in her, her father was the richest man in town."

Their courtship was of the whirlwind variety. On their first date, he proposed. "I thought it was some kind of joke," she said. "He was excessively thin, but very, very good-looking, with lots of black wavy hair, and the most outspoken, straightforward, determined manner I had ever encountered."

At the time, Johnson was working for a congressman. He returned to D.C. but wrote Lady Bird daily. About two months later, he drove back to Karnack so that they could become engaged. Together they continued on to Austin, where Lady Bird wanted to ask a friend's advice. Along the way, Johnson gave her an ultimatum: "We either get married now or we never will." Bypassing Austin, they drove directly to San Antonio, where they were married on November 17. "Some of the best deals are made in a hurry," Lady Bird's father had told her.

As first lady, Lady Bird Johnson prompted comparisons with Eleanor Roosevelt when she visited impoverished areas in Kentucky and Pennsylvania "to see the flesh and blood behind the statistics." She was best known, however, for her efforts to "beautify" public spaces around the country. ("Alas, we never did think of a better word," she said.) Mrs. Johnson encouraged people to spruce up their neighborhoods and businesses, and she was the primary sponsor of the Highway Beautification Act of 1965, which replaced billboards and junkyards along major roads with wildflowers and trees.

MAJOR POLITICAL EVENTS

★ **Civil Rights Act of 1964:** In July 1964, President Johnson signed a civil rights bill that barred discrimination in public places and employment based on race, sex, religion, or national origin. The Civil Rights Act of 1964, which overturned Jim Crow laws, was an expanded version of a bill that Kennedy had failed to pass during 1963. Johnson was able to push this bill through because of his skills as a legislator and his suggestion that the act could serve as a tribute to the fallen president.

★ **Tonkin Gulf Resolution:** In August 1964, Johnson announced that the U.S. destroyer *Maddox* had been attacked by North Vietnamese patrol boats in the Tonkin Gulf off the Vietnamese coastline. The North Vietnamese countered that the attack, which took place in international waters, was justified because the *Maddox* had been protecting South Vietnamese raiders. On August 7, Congress passed the Tonkin Gulf Resolution, which gave Johnson nearly unlimited power to use military force in Vietnam without a formal declaration of war. The White House staff had prepared the resolution in advance, hoping for just such an opportunity. The Tonkin Gulf Resolution passed unanimously in the House, and only Wayne Morse of Oregon and Ernest Gruening of Alaska voted against it in the Senate. On March 2, 1965, the air force began bombing North Vietnam, and six days later, the first U.S. ground troops landed at Danang. According to Johnson, the United States sought "no wider war." However, by 1968, the thirty-five hundred marines who had

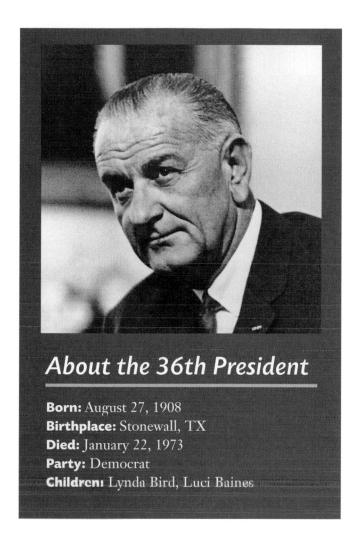

About the 36th President

Born: August 27, 1908
Birthplace: Stonewall, TX
Died: January 22, 1973
Party: Democrat
Children: Lynda Bird, Luci Baines

★ ★ ★ ★ ★ ★ ★ ★ ★ ★ ★ ★ ★ ★ ★

During the Johnson Administration

Jan. 13, 1964 — *The Federal Trade Commission orders tobacco companies to print warning labels on all cigarette packages after a panel of experts appointed by Surgeon General Luther Terry issues a report directly linking cigarette smoking to lung cancer.*

Feb. 7, 1964 — *Beatlemania seizes America when the Fab Four arrive at Kennedy Airport in New York City. Their spot on the Ed Sullivan television show two days later breaks Elvis Presley's record for the largest audience by more than sixteen million viewers.*

Sep. 14, 1964 — *The University of California bans recruiting tables set up by student political groups. When five students defy the ban, the Free Speech Movement begins.*

Feb. 21, 1965 — *Black gunmen assassinate former Nation of Islam leader Malcolm X at the Audubon Ballroom in Harlem.*

Aug. 11, 1965 — *Four days of race rioting begins in the Watts neighborhood of Los Angeles after police beat a black youth for drunken driving.*

Nov. 9, 1965 — *A malfunctioning generator near Niagara Falls causes the largest power failure in history, blacking out thirty million people in seven northeastern states.*

Mar. 1, 1967 — *The Interior Department issues the first endangered species list. It names seventy-eight species facing extinction, including the bald eagle and the grizzly bear.*

Apr. 4, 1968 — *James Earl Ray shoots Martin Luther King Jr. as King leans against a railing outside his room at the Lorraine Motel in Memphis.*

landed at Danang three years earlier had swelled to more than half a million men.

★ **Voting Rights Act of 1965:** In August 1965, Johnson signed a voting rights bill that outlawed poll taxes, literacy tests, and other discriminatory practices that white southerners had been using to keep blacks from voting. The Voting Rights Act of 1965 fulfilled a longtime goal of the civil rights movement, which immediately began organizing registration drives around the country. The new black voters signed up by these drives not only increased minority representation in the South but also helped elect prominent black mayors in such northern cities as Cleveland, Ohio, and Gary, Indiana.

At every turn, we have been beset by those who find everything wrong with America and little that is right. But I am confident that this will not be the judgment of history on these remarkable times in which we are privileged to live.

Richard M. Nixon

37th President • 1969–1974

RICHARD NIXON HAD A WARLIKE VIEW of life that required people to choose sides, vanquish enemies, remain loyal, and root out spies. By various accounts—including his own, if one reads between the lines—he first developed this philosophy during his youth in California. Growing up in the underclass seems to have created in him a bitterness toward people born to wealth as well as an intense desire to join them—one of his many contradictions.

In a candid moment, Nixon once psychoanalyzed himself for aide Ken Clawson:

What starts the process really are laughs and slights and snubs when you are a kid…. But if you are reasonably intelligent and if your anger is deep enough and strong enough, you learn that you can change those attitudes by excellence [and] personal gut performance, while those who have everything are sitting on their fat butts.

The icy heart of this quote—*if your anger is deep enough and strong enough*—suggests both Nixon's secret strength and his ruinous weakness: the anger that flowed through his life like a subterranean river, hidden from public view yet constantly eating away at his stability.

There were moments when the insecurity and paranoia slipped out. After losing the 1960 presidential election and then the 1962 race for governor of California, Nixon momentarily lost control. "You won't have Nixon to kick around anymore," he bitterly told reporters, "because, gentlemen, this is my last press conference."

It wasn't. Six years later, he ran for president again and won. However, the insecurity remained. Obsessed with his "enemies" in the media, Nixon approved the creation of "the plumbers," a covert group operating out of the White House to "plug" news leaks. It was members of this group who staged the Watergate break-in on June 17, 1972.

A different sort of man would have admitted during the Watergate hearings that mistakes had been made and then moved on. But Nixon chose instead to direct a broad cover-up. "Always he lied," historian Fawn Brodie concluded, "and this most aggressively, to deny that he lied."

Nixon was unquestionably one of the most intelligent and thoughtful people ever to hold public office. His pursuit of détente with the Soviet Union and the opening of relations with China proved as much. His ambition as a ten-year-old was to be "an honest lawyer, who can't be bought by crooks." Yet he went on to become the nation's chief crook. According to two presidents, he was "a no-good lying bastard" (Truman) and "the most dishonest president we've ever had" (Carter). In his own private war, Nixon lost.

• Tricky Dick

Nixon picked up the nickname Tricky Dick during his 1950 Senate campaign against Helen Gahagan Douglas. As a congressman from California for three years, he had served on the House Un-American Activities Committee, whose self-appointed task it had been to root out Communist subversives wherever they might have been lurking. Nixon became famous for his crusade against Alger Hiss, a former State Department official who had been accused of spying for the Soviet Union during the 1930s.

In his subsequent campaign for the Senate, Nixon again displayed his instinct for the jugular and masterful ability to manipulate people's fears. Eager to play the Communist card, Nixon had five hundred thousand copies of Douglas's voting record printed up on pink paper. The purpose of this flyer was to show how votes cast by the Pink Lady supported the goals of the worldwide Communist conspiracy. Douglas retaliated by calling Nixon a "pipsqueak" and a "peewee," but it was "Tricky Dick" that stuck.

Dwight Eisenhower picked Nixon as his running mate in 1952 to appease the right wing of the Republican party.

★ ★ ★ ★ ★ ★ ★ ★ ★ ★ ★ ★ ★ ★ ★ ★ ★ ★ ★ ★

• Inner Feelings

Nixon plays piano at the White House. His wife, Pat, helps him keep time.

Like Harry Truman, Nixon was considered a great musical talent as a child. When he was twelve, his mother moved him from one school to another so that he could take daily piano lessons. His teachers encouraged him, but Nixon never lost his lackadaisical attitude toward music. He particularly disliked practicing.

"I sometimes regret that I did not go forward with my musical education," Nixon wrote. "What would have particularly appealed to me would have been to explore the possibilities of being a composer…. I believe I might have done best of all in expressing my inner feelings in music."

Later in life, Nixon used his piano playing as part of his personal campaign to appear outgoing and be "one of the boys." Another way Nixon tried to fit in, despite his awkward personal manner, was to talk sports, especially football. "It doesn't come naturally to me to be a buddy-buddy boy," he once confessed to journalist Stewart Alsop. "I can't really let my hair down with anyone…not even with my family."

• The Berlin Wall

A shy man, Nixon disliked the social aspects of being president. He hated the glad handing and the stroking, preferring to spend his time by himself, thinking. Even cabinet members had a difficult time arranging an appointment.

Nixon's daily schedule was guarded by Chief of Staff Bob Haldeman, domestic policy chief John Ehrlichman, and National Security Adviser Henry Kissinger, who were collectively known as the Berlin Wall.

When not in isolation, Nixon liked to spend hours with these men exploring and analyzing his concerns. "Richard Nixon was like a cow," John Ehrlichman once explained. "He would chew his cud over and over on a subject and turn it over and chew it some more, and turn it over and chew it some more…. Probably you'd grunt at the right times or make some comment or other."

Nixon particularly liked to discuss geopolitical theory with Kissinger during "excruciatingly long conversations" (Kissinger's words) that endlessly went over the same information.

• The White House Tapes

In December 1968, during a tour of the White House, President-elect Nixon learned about Lyndon Johnson's secret tape-recording system. He ordered it removed. However, he later discovered that without a taping system, it was difficult to keep accurate records of meetings. "We would get people going out saying, 'The President says such and such,' when he said no such thing," Bob Haldeman recalled.

In February 1971, Nixon agreed to install a new taping system. Johnson's had been turned on by a secret switch, but Nixon was "notoriously inept in his handling of all things mechanical," according to biographer Jonathan Aitken, and he couldn't be counted

The Nixon White House tape recorder. In July 1973, Nixon said that he wanted the tapes stored under his bed, but the order was never carried out. It would have required raising the ceiling of his bedroom by at least twenty feet because there were so many tapes.

on to press the simplest button correctly. So Haldeman chose a foolproof voice-activated system that turned itself on automatically whenever anyone spoke. Neither he nor Nixon realized at the time the disadvantages of a system that was never turned off.

Many people wondered later why Nixon didn't burn the tapes before they were subpoenaed by the Watergate special prosecutor. The reason was his growing paranoia. "I was prepared to believe that others, even people close to me, would turn against me just as [White House counsel John] Dean had done," Nixon wrote in his memoirs. "In that case, the tapes would give me at least some protection." Evidently, Nixon had rationalized his behavior to such an extreme point that he genuinely believed the tapes would vindicate him.

On July 24, 1974, the Supreme Court ruled that Nixon had to turn over the subpoenaed White House tapes. On August 5, he released a transcript of the "smoking gun" tape that proved his involvement in the Watergate cover-up, admitting that it was "at variance with certain of my previous statements." Nixon is shown here hugging his daughter Julie on August 8, the day he announced that he would resign the presidency.

★ ★

• Pat Nixon

AFTER HIS GRADUATION from Duke Law School, Nixon considered moving to Washington to work for the FBI, but instead he returned to his hometown of Whittier, California, and entered private practice. Soon afterward, he began his one and only serious courtship.

In 1937, the same year that Nixon returned to Whittier, a new teacher of typing and shorthand came to town. Because Pat Ryan, a former movie extra, happened to be interested in acting, Nixon auditioned for a role opposite her at the Whittier Little Theater. He proposed to her the same night. "I thought he was nuts," Pat Nixon said later. She dated Nixon on and off for two years, during which time he demonstrated his almost pathological tendency to become obsessed. Not wanting her to take long trolley rides by herself, Nixon drove Pat to dates with other men and then

waited around for several hours until it was time to drive her home. Finally, she agreed to marry him.

Later, as a political wife, Pat Nixon was content to remain far in the background. She appeared alongside her husband, smiling patiently and waving often but saying very little. Her two daughters, Tricia and Julie, inevitably became the focus of public attention, yet Pat managed to shelter them from the worst political attacks against their father.

Her most memorable moment as first lady came at the end of Nixon's presidency, when she tried to persuade him to remain in the White House. But he had already made up his mind, and Pat somehow knew it. Even before Nixon told her, she had already begun packing for exile. "Very perceptive of her," he noted later. "With us sometimes, as it is between people who are very close, the unspoken things go deeper than the spoken. She knew what I was going to do."

MAJOR POLITICAL EVENTS

★ **Vietnamization:** During the 1968 presidential campaign, Nixon boasted that he had a "secret plan" to end the war in Vietnam. That plan was Vietnamization, or the replacement of U.S. combat soldiers with South Vietnamese troops. Under Vietnamization, Nixon could withdraw U.S. troops yet still keep the war going. To offset the withdrawals, Nixon expanded the bombing of North Vietnam. During a typical week, U.S planes dropped more bomb tonnage on North Vietnam than had been dropped on Germany during all of World War II. Nixon also ordered the secret bombing of Cambodia, where the Communist Vietcong maintained a network of supply bases.

★ **Détente:** Because Nixon's political rise had been founded on outspoken anti-Communism, his August 1971 announcement that he planned to visit the People's Republic of China stunned the world. Since the Chinese revolution of 1949, the United States had backed Chiang Kai-shek's Taiwanese government-in-exile. As a result, there were no formal diplomatic relations between the United States and the Communist mainland. Although relations weren't restored during Nixon's January 1972 trip, "opening the door" to China became an important focus of his policy of détente, or the relaxation of strained relations. Four months after his return from China, Nixon followed up this success with another foreign policy coup. In May 1972, he visited Moscow and signed the SALT strategic arms limitation treaty, which froze the number of nuclear missiles in the arsenals of the United States and the Soviet Union.

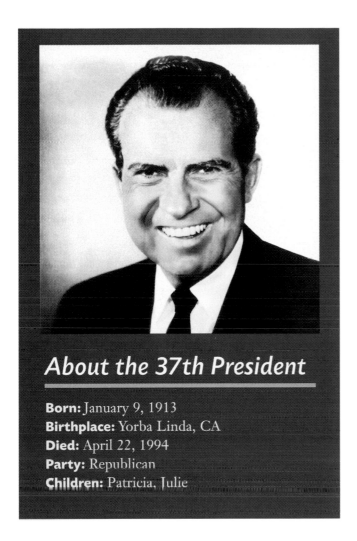

About the 37th President

Born: January 9, 1913
Birthplace: Yorba Linda, CA
Died: April 22, 1994
Party: Republican
Children: Patricia, Julie

★ **Watergate:** In June 1972, police arrested five men, including a former FBI agent, caught breaking into the Democratic party offices at the Watergate building in Washington, D.C. At first, the scandal was limited to Nixon's reelection committee. Then stories began appearing in the *Washington Post* linking the break-in to a larger "dirty tricks" campaign. In February 1973, the Senate appointed a committee to investigate. On July 16, Deputy Chief of Staff Alexander Butterfield revealed that Nixon had been secretly recording Oval Office conversations. The Senate committee subpoenaed the tapes, as did special prosecutor Archibald Cox. Nixon refused to turn them over, citing executive privilege. On July 24, 1974, the Supreme Court ruled that the president had to turn over the tapes. Three days later, the House Judiciary Committee approved the first of three articles of impeachment against him.

During the Nixon Administration

July 20, 1969	*Apollo 11 astronauts Neil Armstrong and Edwin "Buzz" Aldrin land on the moon.*
Aug. 15, 1969	*The Woodstock Music and Art Fair opens in upstate New York.*
Nov. 15, 1969	*The New Mobilization Committee to End the War in Vietnam organizes the largest demonstration yet in Washington, D.C. An estimated eight hundred thousand protesters represent eighty-four antiwar groups, from the Quakers to the Communists.*
Nov. 1969	*The new Public Broadcasting Service begins airing* Sesame Street. *This daily children's educational program, created by the Children's Television Workshop, features Jim Henson's Muppets.*
Apr. 22, 1970	*Environmental groups organize the first Earth Day to call public attention to the growing environmental movement.*
May 4, 1970	*National Guardsmen fire into a crowd of student demonstrators at Kent State University in Ohio, killing four people. The soldiers were summoned after students protesting the bombing of Cambodia set fire to an army ROTC building.*
Sep. 21, 1970	*Howard Cosell, Keith Jackson, and "Dandy" Don Meredith broadcast the first* Monday Night Football *game.*
1972	*Computer scientist Nolan Bushnell invents Pong, the first commercial video game, which mimics the sport of Ping-Pong.*
1974	*Universal Product Code labels, or bar codes, begin appearing on food packages.*

Gerald R. Ford

Gerald R. Ford

38th President • 1974–1977

GERALD FORD'S TERM IN OFFICE SEEMS CERTAIN to go down in history as a curiosity, a brief burlesque that oddly closed the tragedies of Watergate and Vietnam. No one knew what would follow these political dramas, so why not a vaudeville act—a man stumbling down stairs, falling in the snow, and bumping his head into things?

Perhaps the nation needed some comic relief, yet the widespread characterization of Ford as a Keystone Kop was unfair. The hallmarks of his presidency weren't blunders and pratfalls but stability and integrity. These were, after all, the traits that had landed Ford the top job in the first place.

Ironically, Ford's early childhood was anything but stable. His father was an alcoholic and a wife beater. In 1913, after a brief, fear-filled marriage, Ford's mother, Dorothy Gardner, fled with her infant son, Leslie, to her parents' home in Grand Rapids, Michigan. Three years later, she married a paint salesman named Gerald R. Ford. Dorothy renamed her son after her new husband, and he adopted the child. Gerald Jr. later described his step-father as a man whose honesty and integrity made the strongest impression on his life.

Amid the madness of Watergate, Ford stood out as a man who was, in his own words, "disgustingly sane." For that reason, he was chosen to replace Spiro Agnew as vice president after a disgraced Agnew resigned that office in 1973. Less than a year later, Richard Nixon also resigned, and Ford became president. Never having won a national election, he was the first man ever "appointed" to the presidency.

Even so, Americans welcomed Ford with an outpouring of goodwill. Nixon's grim, hunched figure was finally gone from the White House, replaced by an open-faced man who communicated good midwestern common sense. Newspapers gushed about Ford's ordinary lifestyle: He opened his own front door in the morning to pick up his newspaper! He toasted his own English muffins for breakfast! His behavior made the specter of Nixon seem like a bad dream.

And then Ford pardoned Nixon for any crimes Nixon might have committed as president. By all accounts, Ford genuinely believed that the pardon was the right thing to do. He worried, with some justification, that putting Nixon on trial would split the country even more deeply. Yet the scathing reaction to the pardon crippled Ford's presidency. Newspaper editorials condemned him, and people speculated publicly that Ford and Nixon had made a secret deal. A greatly disappointed Ford later wrote, "I began to wonder whether, instead of healing the wounds, my decision had only rubbed salt into them."

Far left: Ford on the football field at the University of Michigan, 1933. Left: Ford's Michigan football helmet.

• Oops!

Although Ford was the most athletic president since Teddy Roosevelt (or at least since Herbert Hoover), nearly everybody thought that he was a klutz. An internal 1976 campaign memorandum ticked off Ford's well-publicized missteps: "Vail, Colorado—ski fall…South Lawn—hitting head on helicopter…San Antonio, Texas—tamale incident…." Comedians, notably Chevy Chase, seized on and magnified the gaffes. Impersonating the president on *Saturday Night Live*, Chase tripped, stumbled, and fell down week after week. One night, he would stab his hand with a fork; another night, he'd pick up a glass of water when the phone rang, dousing himself: "Hello? Hello?… I can't hear you. Where are you? In a pool?"

No one remembered that young Jerry Ford had been a standout athlete in both high school and college. At the University of Michigan, he was the star center of the Wolverine football team that won the 1933 national championship. Both the Detroit Lions and the Green Bay Packers made Ford offers, but he decided that "pro football wouldn't lead me anywhere."

Instead, he took a job coaching football at Yale while he attended the law school there. Among the Yale undergraduates he coached were two future senators, Robert Taft Jr. of Ohio and William Proxmire of Wisconsin. Meanwhile, Ford's law school classmates included future Supreme Court justice Potter Stewart and Jimmy Carter's secretary of state, Cyrus Vance.

Even after his football days, Ford kept in shape, working occasionally as a fashion model to supplement the income from his law practice. He appeared on the cover of *Cosmopolitan* in 1942, the same year he entered the navy.

Working out on the White House tennis court.

• Appointment

Moments after Vice President Spiro Agnew's resignation on October 10, 1973, President Nixon held an unprecedented meeting at the White House with the two most powerful men in Congress: Speaker of the House Carl Albert and Senate majority leader Mike Mansfield. Nixon never admitted as much, but Mansfield and Albert both said later that they knew they were picking the next president of the United States. Nixon began by asking for suggestions. Albert and Mansfield, both Democrats, made their list a short one. "We gave Nixon no choice but Ford," Albert said later. "Congress made Jerry Ford president."

Ford had served in the House since 1949 and as the Republican leader since 1965. In all that time, he had rarely strayed from the Republican party line. And yet these two Democrats were pushing him on Nixon. Why? The answer is that his colleagues in Congress considered him an honest, stable, and sincere man. Albert and Mansfield believed that these traits would prove useful to a country that might be teetering on the brink of a political collapse.

With President Nixon in the Oval Office on August 8, 1974, the day Nixon announced that he would resign the presidency.

★ ★ ★ ★ ★ ★ ★ ★ ★ ★ ★

• Slips of the Tongue

The country could forgive Ford his physical mishaps, but his slips of the tongue were much more difficult to ignore. Former president Lyndon Johnson had once remarked that Ford had played football "too long without a helmet," and many people worried that LBJ, though joking, had been right. Ford's mistakes suggested that he wasn't up to his job.

Some of the errors were embarrassing but insignificant. In one White House meeting, he called Republican senatorial candidate S. I. Hayakawa "Hiawatha" by mistake. A much more important slip came during a 1976 presidential debate with Democratic candidate Jimmy Carter. Answering a question about whether the United States had granted too much latitude to the Soviet Union in Eastern Europe, Ford replied, "There is no Soviet domination of Eastern Europe, and there never will be under a Ford administration." This obviously misguided remark strengthened the view held by an increasing number of Americans that Ford was not merely stable but thick.

Ford chats with Soviet premier Leonid Brezhnev during the president's trip to Vladivostok in November 1974. In foreign affairs, Ford's mantra was "steady as she goes."

★ ★ ★ ★ ★ ★ ★ ★ ★ ★ ★ ★ ★ ★ ★ ★ ★

• Betty Ford

BETTY BLOOMER GREW UP IN Grand Rapids, Michigan, where early on she decided to become a dancer. After high school, she enrolled at the Bennington School of Dance, where she met choreographer Martha Graham. Graham subsequently invited her to New York, and she performed with the Martha Graham Concert Group. (Years later, she persuaded her husband to honor Graham with the Presidential Medal of Freedom.)

In 1941, on the urging of her mother, Betty returned to Grand Rapids, where she took a job as a fashion coordinator for Herpolscheimer's department store. A year later, she married a furniture salesman. This marriage lasted only five years but ended amicably.

Soon after her divorce, Betty met Jerry Ford, who had returned to Grand Rapids after his navy service. They became engaged in February 1948, just as Ford was beginning his first congressional campaign. The wedding took place in mid-October; two weeks after that, Ford won election to the House. For their honeymoon, he drove his bride to Ann Arbor for the Michigan-Northwestern football game.

As first lady, Betty Ford championed women's issues. She lobbied her husband to choose a female vice president and became an outspoken supporter of both abortion rights and the Equal Rights Amendment. In September 1974, after doctors found a lump in her breast, she waged a public battle with breast cancer that increased awareness of the disease and encouraged millions of women to have breast exams.

After her treatment for alcohol and prescription drug dependency in 1978, Mrs. Ford again went public with her problems so that others might benefit from her experience. She became active in raising funds for and planning the Betty Ford Center, which opened in 1982 and quickly became the nation's leading treatment facility for drug and alcohol dependency. She received the Presidential Medal of Freedom herself from George Bush in 1991.

MAJOR POLITICAL EVENTS

★ **Arab Oil Embargo:** In June 1973, Nixon warned Americans that the days of cheap, plentiful energy would soon be over. Those days ended in October 1973, when the Arab states that controlled OPEC (the Organization of Petroleum Exporting Countries) cut off oil shipments to the United States. The Arab oil embargo, which punished Americans for supporting Israel during the recent Yom Kippur War, forced factory closings and produced long lines at the nation's gas pumps. In the aftermath of the embargo, OPEC raised its prices, boosting them 400 percent in 1974 alone. The numerous economic difficulties this caused soon came to be known as the Energy Crisis. As a result,

the Ford administration had to cope with the country's worst inflation and unemployment rates since the Great Depression.

★ **Whip Inflation Now:** During Ford's first year in office, the national rate of inflation rose into double digits, reaching 11 percent by the end of 1974. Unlike Nixon, Ford refused to consider wage and price controls and instead advocated voluntary efforts. However, the Whip Inflation Now (WIN) campaign that Ford launched in October 1974 seemed more like the work of an advertising agency than than that of a presidential administration. Ford handed out WIN buttons and urged moderation with great enthusiasm. Even so, inflation continued to rise. Finally, he adopted the traditional Republican strategy of tightening the money supply and dealing as best he could with the recession that followed.

About the 38th President

Born: July 14, 1913
Birthplace: Omaha, NE
Party: Republican
Children: Michael, John, Steven, Susan

★ **Fall of South Vietnam:** In January 1973, the United States and North Vietnam signed a treaty that called for the removal of all U.S. combat troops in return for the release of U.S. prisoners of war. The South Vietnamese government kept control of Saigon, while the Vietcong remained in place in the countryside. Nixon claimed that he had achieved "peace with honor," yet Henry Kissinger predicted privately that South Vietnam wouldn't last eighteen months. In fact, South Vietnam lasted until late April 1975, when Gen. Duong Van Minh surrendered Saigon to a combined force of North Vietnamese and Vietcong soldiers. During the last few days before the fall of Saigon, Operation Frequent Wind airlifted nearly seven thousand people, including fourteen hundred Americans, from the grounds of the U.S. embassy to navy ships waiting offshore. It was the largest helicopter evacuation in history.

★ ★ ★ ★ ★ ★ ★ ★ ★ ★ ★ ★ ★

During the Ford Administration

Sep. 12, 1974 *Violence disrupts the first day of classes in Boston, where white parents and students refuse to respect a court-ordered integration plan. A federal judge had ordered the busing of black children into all-white schools and white children into predominantly black ones.*

1974 *Students in California start a new fad: running naked through public places. Because they run quickly, they're called streakers.*

Oct. 11, 1975 Saturday Night Live *premieres on NBC. The first guest host is George Carlin.*

Dec. 11, 1975 *Congress asks Americans to switch over voluntarily to the metric system.*

1975 Jaws, *directed by Steven Spielberg, becomes the first movie to sell more than one hundred million dollars' worth of tickets.*

Jan. 10, 1976 *C. W. McCall's song "Convoy" tops the pop music charts, reflecting the country's current fascination with citizen's band, or CB, radio. First Lady Betty Ford even uses a CB at the White House. Her "handle" is First Mama.*

Apr. 22, 1976 *ABC News hires Barbara Walters to be the first woman anchor of a network television news program. Her million-dollar-a-year contract makes her the highest-paid U.S. journalist.*

July 1976 *Nearly two hundred people contract a mysterious illness during an American Legion convention in Philadelphia. Twenty-nine people eventually die of Legionnaire's disease.*

You have given me a great responsibility—to stay close to you, to be worthy of you, and to exemplify what you are. Let us create together a new national spirit of unity and trust. Your strength can compensate for my weakness, and your wisdom can help to minimize my mistakes.

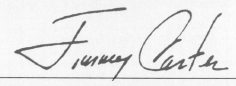

Jimmy Carter

39th President • 1977–1981

JIMMY CARTER WAS an excellent presidential candidate. He preached openness and decency, and people believed him. As an ex-president, he has been even better, pursuing good works without the baggage of partisan politics to weigh him down. The only bump in his road seems to have been the single term he served as president.

In 1976, Carter was just what the people wanted. They longed for a Washington outsider: He came from Plains, Georgia. They wanted an ordinary guy: He was the peanut-farming son of a peanut farmer. They wanted honesty: He was a Sunday school teacher who promised, without irony, "I'll never tell a lie."

It was exactly the right combination of traits to get a man elected in the aftermath of Watergate and Vietnam. However, Carter's skills and qualities, while commendable, weren't as effective as Lyndon Johnson's ruthlessness or Richard Nixon's scheming when it came to running the federal government. After a few years of raging inflation, stagnant growth, and a meandering foreign policy, Americans gave up on their president.

Carter overplayed his outsider role. He ignored procedures for decision making and instead went with his own instincts. He worked late into the night rather than delegate responsibility. Worst of all, he treated Democrats and Republicans on Capitol Hill as though they were his Sunday school students, talking down to them about piety and morality.

It seemed that every political issue became a moral test, and Carter rarely held back from criticizing people who, in his judgment, didn't measure up. Perhaps he thought that he could shame Congress into obedience. If so, he was naive. What Carter created instead was resentment.

In foreign affairs as well, President Carter wanted to do the right thing. Early in his administration, he single-handedly added the phrase *human rights* to the national vocabulary. Later, he helped Egypt and Israel make peace at Camp David. Yet many world leaders, and not just the dictators, came to resent the president for the same reason that members of Congress did: Who was Jimmy Carter to sit in judgment of their moral character?

Carter fought for his policies as best he could. He worked harder and later, gave speeches decrying the nation's "malaise," and reaffirmed his faith in God. Yet none of this helped dispel the image of passivity that enshrouded him after Iranians took fifty-two American embassy workers hostage in November 1979. After 444 days in captivity, the hostages were finally released on Inauguration Day 1981. However, by then the country had elected Ronald Reagan and moved eagerly away from the high standards that Carter had set.

Ensign Carter with his new wife, Rosalynn Smith, on their wedding day in July 1946. After high school, Carter attended the U.S. Naval Academy at Annapolis, graduating just after World War II 59th in his class of 820. In 1951, he joined the navy's nuclear submarine program and was later chosen by Adm. Hyman Rickover to serve as engineering officer aboard the Sea Wolf, *one of the first atomic-powered subs.*

• The Carters of Plains

James Earl Carter Sr., Jimmy's father, took a patch of dusty Georgia soil and turned it into a four-thousand-acre farm, peanut warehouse, and brokerage business. His success, however, came with not only his own sweat and toil but also that of two hundred black sharecroppers. Earl Carter treated these people no better and no worse than any other white Georgia farmer of the 1920s. He didn't allow anyone with dark skin into his house, for instance.

Earl's wife, Lillian, had her own ideas about race. In defiance of local custom, she preached racial equality and made an issue of it with her husband. Earl Carter finally relented, allowing her to invite black friends into the house, but he made a noisy point of going out whenever she did.

Of course, Carter sided with his mother, yet it took some time for him to grasp the extent of the problem. "It seems hard to believe now," he said later, "but I was actually a member of the county school board for several months before it dawned on me that white children rode buses to their schools and black students still walked to theirs."

★ ★

• Born Again

In 1966, Carter ran for governor of Georgia—and lost. A deep depression followed. "When you run for an office and you've failed," he once said, "there's a requisite reassessment of your life's future. Are you going to lower your standards, lower your aspirations,…or are you going to just dig in?"

On the outside, Carter picked himself up and went back to work. On the inside, however, he remained troubled. One Sunday at church in his hometown of Plains, he listened to a sermon entitled "If You Were Arrested for Being a Christian, Would There Be Enough Evidence to Convict You?"

"I was going through a state in my life then that was a very difficult one," Carter later said. "Everything I did was not gratifying…. I was always thinking about myself."

Although he had been only a superficial Christian most of his life, he sought the counsel of his evangelist sister, Ruth Carter Stapleton. The result was a religious experience that lifted his depression and gave a new shape to his public life. He was born again. "I formed a very close, intimate personal relationship with God, through Christ," Carter said, "that has given me a great deal of peace, equanimity, and the ability to accept difficulty without unnecessarily being disturbed."

An avid angler, Carter takes a break from the 1980 presidential campaign to fly-fish in Pennsylvania's Spruce Creek.

• The Camp David Accords

Carter's most lasting achievement as president was the Middle East peace treaty that he helped negotiate between Egypt and Israel in September 1978. Despite warnings that only failure would result, he personally invited Egyptian president Anwar el-Sadat and Israeli prime minister Menachem Begin to Camp David for two weeks of direct face-to-face talks.

There were many problems for Carter to overcome at Camp David, one of which was the food. Because of his poor health, President Sadat traveled with his own chef, who prepared for him special meals of boiled meat and vegetables served with honey-flavored mint tea. Prime Minister Begin didn't bring a cook, but he and several other Israelis preferred kosher food. A third team of stewards prepared food for everyone else. "We marveled at the ease with which Sadat's chef, our regular stewards, and the kosher cooks shared the same kitchen," First Lady Rosalynn Carter remembered. "And we had a lot of laughs about the food."

Carter with Sadat (left) and Begin (right) at the White House in March 1979. According to Mrs. Carter, "Everybody who ate with the Begins [at Camp David] ordered kosher food. But when the prime minister ate [alone] in his cabin, there were few requests for it."

• After the Presidency

As Douglas MacArthur once observed about generals, most presidents tend to fade away after their terms have ended. There are exceptions: John Quincy Adams's service in the House, Teddy Roosevelt's independent run for president, William Howard Taft's appointment to the Supreme Court. Now another exception can be made.

Jimmy Carter's post-presidential career has been one of the most extraordinary in history. Putting to work the enormous prestige enjoyed by a former president, he has pursued the same goals that he set for himself in the White House—but now he succeeds.

Carter with his wife, Rosalynn. His skill as a carpenter was well enough known that when he left office, his White House staff gave him tools as a parting gift.

Carter has personally traveled to trouble spots all over the world, from Haiti to Bosnia to North Korea, making peace. At home, he has been supportive of the Christian housing ministry Habitat for Humanity. Each year, Jimmy and Rosalynn Carter spend a week of their time helping other Habitat volunteers build homes as they raise awareness of the need for affordable housing.

"I get a lot more recognition for building houses in partnership with people than I ever got for the Camp David Accords or for SALT II," the former president has said.

★ ★ ★ ★ ★ ★ ★ ★ ★ ★ ★ ★ ★ ★

• Rosalynn Carter

MOST OF THE TIME JIMMY CARTER was a patient, methodical person. He had carefully planned his Annapolis career since age four, yet he decided to marry Rosalynn Smith on their first date, almost as a whim.

Rosalynn was his sister Ruth's best friend. He had known her for many years but had shown no interest in her until the summer of 1945, when he returned to Plains after his second year at the naval academy. Out of the blue, he asked Ruth to fix him up with Rosalynn, and when he came home that night, he announced that he had found the girl he was going to marry.

The valedictorian of her recently graduated high school class, she was quiet, shy, hardworking, independent, and determined to do something better with her life than stay in Plains forever. As most biographers have pointed out, Rosalynn was very much like Carter himself.

The Carters were married in July 1946, and immediately after the wedding they drove off to Norfolk, Virginia, where Jimmy began his first tour of naval duty. Some Carter watchers have speculated that marrying a hometown girl may have been his way of taking some of Plains with him as he ventured out into the wider world.

When Carter returned to Plains to run his father's business, Rosalynn learned accounting so that she could keep the books for the peanut warehouse. When her husband entered politics, she suppressed her fear of public speaking and made appearances for him at smaller meetings so that he could attend larger ones.

She continued to meet and overcome similar challenges as first lady. Like Eleanor Roosevelt, she worked hard to conquer her basic shyness so that she could promote issues of concern to her. She became the first presidential wife since Mrs. Roosevelt to testify before Congress when she appeared in support of increased funding for mental health programs. She also became a champion of the Equal Rights Amendment.

MAJOR POLITICAL EVENTS

★ **Panama Canal Treaties:** In September 1977, President Carter negotiated with Panamanian leader Omar Torrijos two treaties that transferred control of the Canal Zone to Panama by the year 2000, provided that Panama maintained the canal's neutrality. Criticism of the treaties was intense—particularly among conservative Republicans, who claimed that Carter was giving away the canal. Led by former California governor Ronald Reagan, these opponents nearly blocked Senate ratification of the treaties. The final vote, after months of determined White House lobbying, was 68–32, or just one vote more than the necessary two-thirds majority.

★ **SALT II:** Carter continued Nixon's policy of détente with the Soviet Union. He also supported the Strategic Arms Limitation Talks, which produced a second treaty in June 1979. Although prospects for Senate ratification of SALT II weren't good to begin with, the Soviet invasion of Afghanistan in December 1979 caused the president to withdraw the treaty. Later, Carter halted all U.S. grain exports to the Soviet Union and organized an international boycott of the 1980 Summer Olympics in Moscow. Meanwhile, the Red Army spent nine frustrating years in Afghanistan waging a war against Islamic rebels that resembled the Vietnam conflict in its cost and futility.

★ **Iranian Hostage Crisis:** Early in 1979, Islamic revolutionaries in Iran led by the Ayatollah Ruhollah Khomeini toppled the U.S.-supported government of Shah Mohammed Reza Pahlevi.

About the 39th President

Born: October 1, 1924
Birthplace: Plains, GA
Party: Democrat
Children: John, James Earl III, Jeffrey, Amy

In November, a mob attacked the U.S. embassy in Teheran, taking ninety people hostage. The Iranians demanded that the shah, then undergoing cancer treatment in New York City, be returned to Iran in exchange for the hostages' release. Shortly after the standoff began, the Iranians released twenty-four non-American hostages and fourteen others, including several ill hostages, women, and blacks. The fifty-two embassy workers who remained in captivity were repeatedly blindfolded and paraded in front of TV cameras. At first, Carter tried to free the hostages through diplomatic efforts, all of which failed. In April 1980, he approved a military rescue mission, but this also failed when helicopter problems led to a crash and the death of eight servicemen. Carter finally obtained the hostages' release on January 19, 1981, his last full day in office.

During the Carter Administration

Jan. 1977 — *An estimated 130 million people watch the miniseries* Roots, *based on Alex Haley's best-selling book about his family's history from slavery to modern times.*

Apr. 26, 1977 — *Steve Rubell and Ian Schrager open Studio 54 in New York City. The nightclub sets a new standard for celebrity flamboyance and becomes a symbol of the disco lifestyle.*

May 1977 — *Apple Computers introduces the Apple II, the first commercial personal computer. The Apple II uses a television set for a monitor and a cassette recorder for data storage.*

Aug. 16, 1977 — *Elvis Presley dies at age forty-two from drug-related causes. Television stations all over the world interrupt their programs to announce the news.*

1977 — *The* Complete Book of Running *by James F. Fixx sparks a fitness craze that turns jogging into a popular sport.*

Mar. 28, 1979 — *Human error causes the Unit 2 reactor at Pennsylvania's Three Mile Island nuclear power plant to overheat. Some radioactive gases are released, requiring the evacuation of pregnant women and children from a five-mile area around the plant.*

May 17, 1980 — *Miami suffers the country's worst race riots since 1967 after an all-white jury acquits four white policemen in the beating death of a black businessman.*

Dec. 8, 1980 — *A deranged fan murders former Beatle John Lennon outside his New York City apartment building. Mark David Chapman says that he shot Lennon to become famous.*

It is not my intention to do away with government. It is, rather, to make it work—work with us, not over us; to stand by our side, not ride on our back. Government can and must provide opportunity, not smother it; foster productivity, not stifle it.

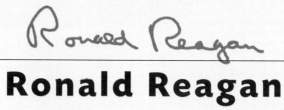

Ronald Reagan

40th President • 1981–1989

I N LATE 1979, WHEN RONALD REAGAN announced his campaign for the presidency, some people made bad jokes about the aging former actor wanting to "star" one last time. Others recalled how close he had come to stealing the Republican nomination from Gerald Ford in 1976 and realized that his campaign was no joke.

During an interview that fall on *Today*, host Tom Brokaw noted that if Reagan won he'd be the oldest president ever elected. Reagan replied, "I would be younger than all the heads of state I would have to deal with, except Margaret Thatcher." (In fact, at sixty-eight, Reagan would have been older than most Western heads of state.) A puzzled Brokaw pointed out, "Giscard d'Estaing of France is younger than you." "Who?" asked Reagan.

Did Reagan not know the French president's name? Or, as his aides later insisted, did he not hear Brokaw's question? Was his confused reply a hint of the Alzheimer's disease that would later fell him? Whatever the case, voters didn't seem to care. Ronald Reagan could say and do just about anything, and people still loved him.

"There's just something about the guy that people like," Speaker of the House Thomas P. "Tip" O'Neill once observed. "They want him to be a success. They're rooting for him, and of course they're rooting for him because we haven't had any presidential successes for years."

Because none of his gaffes seemed to faze voters, reporters called him the "Teflon president"—nothing stuck to him. Even when flaws of character or judgment were reported—flaws that would have ruined an ordinary politician—people chose to shrug them off.

The most notable of these was the Iran-contra scandal. Unlike Carter, Reagan was a passive president, broadly delegating authority to his aides. Content to be a communicator of grand themes, he trusted subordinates to translate these ideas into action. It should have been no surprise, therefore, when two of his aides decided, largely on their own, to use money from covert Iranian arms sales to fund weapons for the Nicaraguan contras.

Those who already despised Reagan waited for the hue and cry, but it never came. In a certain sense, Americans might as well have blamed themselves. On election eve in 1980, a radio reporter asked Reagan what it was that Americans saw in him. "Would you laugh if I told you that I think, maybe, they see themselves and that I'm one of them?" Reagan said. "I've never been able to detach myself and think that I, somehow, am apart from them."

• Movie Star

Reagan moved to Hollywood in 1937 after spending his first five years out of college working as a radio announcer and sportscaster in Iowa. He did well enough in his debut film, *Love Is on the Air*, to become a regular player in Warner Brothers "B" pictures (the low-budget films that accompanied "A" features on movie-house double bills).

Reagan's friendliness and optimism formed the basis for his good-natured screen personality. Like the actor himself, the characters he played were likable, easygoing, and idealistic.

Although he made more than fifty films during his three-decade-long career, Reagan never became the sort of solid leading man whose name alone could sell tickets. He made several "A" features but always in supporting roles, most notably those of George Gipp ("the Gipper") in *Knute Rockne—All American* (1940) and Drake McHugh in *Kings Row* (1941).

When Reagan's former boss, Jack Warner, learned that the actor was running for governor of California in 1966, he protested. "No, no!" the studio chief said. "*Jimmy Stewart* for governor, Ronald Reagan for best friend."

The Reagans during the 1970s with his four children (from left to right): Patti, Michael, Maureen, and Ron.

• Family Values

Throughout his political career, Reagan attacked "permissive" parents for contributing to the decline of the American family. The presumption was that his own family embodied the traditional values that he championed. This wasn't so. Reagan was the first divorced man elected president, and he had an uncomfortable relationship with his children.

Reagan had four children in all: two (Maureen and Michael) by his first wife, actress Jane Wyman, and two (Patti and Ron) by his second wife, Nancy Davis. After his marriage to Wyman ended in 1949, he spent less and less time with Michael and Maureen, especially after marrying Nancy in 1952 and beginning a new family with her that same year. Michael, for example, quarterbacked his high school football team, yet Reagan, a lifelong football fan, never saw his son play.

His second family wasn't closely knit either. When Nancy Reagan underwent surgery for breast cancer in 1987, a White House spokesman was forced to confirm that her only daughter, Patti, never telephoned her to find out how she was doing.

• Rancho del Cielo

Although the Sierra Club disagreed, President Reagan thought of himself as an environmentalist because he loved the outdoors. Most of his immediate predecessors in the White House had relaxed by swimming or playing golf, but Reagan preferred riding horses and doing ranch chores at his California retreat, Rancho del Cielo.

According to one biographer, "Reagan was in many ways a frustrated cowboy." As an actor, he repeatedly pleaded with Warner Brothers to give him roles in westerns. Later, as president, he was appalled to learn that Richard Nixon had ordered most of the Camp David riding trails paved over.

Of his eight years in office, Reagan spent about one of them—345 days, to be exact—at his 688-acre spread in the Santa Ynez Mountains. White House staffers knew that the first lady much preferred Beverly Hills, but for her husband's benefit she made a show of liking the ranch outside Santa Barbara. "When you get in there," he said in a 1985 interview, "the world is gone."

Above right: Reagan was a compulsive doodler. His aides thought that it helped him to think. "I never understood it," said one. "You could talk to him about options, and he might or might not get interested. But if you gave him a pencil and said these are the options but maybe we're missing something, he would start doodling around, making out words, and the first thing you knew he had taken a little of option one, and a little of option two, and added something of his own, and you had a whole new option."

★ ★

• The Great Communicator

Reagan was called the Great Communicator by the press because reporters marveled at his ability to transmit his political "message" to the public. Of course, the skills that he had honed as an entertainer helped him appear likable and sincere, but Reagan's gift went beyond that. He made people *want* to believe him.

Highly aware that he possessed this talent, Reagan casually ignored facts when they got in the way of his points. As an announcer for Chicago Cubs baseball games in Iowa, he had learned to make up colorful details to enliven the brief pitch-by-pitch reports that came over the telegraph wire. Later, according to CBS White House correspondent Bob Schieffer, "The old actor looked upon facts in a speech much as he had lines in a movie script: that is, it was perfectly all right to make changes as long as the revisions improved a scene or strengthened the overall performance."

A press briefing in February 1985.

Often Reagan made up quotes that supported his ideas. In 1982, he declared, "Justice Oliver Wendell Holmes once said, 'Keep the government poor and remain free.'" Journalists who did some checking learned that Holmes had said no such thing. By that time, however, Reagan's speech had already had its intended effect.

★ ★ ★ ★ ★ ★ ★ ★   ★ ★ ★ ★ ★ ★ ★ ★

• Nancy Reagan

WHEN RONALD REAGAN'S first wife, actress Jane Wyman, divorced him in 1949, gossip columnists blamed professional jealousy: Wyman's film career was flourishing, while Reagan's was declining. However, the genuine reason was that Reagan had become active in the anti-Communist hysteria then sweeping Hollywood. "Perhaps I should have let someone else save the world and saved my own home instead," he later admitted.

In 1951, he began dating another actress, Nancy Davis, whom he married in March of the following year. Unlike Wyman, Nancy never complained about Reagan's political activities. Instead, she gave up her career to become his most loyal supporter. Thirty years later, as one White House correspondent remarked, First Lady Nancy Reagan still looked on her husband with "a kind of transfixed adoration more appropriate to a witness of the Virgin Birth."

Because Reagan liked to appear the well-meaning bumbler, people often assumed that there must be someone feeding him his lines. Tough, shrewd Nancy was a likely suspect. Reagan's friends regularly complained about her influence whenever his views moved away from theirs. During the late 1950s, when Reagan left the Democratic party, liberals blamed Nancy for his shift to the right. During his presidency, conservatives blamed her for his acceptance of détente with the Soviets. In each case, it was much easier to fault Nancy than Reagan himself.

Like her husband, Nancy was superstitious. The president knocked on wood, threw salt over his shoulder, and carried a good-luck penny. The first lady was less casual: She insisted that all trip schedules be submitted to her in advance so that she could consult astrologer Joan Quigley. "By 1985," wrote journalist Lou Cannon, "Nancy Reagan had long become convinced that Quigley's advice had protected her husband from a repetition of the [1981] assassination attempt." When Quigley's charts showed a problem, the president's schedule was changed.

MAJOR POLITICAL EVENTS

★ **Reaganomics:** During the 1980 primary campaign, George Bush called Reagan's budget plan "voodoo economics" because of its controversial assumption that lowering tax rates would boost the economy and therefore increase tax revenue. When he became president, Reagan quickly lowered taxes, raised defense spending, and cut everything else, especially social welfare programs. His tax cuts, which favored the rich, included a 25 percent reduction in individual tax rates over three years. The spending cuts didn't come close to offsetting the drop in government revenue, much less the new defense spending. The result was a string of enormous budget deficits.

★ **Nicaragua:** Under Carter, the United States withdrew its support for Nicaraguan dictator Anastasio Somoza because of his poor human rights records. After the leftist Sandinistas deposed Somoza in July 1979, Carter offered aid to the new government. Immediately upon taking office, however, Reagan suspended this aid, charging that the Sandinistas were helping Communist rebels in nearby El Salvador. Instead, Reagan began arming the contras, a coalition of anti-Sandinista groups that included many former members of Somoza's police and military forces. In 1984, after learning that the CIA had been secretly mining Nicaraguan harbors and giving lessons in political assassination, Congress passed the Boland Amendment, which forbade further U.S. military aid to the contras. To evade this law, the White House assigned National Security Council staffer Oliver North to help the contras raise money quietly from private sources.

About the 40th President

Born: February 6, 1911
Birthplace: Tampico, IL
Party: Republican
Children: Maureen, Michael, Patricia, Ronald

★ **Iran-Contra Scandal:** In November 1986, a small Lebanese magazine exposed secret U.S. arms sales to Iran. Although the Reagan administration had publicly refused many times to negotiate with terrorists, members of Reagan's national security staff had indeed arranged the arms deals, hoping to win the release of U.S. hostages being held in Lebanon. Meanwhile, profits from the illegal arms deals were being used to buy weapons for the contras, also illegally. Reagan ordered Attorney General Edwin Meese to investigate, but Meese badly bungled the job: While Meese's aides conducted interviews in one room, Oliver North and National Security Adviser John Poindexter shredded documents in another. Poindexter later admitted that he destroyed Reagan's signed authorization in order to save the president from embarrassment. Reagan himself claimed that he hadn't known what was happening.

★ ★ ★ ★ ★ ★ ★ ★ ★ ★ ★ ★ ★ ★ ★

During the Reagan Administration

Aug. 1, 1981   *MTV, the first all-music-video cable network, begins serving subscribers nationwide.*

1983   *Sony and Philips begin marketing music on compact discs, a technology they have jointly developed. CDs catch on quickly, and by 1991 they outsell vinyl albums.*

Apr. 23, 1984   *Government researchers announce that they have found the virus thought to cause AIDS. This fatal disease first appeared in the United States three years ago.*

July 13, 1985   *British musician Bob Geldof organizes the Live Aid concerts held simultaneously in London and Philadelphia. Featuring the biggest names in the music business, the concerts raise seventy million dollars to feed starving Africans.*

Jan. 28, 1986   *The space shuttle* Challenger *explodes seventy-three seconds after takeoff. A special commission later blames the accident on a leak caused by extremely cold weather.*

Nov. 14, 1986   *Wall Street tycoon Ivan Boesky admits to illegal insider trading and agrees to pay a one-hundred-million-dollar fine. Boesky also agrees to help the government prosecute other insider traders.*

Oct. 19, 1987   *Just two months after a record-setting high, the stock markets drops 508 points in a single day. Shares lose more than five hundred billion dollars in value.*

1987   *Tom Wolfe's first novel,* The Bonfire of the Vanities, *captures the greed and arrogance of the decade, in part because many of its characters bring to mind real people.*

America *is never wholly herself unless she is engaged in high moral principle. We as a people have such a purpose today. It is to make kinder the face of the Nation and gentler the face of the world.*

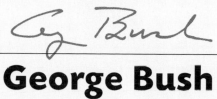

George Bush

41st President • 1989–1993

WHEN GEORGE BUSH BECAME PRESIDENT in 1989, the United States had most recently been led by a peanut farmer and then an actor. Bush was something quite different—a member of the country's traditional ruling class. One historian has even described him as a throwback to the eighteenth century, when children of wealth and influence were routinely trained for careers in public service.

Bush may have made his money as a Texas oilman, but his background was quintessentially Connecticut. He was related by birth to four U.S. presidents (as well as to Benedict Arnold and Winston Churchill), and his father was a U.S. senator. According to Bush, whenever he or his siblings misbehaved, the usual punishment was a spanking delivered with a squash racket.

Bush grew up in Greenwich and prepped at the Phillips Academy in Andover, Massachusetts. After World War II, he followed nearly half of his Andover classmates to Yale, where he was tapped for membership in the exclusive Skull and Bones secret society.

After making enough money in the oil business to provide for his family, Bush began to build his political résumé. He represented Houston for two terms in the House before losing a Senate race in 1970. During the next six years, he served as U.S. ambassador to the United Nations, chairman of the Republican National Committee, unofficial U.S. ambassador to China, and director of the Central Intelligence Agency.

Bush's personality and temperament were obviously better suited to the boardroom than to the modern campaign trail. The refined manners taught him by his mother—don't brag, don't cause a stir—made him feel awkward in the strip show of contemporary politics. Yet he managed to succeed in Washington because of another trait his parents had instilled in him: loyalty, first to Richard Nixon and later to Ronald Reagan as his vice president. "I'm for Mr. Reagan blindly!" he once declared.

Bush was also a devout believer in noblesse oblige—the duty of the privileged classes to return to society some of the benefits they enjoy. As a result, he spent much of his adult life serving the American people. However, he rarely seemed to be one of them.

Sometimes he could make wobbly connections. As a junior officer in the navy, he often pulled mail duty, which required him to read the outgoing letters of enlisted men to make sure that they didn't reveal important information. "We'd sit there and read these damn things," Bush said later. "They could hardly write. [But] it gave you a real feel for people and what they cared about. It was very helpful in understanding the truth about private lives."

• In the Navy

Within hours of the surprise attack on Pearl Harbor, seventeen-year-old George Bush made up his mind to enlist. His father, who opposed the decision, confronted him five months later at his graduation from Phillips Andover Academy. Bush repeated his intention to join the navy on his eighteenth birthday, only weeks away. It was "the first I had ever seen my dad cry," he later said.

Bush chose naval aviation, and when he got his wings on June 9, 1943, he became the youngest commissioned pilot in the navy. He flew a carrier-based torpedo bomber known as the TBF Avenger. His squadron, VT-51, was posted to the aircraft carrier *San Jacinto* in early 1944. On active duty in the South Pacific, the *San Jacinto* took part in the attacks on Wake Island and Saipan. According to biographer Herbert S. Parmet, Squadron Leader Bush "was notable for instilling his men with the sort of confidence that almost artificially bolsters a potentially ominous outlook."

For forty years, Bush carried in his wallet a shamrock, a photograph of Barbara clipped from their engagement announcement, and a remembrance of their daughter Robin, who died of leukemia at age three in 1953.

Bush's squadron aboard the San Jacinto. *Inset: Bush in the cockpit of his torpedo bomber.*

On September 2, 1944, Lieutenant Bush was assigned to bomb several radio towers on Chichi Jima, one of the Bonin Islands. As he approached the well-defended target, he recalled, "Suddenly, there was a jolt, as if a massive fist had crunched into the belly of the plane. Smoke poured into the cockpit, and I could see flames ripping across the crease of the wing, heading toward the fuel tanks."

Despite the chaos, Bush stayed on his run, delivered his bombs, and then headed his plane out over the ocean. His plane was very low, but a water landing, given the fire and the risk of explosion, was impossible. As he jumped, his parachute caught on the plane's fuselage and ripped. The hole that this created made him descend quickly, so he hit the water hard. Meanwhile, he had hit his head on the horizontal stabilizers, opening a gash in his forehead.

Japanese boats were on their way to pick him up, but Bush had heard rumors about the atrocities to which captured pilots were subjected. "I swam like hell," he recalled. "I got to my sea pack and unleashed the inflatable raft and got in, and then I started paddling out to sea." After three hours in the water, he was picked up by the submarine *Finback*, which was on "lifeguard" duty. (Subs were often assigned to bombing missions to pick up downed pilots.) For completing his mission, Bush was awarded the Distinguished Flying Cross.

• Horseshoes

In his youth, Bush captained both the soccer and the baseball teams at Andover, and twice he led his Yale baseball team to the College World Series. "I love the adrenaline factor, competition," he once said.

As president, Bush popularized the sport of horseshoe pitching, which he learned to play at a farm camp as a boy. He had horseshoe pits installed at both the White House and Camp David, where he taught Soviet premier Mikhail Gorbachev how to play. On his first attempt, Gorbachev tossed a ringer.

At the White House, Bush held annual horseshoes tournaments. Invariably, his toughest competition came from the permanent White House staff—the cooks, house-men, groundskeepers, and military aides.

"My mother taught me to lose with class," Bush remembered. "'Be a good sport, George. Don't ever throw your racket again. Stop crying and go out and practice!'"

Bush, a left-hander, used the standard flip toss. He stepped forward once with his left foot and once with his right foot before releasing the shoe with his arm straight and his eyes aimed at midstake.

★ ★

Bush with Gen. Norman Schwarzkopf during the president's Thanksgiving 1990 visit to Saudi Arabia, where he visited U.S. troops taking part in Operation Desert Shield.

• The Wimp Factor

Bush's biggest problem as a candidate was the perception that he was a wimp. In 1986, columnist George Will quoted First Lady Nancy Reagan's opinion that Bush was "whiny," weak, and spineless. Even worse, according to presidential aide Lyn Nofziger, Ronald Reagan thought so, too. In October 1987, *Newsweek* ran a cover story on Bush entitled "Fighting the Wimp Factor."

Bush fought back by devoting an afternoon a week to working with media consultant Roger Ailes. Using video-tape, Ailes taught Bush to project strength rather than weakness. Ailes also trained him to avoid lapsing into a tone of voice that reporters often described as "squeaky."

In January 1988, Bush earned some measure of revenge during a live television interview with Dan Rather of CBS News. When Rather questioned Bush pointedly about his involvement in the Iran-contra scandal, the vice president shot back, "How would you like it if I judged your whole career by those seven minutes when you walked off the set in New York?" (Bush was referring to the time when a U.S. Open tennis match delayed the start of Rather's broadcast and an infuriated Rather stormed out.) "If George Bush is a wimp or a lapdog," William Safire wrote two days later in the *New York Times*, "beware of wily wimps and ferocious lapdogs."

★ ★ ★ ★ ★ ★ ★　　　　　　　　　　　　　★ ★ ★ ★ ★ ★ ★

• Barbara Bush

GEORGE BUSH MET BARBARA Pierce at a country-club dance during the 1941 Christmas holidays. She was sixteen, he a year older. "I married the first man I ever kissed," Barbara admitted later. "When I tell this to my children, they just about throw up."

That first night, Bush had Pearl Harbor on his mind, but the sight of the dark-haired, stately Barbara dancing in her off-the-shoulder dress changed his mind immediately. Barbara was equally smitten: "I could hardly breathe when he was in the room."

Their romance developed quickly through letters and during occasional visits. Sometime before Bush reported to his squadron in September 1943, he and Barbara became secretly engaged—although, Bush said later, their engagement was "secret [only] to the extent that the German and Japanese high commands weren't aware of it." They were married on January 6, 1945, just four months after Bush's plane was shot down over the South Pacific.

As first lady, the warm, grandmotherly Barbara rarely overshadowed her husband. "She remained the Victorian wife and mother," biographer Herbert S. Parmet has written, "while hinting, sometimes in devilish ways, that not far below that matronly figure was a modern woman."

She consistently avoided any policy-making role, yet her tongue did slip once, shortly before Bush's inauguration, when she told some reporters that she thought assault weapons should be illegal. This remark caused a fuss because it contradicted the president's view. Her press secretary subsequently announced that Mrs. Bush would no longer discuss gun control or any other controversial issue.

Instead, the first lady promoted literacy and education. She wrote *Millie's Book*, a view of the White House through the "eyes" of the first dog. It raised more than one million dollars for reading programs. She also continued to champion her husband. "It takes guts to be George Bush," she liked to say.

MAJOR POLITICAL EVENTS

★ **Savings-and-Loan Scandal:** One of Reagan's priorities as president was deregulation. Savings-and-loan institutions, in particular, benefited from the relaxation of federal oversight. Many made risky loans in the hope of gaining large profits. Others simply used their new freedom to cheat depositors. One of the worst offenders, Charles Keating, was later charged with making sizable campaign donations to five senators in exchange for their help in stalling federal investigations of his banking practices. President Bush's son Neil was also caught in the scandal when a Colorado savings-and-loan on whose board he sat failed in late 1988, costing the taxpayers one billion dollars. By 1989, hundreds of billions of dollars in government-insured accounts had disappeared. In August 1989, Bush committed $166 billion in public money to close the failed savings-and-loans and pay off depositors.

★ **"No New Taxes" Pledge:** "Read my lips, no new taxes!" Bush told the Republican national convention in August 1988 as he accepted its nomination for president. Although the no-new-taxes pledge proved to be good politics, it limited Bush as president. The mounting budget deficits that he had inherited from Reagan forced him to admit in June 1990 that a tax increase might be necessary. Then, during negotiations with Congress over the 1991 budget, he broke his central campaign promise by agreeing to a compromise that included increases in the gasoline tax, Medicare premiums, and the top income tax rate.

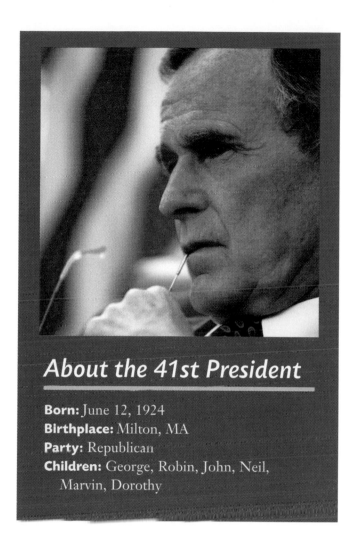

About the 41st President

Born: June 12, 1924
Birthplace: Milton, MA
Party: Republican
Children: George, Robin, John, Neil, Marvin, Dorothy

★ **Persian Gulf War:** In August 1990, Iraqi troops invaded the Persian Gulf nation of Kuwait. Although a tiny country, Kuwait controlled about 10 percent of the world's oil reserves. Using the United Nations, Bush built an international coalition to oppose Iraq's "naked aggression." At first, as Bush sent troops to defend Saudi Arabia, economic sanctions were imposed. In November, the UN Security Council set a deadline of January 15, 1991, for the complete withdrawal of Iraqi troops from Kuwait. Seven hours after the deadline passed, Bush began Operation Desert Storm. For nearly six weeks, coalition bombers targeted Iraq's military infrastructure. In late February, after more than one hundred thousand bombing missions, the ground war began. In less than one hundred hours, troops under Gen. Norman Schwarzkopf overwhelmed the Iraqi army and liberated Kuwait.

★ ★ ★ ★ ★ ★ ★ ★ ★ ★ ★ ★ ★ ★ ★

During the Bush Administration

Mar. 24, 1989
The tanker Exxon Valdez *runs aground on Bligh Reef, off the coast of Alaska. The accident punctures the supertanker's hull, causing the worst oil spill in U.S. history.*

Oct. 17, 1989
An earthquake measuring 7.1 on the Richter scale rocks the San Francisco Bay area. Highways and bridges collapse, killing more than one hundred people. The quake hits minutes before the start of a World Series game at Candlestick Park.

Dec. 17, 1989
A cartoon series called The Simpsons *premieres on the new Fox television network. Its success helps establish Fox as a legitimate alternative to CBS, ABC, and NBC.*

Mar. 22, 1990
President Bush bans broccoli from the White House because he says he doesn't like the way it tastes.

Sep. 1990
Public television airs The Civil War, *an epic documentary series that wins critical praise for its inventive use of still images, period music, and excerpts from the diaries and letters of ordinary Americans.*

Nov. 7, 1991
Popular basketball star Earvin "Magic" Johnson announces that he has tested positive for HIV, the virus that causes AIDS. Before Johnson's disclosure, most Americans thought that only homosexuals and drug users could get AIDS.

June 1992
Delegates from 153 countries meet at the first Earth Summit in Rio de Janeiro, where treaties are signed concerning such environmental issues as global warming, the greenhouse effect, and biodiversity.

My fellow citizens, this is our time. Let us embrace it. Our democracy must be not only the envy of the world but the engine of our own renewal. There is nothing wrong with America that cannot be cured by what is right with America.

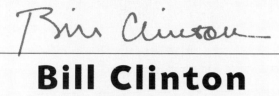

Bill Clinton

42nd President • 1993–

BILL CLINTON HAS ALWAYS SEEMED to be running for something. During the summer of 1963, after finishing his junior year of high school, he attended Arkansas Boys State, a weeklong political training camp sponsored by the American Legion. At the end of the week, the boys were expected to elect two "senators" to represent the state at Boys Nation in Washington, D.C. Clinton was determined to become one of these senators.

He carefully studied the makeup of each barracks at the camp, learning which boys were staying where, what their likes and dislikes were, and especially whom they might know in common. Always he was in campaign mode, his big right hand extended again and again as he introduced himself to potential supporters. He canvassed the barracks at night and posted himself beside the cafeteria at six-thirty each morning to greet the incoming breakfast crowd. Typically, Clinton won.

From that point on, the line between the candidate and the man became thinner and thinner. Whenever he met people in the years ahead, he would ask them as a matter of course where they were from and what they were interested in. Then he'd work the conversation around to his own roots in Arkansas and his ambition to govern the state one day. Like many other Clinton classmates at Yale Law School, Hillary Rodham was impressed by his strong sense of place. "He cared deeply about where he came from, which was unusual," she said. "He was rooted, and most of us were disconnected."

Throughout his life, Clinton has been quick with a handshake, eager and friendly, showing little reserve. According to one Clinton biographer, "He [has] an ability to walk into any conversation…and immediately place himself at the center of it."

Certainly since college he has systematically collected people—Friends of Bill, or FOBs for short—who might one day be able to help him politically. Taken together, these FOBs now comprise a vast personal network of influential advisers and supporters. They have helped their friend get elected, and now they help him run the country.

Clinton has always impressed people with his great energy. He talks so much and so often because he's curious about people and wants to know what they think. For Clinton, conversations are the point at which his gregarious personality meets his political ambition. Even as a twenty-two-year-old at Oxford, one of his fellow Rhodes scholars remembered, Clinton was "always the character who wanted to do one more thing, go one more place, stay up one more hour, have one more drink. He came across as somebody with a great appetite for life."

• Boyhood

Clinton's natural father, a heavy-equipment salesman named William Jefferson Blythe, was killed in an automobile accident three months before Bill was born. He and his mother, Virginia Cassidy Blythe, lived with her parents in Hope, Arkansas, until she married a freewheeling car dealer from Hot Springs in 1950.

Roger Clinton liked to drink, gamble, and womanize, all to excess. He was an alcoholic, and in drunken rages he would sometimes abuse his wife. In the spring of 1962, she filed for a divorce, which was granted. But then she began to feel sorry for Roger and took him back.

William Jefferson Blythe III (later William Jefferson Clinton) in 1950.

Psychologists who treat the children of alcoholics often speak of a Family Hero, usually the oldest child, who assumes adult responsibilities and redeems the family unit. Bill Clinton was a textbook example. Once when he was fourteen years old (and about the same size as his stepfather), he heard his parents fighting. Storming into their bedroom, he demanded that his stepfather stand and face him. Then he told Roger never to hit his mother again. "I was the father," Bill Clinton later said of his role in the family.

★ ★

Sixteen-year-old Bill Clinton was already six foot three and two hundred pounds when he met President Kennedy. One of the few Democrats in his conservative hometown of Hot Springs, Arkansas, Clinton was the only Kennedy supporter in a 1960 election debate organized by the teacher of his ninth-grade civics class.

• Meeting the President

Clinton's mother, Virginia, often said that her son's political aspirations began on the day in July 1963 that he met President John F. Kennedy at the White House. That summer, Clinton had traveled to Washington with ninety-nine other high school seniors-to-be to participate in Boys Nation, a program of mock debates, speeches, and elections run by the American Legion.

For five days, senior politicians had called the boys, who were being rewarded for academic achievement, the "future leaders of the free world." On July 24, they met the current leader of the free world. As the boys left their air-conditioned buses, they were reminded not to run, push, or throw elbows, so several of the most eager boys tried to look casual as they speed-walked to the Rose Garden. Clinton's long strides enabled him to reach the reception area first and place himself in the front row, just to the right of the podium. After the president's speech, Kennedy paused to shake some hands before returning to the Oval Office. Clinton's was the first hand that he encountered.

Thirty-four-year-old Bill Clinton, the boy governor of Arkansas, in October 1980.

• Clinton Time

Friends of Clinton from his days as an aide to Arkansas senator William Fulbright have said that he adapted to life on Capitol Hill by becoming chronically late. "Oh, sorry," he'd say, "I was talking to somebody."

As governor of Arkansas, Clinton was famous for running hours behind schedule. "We'd drive through a precinct...and we'd pass by a store," recalled his travel aide, Randy White, "and he'd say, 'Oh, stop here' for Miss so-and-so, 'I've known her forever.' He'd go in and drink a Coke and stay. It went all day like this. Good Lord, we were off schedule. Way off."

His staff operated on what they called "Clinton time." According to Clinton biographer David Maraniss, "They would often lie to him about when he was due somewhere, giving him an earlier time than the actual one,...but by the end of the day he could still be an hour or two behind." Always an egalitarian, the governor was just as likely to show up late for a lunch with big donors as he was to delay a meeting with poor farmers.

• Playing the Sax

Clinton began playing the saxophone when he was a boy. He practiced every night because, he later said, it gave him "the opportunity to create something that was beautiful, something that I could channel my sensitivity, my feelings into." By the time he entered high school, he was the best saxophone player in Hot Springs and one of the best in the state. He formed a trio called the Kingsmen, but his classmates preferred to call the group the Three Blind Mice because they always wore dark sunglasses when they performed.

As a candidate, Clinton made clever use of his photogenic musical ability. On June 3, 1992, the day after the final Democratic primaries, he appeared on Arsenio Hall's late-

A Wisconsin farmer sings "Danny Boy" at a Clinton rally in late October 1992. "A gentleman," Mark Twain allegedly said, "is someone who knows how to play the saxophone— but doesn't."

night TV talk show playing "Heartbreak Hotel." The spot made headlines: Never before had a presidential candidate courted the youth vote directly by appearing on one of its own programs. Clinton's aides quickly booked him onto other talk shows, including one on MTV. Some older commentators chastised him for sacrificing his dignity, but the appearances helped many voters understand emotionally what Clinton meant by "change."

★ ★ ★ ★ ★ ★ ★ ★ ★ ★ ★ ★ ★ ★

• Hillary Rodham Clinton

THE COURTSHIP OF BILL CLINTON and Hillary Rodham was, in the words of one Clinton biographer, "a fair fight." They were both smart, ambitious, socially conscious, and politically inclined. They also complemented each other: Her sharp midwestern directness offset his syrupy southern charm.

They met in the fall of 1970 at Yale Law School, where Hillary was in her second year and Clinton beginning his first. (Clinton was fourteen months older than Hillary, but he had spent his first two years out of college in Oxford on a Rhodes scholarship.)

After her graduation from Yale, Hillary worked for the Children's Defense Fund, pursuing her long-standing interest in child welfare and children's rights. Next, she landed a prestigious job with the House committee preparing to impeach President Nixon. Following Nixon's resignation in August 1974, she moved to Fayetteville, Arkansas, where she joined Clinton on the faculty of the University of Arkansas Law School. They were married a year later, but not without some soul searching on Hillary's part. Friends told her that she was selling short her own ambitions, and she understood that Clinton, who was noticeably flirtatious, might not be faithful to her, but she finally decided that she was willing to bind her life to his.

Their relationship is unique among presidential couples. According to Clinton aide George Stephanopoulos, "One thing was evident: Hillary was his most important advisor, and she wanted a senior post in the White House." To begin with, she got an office in the West Wing, the center of policy, rather than the traditional first lady's office in the East Wing, where social arrangements were made. Later, Clinton did something else unprecedented: He put his wife in charge of a presidential task force (on health care reform). Among the reporters covering the White House, none doubted that Hillary's power was second only to the president's.

MAJOR POLITICAL EVENTS

★ **Gays in the Military:** During the 1992 presidential campaign, Clinton appealed to the gay community by promising to lift the ban on homosexuals in the military. After taking office, however, he found out that important congressmen, military officers, and even most of the public supported the ban. In July 1993, Clinton agreed to a compromise that satisfied the Joint Chiefs of Staff, if not the gay community. Under this policy, called "don't ask, don't tell," the military would no longer ask soldiers whether or not they were homosexual. That way, gays could continue to serve in the military as long as they didn't reveal their sexual preference.

★ **Trade Agreements:** Clinton won a major political victory when Congress narrowly approved the North American Free Trade Agreement (NAFTA) in November 1993. NAFTA removed all trade barriers among the United States, Mexico, and Canada. Ross Perot had led a vigorous campaign against NAFTA that had included a televised debate with Vice President Al Gore. Perot claimed that NAFTA would result in the loss of many American jobs to Mexico, where wages were lower. A month after the approval of NAFTA, the director of the General Agreement on Tariffs and Trade (GATT) announced the end of the Uruguay Round of talks. The complex agreement that the Uruguay Round produced, negotiated by representatives of 117 nations, summed up seven years of global trade talks. With much less debate than NAFTA had caused, Congress approved the GATT treaty in November 1994.

About the 42nd President

Born: August 19, 1946
Birthplace: Hope, AR
Party: Democrat
Children: Chelsea

★ **Contract with America:** In September 1994, at the height of the congressional campaign, Rep. Newt Gingrich of Georgia gathered more than three hundred Republican candidates at the Capitol to sign the Contract with America. This document promised that a Republican majority in the House would approve a line-item veto, make all federal laws applicable to members of Congress, and end unfunded mandates (federal laws that required states to pay for federal programs). The contract also promised passage of a balanced-budget amendment and a slate of legal reforms. The following spring, during the first hundred days of the new Republican-controlled Congress, the first three measures passed both the House and the Senate. The last two, however, like many other parts of the contract, stalled in the Senate, where the Republicans were much less radical than those in the House.

During the Clinton Administration

Feb. 26, 1993 *An explosion nearly topples the World Trade Center in New York City. The bomb, placed by radical Muslim terrorists, kills five people and injures more than one thousand. The attack is the worst terrorist incident yet to have taken place on U.S. soil.*

Apr. 28, 1993 *The Ms. Foundation sponsors the first Take Our Daughters to Work Day. Hundreds of thousands of young girls accompany their parents to work, where they learn about jobs and observe office procedures.*

Aug. 12, 1993 *President Clinton signs a multibillion-dollar relief bill to help victims of the Great Flood of 1993. Fifty people have died in states bordering the Mississippi River, and more than seventy thousand people are homeless.*

Dec. 5-9, 1993 *Astronauts aboard the space shuttle repair the $1.5-billion Hubble Space Telescope, which begins transmitting incredibly detailed images of the solar system, the galaxy, and the universe beyond.*

Sep. 6, 1995 *Baltimore Orioles shortstop Cal Ripken plays in his 2,131st consecutive game, breaking Lou Gehrig's record of 2,130 consecutive games set in 1939.*

Oct. 3, 1995 *Jurors in Los Angeles find O. J. Simpson not guilty of murdering his ex-wife, Nicole Brown, and her friend Ron Goldman.*

June 13, 1997 *Timothy McVeigh receives the death penalty for his role in the April 19, 1995, bombing of the Murrah Federal Office Building in Oklahoma City. The bomb, which had been hidden in a rented van, collapsed the front half of the building, killing 168 people.*